TO CDR FRED DRAKE,

THANKS FOR YOUR SUPPORT
OF CCE ... you've DONE A
GREAT JOB IN A TOUGH
ASSIGNMENT.

I hope you ENJOY ALL OF
THE GREAT "LOGGIE - STUFF"
IN THIS BOOK.

LOGISTICS
IN THE
NATIONAL DEFENSE

Naval War College

Logistics Leadership Series

Book Two

This is the second book in the U.S. Naval War College Logistics Leadership Series.

For additional research in this area, refer to the first book in the series: *Pure Logistics* by George C. Thorpe, published by the Naval War College Press

Research assistance provided by Marguerite Rauch, Reference Branch, Naval War College Library.

Cover: U. S. Navy and U. S. Marine Corps personnel move supplies and equipment across the beach at Iwo Jima in 1945. Painting by Andrew Small, Newport, Rhode Island.

HENRY E. ECCLES

LOGISTICS
IN THE
NATIONAL DEFENSE

A Naval War College Press Edition
in the
Logistics Leadership Series

Foreword
by
Vice Admiral William J. Hancock, U.S. Navy
Deputy Chief of Naval Operations (Logistics)

Introduction
by
Captain John E. Jackson, SC, U.S. Navy
Military Chair of Logistics
U.S. Naval War College

Naval War College Press
Newport, Rhode Island
1997

Reprinted in 1981 by Greenwood Press
An imprint of Greenwood Publishing Group, Inc.

Naval War College Press, Newport, R.I.
First printing 1997

Library of Congress Cataloging-in-Publication Data

Eccles, Henry Effingham, 1898-
    Logistics in the national defense / by Henry E. Eccles ;
foreword by William J. Hancock ; introduction and comments
by John E. Jackson. — A Naval War College Press ed. in the
logistics leadership series.
        p.   cm. — (Naval War College / Logistics leadership
series ; bk. 2)
    Originally published: Harrisburg, Penn. : Stackpole Co.,
1959.
    Includes bibliographical references and index.
    ISBN 0-313-22716-0
    1. Logistics.   I. Title.   II. Series: Logistics leadership
series ; bk. 2.
U168.E22   1997
355.4' 11—dc21
                                                            97-35560
                                                                 CIP

Printed in the United States of America

Contents

vii

ix

Illustrations

Foreword

We live in very challenging times, and every day I find myself confronted by a highly technical and rapidly evolving world. Change comes fast and furious, and it seems that today's innovation is tomorrow's surplus gadget. One indicator of the pace necessary to keep up with technological change is the state-of-the-art computer on my desk that will be virtually obsolete long before my tour in this job is over! You may ask, in this fast-paced world, is there any value in reading some forty-year-old ideas from a World War II logistician? **You bet there is!** Shortly after assuming my duties as the Navy's senior logistician, I visited the Naval War College, where I was introduced to the work of the late Rear Admiral Henry E. Eccles. As I browsed with mild curiosity through one of his books, I soon recognized that the things he had written four decades ago were directly relevant to the problems I had left only hours earlier in the Pentagon. I found that his fundamental truths were still true . . . his basic assumptions were still valid . . . and his cautions and recommendations were still applicable to the Navy of today.

Eccles writes from a wealth of personal experience, having served as a combat-tested commander, a theater-wide logistician, and a world-class educator. When he makes a statement, you can be sure it is backed by either personal experience or scholarly research. I know of no one with more credibility as a logistician than Henry Eccles. The book that follows, *Logistics in the National Defense*, is one of his most renowned works. While its value has long been recognized, it has not been readily available to modern day scholars or practitioners. I applaud the Naval War College for selecting this book as the second volume in its Logistics Leadership Series, and I recommend it to every military leader (officer and civilian) who wants to ensure that his operational plans are supportable. I commend it to all defense leaders interested in deriving the maximum benefit from each defense dollar spent. If you do no more than read

Eccles' discussion on the so-called "logistics snowball" and gain an increased appreciation for the finite nature of logistic resources, you will have gained a great deal—and in the process, the spirit and ideas of the "Grand Old Man of Logistics" will have benefited yet another generation of military professionals.

William J. Hancock
Vice Admiral, U.S. Navy
Deputy Chief of Naval
Operations (Logistics)

Introduction

Logistics provides the physical means for organized forces to exercise power.

Rear Admiral Henry E. Eccles, USN

The quotation above, by one of the most respected logisticians of all time, is both elegant in its simplicity and accurate in its scope. In only a dozen words, Eccles manages to convey the essence of a complex and often misunderstood branch of military science. The statesmen and generals can devise a military strategy detailing the objectives of a given military action, and the planning staffs can develop specific tactics to explain how to achieve these objectives, but without logisticians to provide the "physical means" to wage war, the battle cannot be joined. History has often shown that even the most brilliant tactical or strategic plan will fail unless it can be logistically supported. The most highly armored tank, the most maneuverable ship, and the most agile aircraft mean nothing without the ammunition, fuel, and manpower provided by the "logistical tail." In the pages that follow, H.E. Eccles makes a strong case for the role and importance of this oft-neglected art.

Captain John E. Jackson, Supply Corps, United States Navy, has served in a series of logistics assignments both afloat and ashore over the past 26 years. A Distinguished Naval Graduate from the Naval Reserve Officer Training Corps at the University of New Mexico, he holds graduate degrees in education and in management and is currently a doctoral candidate at Salve Regina University. He is also a graduate of the Management Development Program at Harvard University. In 1994 he was appointed by the Deputy Chief of Naval Operations (Logistics) to hold the **Frederick J. Horne Military Chair of Logistics** at the U.S. Naval War College. An author, logistician, and educator, he is listed in *Who's Who in America*.

About the Author

Henry Effingham Eccles was born in Bayside, New York, on 31 December 1898 to George and Lydia Eccles. George was an Episcopal priest, and he and his wife "home-schooled" young Henry until the age of twelve, at which time he enrolled in Trinity School in New York City. His nontraditional early education included considerable travel, and he made ten crossings of the Atlantic Ocean before the age of thirteen. This early exposure to the joys and rigors of the sea no doubt contributed to his desire for a career as a naval officer. Eccles completed one year at Columbia College, New York, and was appointed to the U.S. Naval Academy in 1918. He graduated in the class of 1922, and served aboard the battleships USS *Maryland* and USS *New York* before transferring to the submarine service. In 1930 he earned a master of science degree in mechanical engineering from Columbia University, then returned to sea to command the submarines USS *O-1* and USS *R-13*. In the mid-1930's he returned to duty aboard surface ships, and was in command of the destroyer USS *John D. Edwards* on the China Station during the time when Pearl Harbor was attacked. In the months that followed America's entry into the war, Eccles commanded *John D. Edwards* through thirteen intense combat engagements. He saw action in the Battle of the Badoeng Strait, earning the Navy Cross for "especially meritorious conduct in action with a greatly superior Japanese Naval force" and in the Battle of the Java Sea in which he earned the Silver Star "for conspicuous gallantry and intrepidity in offensive daylight action against the Japanese Battle Line of heavy and light cruisers." After relinquishing command of his destroyer, Eccles completed a tour in the base Maintenance Division of the Office of the Chief of Naval Operations in Washington, followed by completion of the Command Course at the Naval War College, Newport, Rhode Island. He was then ordered to the position that placed him the midst of the largest logistics operation ever conducted in the Pacific theater.

In December 1943, he reported to Pearl Harbor as Officer-in-Charge of the Advanced Base Section on the staff of the Commander Service Force, U.S. Pacific Fleet. The scope of his task and the manner in which he carried it out is best described by quoting from the award citation that accompanied the presentation of the Legion of Merit in 1945:

> ... Commencing with no precedent to guide him and no experienced staff to assist him, Captain Eccles skillfully developed and directed the establishment, administration, and logistic support for the construction and maintenance of all advanced base units in the Central Pacific Ocean area. During this period of tremendous expansion and resultant taxation of personnel and material, he displayed an outstanding degree of resourcefulness, ingenuity, sound judgment and planning and clear and realistic concept of the task to be accomplished coupled with the possession of the necessary professional skill and experience with which to accomplish it. His untiring efforts and unswerving devotion to duty contributed substantially to the successful prosecution of the war against the enemy in the Pacific.

After the war, Eccles served on the prestigious Joint Operations Review Board, which was tasked with developing a series of "lessons learned" from the Second World War. Thereafter, he briefly commanded the battleship USS *Washington* prior to its post-war decommissioning in 1947.

Henry Eccles' reputation as the "Grand Old Man of Logistics" derives in great part from his decades of work educating military and civilian personnel in the "secrets" of the logistical art. He did this in ways that ranged from formal classroom settings to scholarly books and thought-provoking articles, and in countless speeches and presentations at war colleges, universities, and civic groups. His opportunity to be a full-time logistics educator came as he prepared to decommission the battleship USS *Washington*. The story of his many productive years at the Naval War College is perhaps told best in the paragraphs that follow (adapted from John B. Hattendorf et al., *Sailors and Scholars: The Centennial History of the U.S. Naval War College*, published by the Naval War College Press in 1984).

Henry Eccles and the Logistics Course

Eccles returned to the Naval War College in the late spring of 1946 to lecture on advanced base development. A few months later he received orders to command the battleship *Washington*. Shortly after he assumed command, the Navy Department decided to decommission the ship within a few months and she proceeded to the New York Naval Shipyard in Brooklyn to make the necessary preparations. Eccles, then a senior captain, started looking for his next billet. He soon found it.

On a trip to Washington a friend showed him the directive signed by the Chief of Naval Operations, Fleet Admiral Chester Nimitz, which established the logistics course at the Naval War College and called for a flag officer to head the course. Eccles was asked if he could suggest anyone for the job. When he mentioned two or three names, he was told those officers were either not available or not interested. Finally, he was asked if he might be interested. He was. He said he would take either the number one or the number two position. Admiral Spruance knew Eccles and, believing that commitment and knowledge were more important than rank, eagerly approved assigning him to lead the course even though he was not a flag officer.

There was important high-level interest in establishing the course. The Deputy Chief of Naval Operations for Logistics, Admiral Robert B. Carney, who supported the idea, made $90,000 available to convert the then unused Training Station Barracks "C" (later named Sims Hall) into suitable spaces. For more than two months, Eccles alternated his weekends, commuting from his ship in Brooklyn to either the college in Newport or to Washington in his efforts to recruit qualified officers for his staff and to oversee the renovation of the barracks.

Eccles was able to gather a competent staff and have them on board in sufficient time to prepare for the opening of the course in July 1947. He received unqualified assistance and support from the Bureau of Supplies and Accounts, which assigned several outstanding Supply Corps officers.

By early July 1947, 46 officer students, representing all branches of the U.S. armed forces as well as Britain's Royal Navy, reported for the logistics course. This new course was co-equal with the regular course in strategy and tactics. Both courses were integrated for the first two months, which were devoted to common background work in general principles and in the capabilities of ships, planes, and weapons, and other combat forces. There was also study of weather, communications, and intelligence.

Then the logistics students broke off and concentrated for eight months on their subject. A considerable amount of time was devoted to joint amphibious operations. Moreover, the logistics students solved naval problems, working them out on the game board. These ranged from a quick tactical problem to a major one involving a global war. In addition, each student was required to write papers on two subjects, "A Comparison of the War Potential of the United States and the U.S.S.R." and "The Effect of New Weapons on Naval Logistics." Besides the obvious educational benefits of research, arriving at conclusions, and reducing thoughts to writing, the thesis topics had the additional virtues of requiring every student to look forward in regard to the most likely enemy and of requiring each one to focus on problems that logisticians might have to face in the future.

Among other things, the logistics war games examined the concept of a "one-stop" replenishment ship. As early as 1948, Eccles proved the effectiveness and efficiency of a concept that did not become an operational part of the fleet until 1964 when USS *Sacramento* (AOE-1) was commissioned. In addition, Eccles wrote the Navy's first logistics manual, *Operational Naval Logistics*, which was published in 1950. It was a philosophical approach to the study of logistics as a command responsibility "devoted to the thesis that while we can expect to make new mistakes in the logistics of future war, we should not repeat the old ones."

In the succeeding three years refinements were made to the logistics course, but the basic concept remained the same: to teach logistics from the point of view of command. In 1950, the name of the course was changed to strategy and logistics in recognition of their close relationship. Considerable difficulty attended the search for qualified relief for Eccles in 1951. Although logistics was a responsibility of the line, officers of the line failed to support the course. Thus, shortly after Eccles' reassignment, the logistics course was fully integrated into the regular college curriculum and the subject was once again relegated to a position of secondary importance.

After nearly five productive years of teaching logistics, Eccles was given the opportunity to put his theories into practice. In April 1951, he became Assistant Chief of Staff for Logistics for the Commander-in-Chief, U.S. Naval Forces Northeastern Atlantic and Mediterranean. He performed the same function for the Commander-in-Chief Allied Forces Southern Europe when that North Atlantic Treaty Organization (NATO) command was established. He held that position until his retirement on 30 June 1952, and at that time, he was promoted to the rank of rear admiral on the retired list.

After retirement from active duty, Rear Admiral Eccles established a residence in Newport, Rhode Island, and renewed his close relationship with the Naval War College. He lectured frequently and taught several elective courses there, although he was never formally employed by the college during these years. During the nearly three decades that followed his departure from active service, he wrote and published three of his landmark works on logistics and military theory: *Logistics in the National Defense* (1959); *Military Concepts and Philosophy* (1965); and *Military Power in a Free Society* (1979). He also published dozens of articles in various journals and magazines. In recognition of his many years of outstanding support to the Naval War College, the school's library was named in his honor in 1985. In June of 1985, Rear Admiral Eccles and his wife, Isabel, moved to a retirement home in Needham, Massachusetts. Less than a year later, following a brief illness, he passed away, on 14 May 1986 at the age of 87.

The Essence of Eccles

Logistics in the National Defense was first published in May 1959 by the Stackpole Company (formerly the Military Service Publishing Company) of Harrisburg, Pennsylvania. The book represented a compilation of a series of research papers and lectures prepared by Eccles while at the Naval War College and while involved with the George Washington University Logistics Research Project, a massive project that was funded by the Office of Naval Research and took place during the period 1952-1970.

The book is divided into three major sections: Part I: *Basic Considerations*; Part II: *Operational Factors*; and Part III: *Organization and Readiness*. Each part builds upon the previous, and collectively, they address the issue of logistics from its theoretical basis through practical application, in a remarkable level of detail.

The first one-third of the book, *Basic Considerations*, lays a firm foundation for the subsequent discussion. In this initial section, Eccles identifies the recurring themes that are interwoven throughout the ensuing chapters. These themes are:

(1) Modern war covers an entire spectrum of human conflict.

(2) Strategy should be considered the comprehensive direction of power for the purpose of exercising control of a field of action in order to attain objectives.

(3) Logistics is the bridge between our national economy and the actual operations of our combat forces in the field.

(4) Unless restrained by wise, adequate, and timely planning, logistics installations and operations tend to snowball out of proportion to the true needs of combat support.

(5) Sound logistics forms the foundation for the development of strategic flexibility and mobility. If such flexibility is to be exercised and exploited, military command must have adequate control of its logistic support.

(6) The understanding of the nature and degree of logistic control that command should exercise is essential to the attainment of combat effectiveness.

This section also engages the reader in a preliminary discussion of the nature of war and the relationship between strategy, tactics, and logistics. He sights numerous historical examples to demonstrate the manner in which strategic/logistical relationships have shaped the outcome of major events. Part I also discusses logistical planning in significant detail and touches upon everything from the two broad categories of planning (mobilization planning and operational planning) to the discussion of planning for consumption and usage of specific line-items of supply.

Part II opens with a discussion of one of the most famous of Eccles' logistical concepts, the so-called logistic snowball. Here he expands on his fourth major theme, which he labels as "perhaps the most important single thesis of this book." The "snowball theory" holds that logistical operations have a tendency to grow in size and complexity far beyond the minimum level needed to support the operations at hand. He cautions commanders to carefully monitor the level of support being planned for a given operation, and when a growing "snowball" is detected, attempt to curtail excesses before they become burdensome and threaten to crush the operation. He cites a number of reasons for the growth of the "snowball," some of which are primarily psychological in nature. He reasons that commanders may discover some aspect of logistical support that they consider inadequate, and once such logistic "under-planning" is identified, there becomes a tendency to "over-plan." Thus, for example, if a truck convoy is slowed because all ten replacement tires have been consumed in a given period of time, requisitions might go out for *100* tires—just to ensure that this type of shortage never happens again! If other logistic planners subsequently notice a ten-fold increase in tire usage in this unit, they may see it as an indicator of future demand and move ten-times more tires into the theatre than are actually needed. Thus the "snowball" grows larger and becomes even more dysfunctional.

Some modern historians sarcastically report that the Gulf War of 1991 really had three phases: Desert Shield, Desert Storm, and Desert *Surplus*. The tremendous tonnage of unused material that was ultimately returned from the Gulf was largely the result of the shorter than expected war, but it is reasonable to believe that the excesses were (at least partially) the result of the "snowball" effect Eccles speaks to so eloquently. The "snowball" was also apparent during the Vietnam war. With 20/20 hindsight, a lecturer at the U.S. Air Force's Air Command and Staff College stated:

If there is one thing that surfaces again and again to characterize our logistical effort in Southeast Asia, it is *lavishness*, aggravated by a lack of priorities and mammoth waste. The characteristics refer to a *style of war*, a logistical doctrine if you will, that violated important principles of economy, security, and objective. The Secretary of Defense testified that, while the North Vietnam forces used 100 tons per day of non-food supplies, we were bringing in 1,350 tons per day of goods for the base exchanges alone! Good logistics is sustaining the needed level of combat at least cost, so that resources can be used elsewhere, and so the home economy isn't bankrupted or inflated out of proportion.

The existence of the "snowball" phenomena, however, should *not* be interpreted as evidence of misbehavior or miscalculation on the part of the many dedicated and hard-working logisticians who served during the Vietnam war and in other conflicts. Instead, the concept simply acknowledges a number of tendencies of large organizations in times of stress, which, left unchecked, can lead to excesses. Eccles' intention in highlighting this phenomena was simply to alert commanders to the potential for logistical overreaction in hopes that this knowledge would help keep obvious excessive growth in check. In the grand scheme, however, the greatest danger is to be too conservative (in an attempt to prevent the "snowball") and fail to provide the necessary support to the combat forces when and where it is needed.

In Part III, Eccles turns to issues of organization and readiness. He discusses issues of centralization vs decentralization; the balance between quality, quantity, and time; and the need for simplicity and conformity (when the conditions dictate). He also offers thoughts on the relationship between logistics and the theory of war. In one often quoted passage he states:

Logistics provides the means to create and support combat forces. Logistics is the bridge between the national economy and the operation of combat forces. Thus, in its economic sense it limits the combat forces which can be created; and in its operational sense it limits the forces which can be employed. Thus strategy and tactics are always limited and at times are determined by logistic factors. Obviously, therefore, in order to support the combat requirements of strategy and tactics **the objective of all logistics efforts must be the attainment of sustained combat effectiveness in operating forces.**

It is clear that today's world is far different from the one in which Henry Eccles worked and lived. He would no doubt be astounded by the military and political realities we now take for granted, but he would still recognize much within the world of military logistics. In fact, the task of today's logistician has not changed that much from the one faced by the quartermasters of Caesar's legions. The task includes assembling and equipping a military force, procuring the materials to sustain that force, transporting the force and its supplies to the field of action, sustaining the force while in combat, returning the force to its garrison after victory, and reconstituting the force for its next engagement. Logistics is not magic, nor is it glamorous, but it *is* critical to the success of every military operation.

Logistics in the National Defense is designed to be a helpful tool for both the logistician and for the commander he or she serves. As a team, and **only as a team**, the logistician and the war-fighter can provide the nation with the kind of military force it demands and deserves.

John E. Jackson
Captain, Supply Corps
United States Navy

U.S. Naval War College
Newport, Rhode Island
October 1997

The pages that follow represent a total reprint of the original 1959 edition. This printing follows the original edition, retaining the style of the author. The only changes made are corrections of typographical errors and minor modifications of format.

Author's Preface

For more than a decade the problems of National defense, its organization and its control, have been recognized as vital to this country and to the free world. The differences of opinion both in civilian and military areas have been very marked. These differences have been apparent in the determination of strategy and in the creation of military forces to support it. The Hoover Commission Reports, The Rockefeller Reports, and many other prominent commentaries place major emphasis on the problems at the top of our command structure. They usually ignore consideration of the manner in which the top level arrangements and decisions influence the effectiveness of the combat units whose efficient employment constitutes the sole purpose of this enormous effort. In the welter of controversy over high command organization and the allocation of the budget dollar, the vital factor of logistics has received inadequate analytical effort. And, yet, in the understanding of this relatively unknown subject lies the key to relating the creation of armed forces to the effectiveness of their employment.

My first book *Operational Naval Logistics*[1] discussed the basic structure of logistics and some of its more important operational features. It now seems appropriate to look more deeply into the subject and its relationship to other elements of modern conflict.

Logistics in the National Defense evolved out of a series of research papers prepared for the George Washington University Logistics Research Project and a group of lectures delivered at the Naval War College, The Command and General Staff College, The National War College, The Air University, The Industrial College of the Armed Forces, The Armed Forces Staff College, and at the U.S. Air Force School of Logistics.

As the studies developed it soon became apparent that the technical aspects of logistics were so vast and so complicated

---

[1]Published by Bureau of Naval Personnel, NAVPERS 10869, APRIL 1950.

that they obscured the main issues and principles. Therefore, the emphasis has been placed on the command aspects of the subject as providing the only perspective by which the complexity of technical details could be penetrated and the major factors brought into focus.

These studies and lectures were based on active experience in the planning and management of logistic work and, while many official sources have been studied, no attempt is made to express official opinion. To a very great degree my conclusions have been influenced by correspondence and discussion of an unofficial nature with officers of all services and many nations and with historians and military analysts of widely different background and interests.

In particular, it has been a great privilege to have served and studied in the U.S. Naval War College where the encouragement of its presidents and the close association with the students and civilian and military members of the staff have contributed to my understanding and stimulated my efforts.

HENRY E. ECCLES

101 Washington Street
Newport, Rhode Island
January 1959

Acknowledgements

Obviously extensive help has been required to prepare a book of this scope. Over the years I have been fortunate in the friends who have helped me with their experience and advice. I have appreciated the long discussions where difficult points have been presented and argued. It is impractical to list all to whom I am indebted but it would be a gross ingratitude not to mention a few who have been particularly stimulating and helpful.

I am deeply grateful to Doctor Henry Wriston, President of The American Assembly, for his gracious and understanding preface.

I owe special gratitude to Admiral Robert B. Carney who gave me my major opportunity to study logistics and thereafter has supported and encouraged me in all my work.

Under the wise guidance of Admiral Raymond Spruance, then President, I started my work at the Naval War College in 1947. Since then I have had the continued support of his successors. The hospitality of the Naval War College has presented a unique opportunity. Here I have found able and dedicated military leadership, distinguished civilian scholars and scientists—both resident and visiting, a selected and alert staff and student body, devoted and experienced permanent civilian staff, and a superb library. Above all it has provided the vital atmosphere of free discussion based on immense variation in personal background and the point of view of high military command. The combination is ideal for idea research.

I wish to thank the publishers listed in the bibliography for their permission to use the quotations necessary to illustrate the ideas expressed.

In addition I must acknowledge a special debt to three who through long discussions and specific suggestions have made vital contributions to my work: Rear Admiral Robbins, Dr. Rosinski, and Rear Admiral Bates.

Rear Admiral Thomas H. Robbins, Jr., USN, while President of the Naval War College and subsequently, gave me unstintingly of his time and experience in criticising many of my early "working" papers. His wide experience in naval and joint planning at high levels gave him a unique understanding of what I was attempting to explore. He gave me every positive help and encouragement in my studies at the Naval War College. Finally, he read my manuscript with great care, pointing out important elements of possible misinterpretation.

Doctor Herbert Rosinski has given freely of his vast historical knowledge and his special insight. His expositions of the need for and the nature of comprehensive theory have illuminated my whole study of war, of strategy, and of logistics.

I have tested many of the ideas in this book against the stubborn but friendly skepticism of Rear Admiral Richard W. Bates, USN, Retired, whose own battle analyses are a monument to scholarly rigor and historical integrity.

Rear Admiral Bern Anderson, USN, Retired, has drawn my attention to pertinent facets of his own research and has made many helpful suggestions.

I am thankful for the continued, essential support of the Office of Naval Research, especially Dr. Fred D. Rigby, and to Dr. William H. Marlow of The George Washington University Logistics Research Project and his predecessors Doctors C. H. Tompkins, E. M. Cannon, and Max Woodbury.

I am indebted to Mrs. Lucille Rotchford of the library staff of the Naval War College for experienced editorial advice and for her invaluable aid in preparing the index.

Finally, I offer my sincere thanks to my secretary, Mrs. Erma King, for her cheerful competence and patience shown not only in handling all dictation and repeated typing of the manuscript, but also in bringing intelligent order out of the chaos of my rough notes.

H.E.E.

PART I

BASIC CONSIDERATIONS

Chapter 1

The Background

The wars of peoples will be more terrible than those of kings.[1]

—WINSTON CHURCHILL

Military Background

In Washington on 13 March 1942 Major General Dwight D. Eisenhower, head of the Operations Division of the War Department, made a notation relative to his attempts to furnish logistic support to the American forces in the Philippines: "For many weeks—it seems years—I have been searching everywhere to find any feasible way of giving real help to the P.I. . . . . I'll go on trying, but daily the situation grows more desperate." [2]

On 9 April 1942 the American forces on Bataan surrendered: "The battle for Bataan was ended. . . . . The men who had survived the long ordeal could feel justly proud of their accomplishment. For three months they had held off the Japanese, only to be overwhelmed by disease and starvation." [3]

On 6 May 1942 when General Wainwright on Corregidor unconditionally surrendered all forces in the Philippines, his only consolation was a message from the President of the United States:

[1] Winston Churchill, speech in House on Army Estimates, 1901. *Maxims and Reflections,* Houghton Mifflin, New York, 1949.

[2] Richard M. Leighton and Robert W. Coakley, *Global Logistics and Strategy 1940-1943,* Office of the Chief of Military History, Department of the Army, Washington, D.C. 1955, p. 172.

[3] Louis Morton, *The Fall of the Philippines.* Office of the Chief of Military History, Department of the Army, Washington, D.C. 1953, p. 467.

1

In spite of all the handicaps of complete isolation, lack
of food and ammunition you have given the world a shining
example of patriotic fortitude and self sacrifice.[4]

In early September 1944 the immense forces of General
Dwight D. Eisenhower, Supreme Commander Allied Expeditionary Forces, after brilliantly exploiting the tactical victories of
the Falaise Pocket from August 10th to 22d, seemed on the
verge of driving through to victory in Germany.

By the end of September this offensive under Generals Bradley and Patton, an offensive which if successful might have
changed the whole post-war political situation in Europe, was
halted by lack of gasoline and ammunition. "For the next two
months supply limitations were to dominate operational plans
and the allies were now to learn the real meaning of the tyranny
of logistics." [5]

On 1 May 1945 at 3:30 p. m. Adolph Hitler, his armies
crushed by allied forces supported by the industrial might of
the United States, shot himself in his Berlin bunker. On Monday,
7 May, Germany surrendered unconditionally. At four o'clock
on the morning of 22 June 1945 on Hill 89 of Mabumi, General
Ushijima the Commander of the Japanese Forces on Okinawa,
committed suicide and the last organized resistance of the Japanese Army in the Pacific Campaign ended. General Ushijima
had been cut off from support for months; his fortifications had
been smashed by air, sea, and land bombardment; his positions
were overrun; and many of his troops had been destroyed in
bitter close-in fighting by joint forces which employed enormous
quantities of new weapons brought 6000 miles across the Pacific.

During the summer of 1945 the U.S. Army Air Force
mounted a devastating bombardment of Japan from great advanced bases built with incredible speed by massive mobile
engineering forces.

The bases were captured by the assaults of amphibious forces
whose power and speed were made possible by novel logistic

---

[4] Morton, *op cit*, p. 572.

[5] R. G. Ruppenthal, *Logistical Support of the Armies*, Office of the Chief
of Military History, Department of the Army, Washington, D.C. 1953, p.
583.

techniques. The amphibious operations were made possible by protection of naval striking and covering forces which were maintained in the combat zone by versatile and mobile logistic support.

All the while the strangulation of Japan's logistic capability was accomplished by the great naval forces, submarine and air, whose sustained operations were wholly dependent upon naval advanced bases, the mobile floating bases, and the underway replenishment forces. Under this pressure Japan indirectly sought peace before the atomic bomb brought on the final surrender in Tokyo Bay on 2 September 1945.

Thus, the United States Forces, although beaten in 1942, and thwarted in 1944, finally triumphed in 1945 in a series of campaigns which emphasized the vital influence of logistics in modern war.

After this dramatic evidence of the dominant influence of logistics in World War II it is necessary that we look ahead and ask how the recent tremendous burst of technological progress will in the future affect the nature, conduct, and influence of logistics.

In recent years, in the fascinated contemplation of the power of new weapons, many persons have concluded that no protection other than that of the hydrogen bomb was necessary to our security. However, the thought that we could place our sole dependence on the security of thermonuclear weapons was abandoned in the mid-fifties in a series of statements by authoritative government officials. A representative example of these is:

> The protection of the free world absolutely demands that two dangers be avoided. One danger is the so-called "war of survival," waged with the immense new thermonuclear weapons. . . .
> However, this heavy emphasis on megaton bombs has itself created the second danger, namely, the possibility of piecemeal defeat at the hands of international Communism. . . .
> Sudden destruction or slow defeat—both of these alternatives must be ruled out with all the certainty that human prudence can achieve. . . . The problem is to find the

path of policy that will lead us between these dreadful alternatives.[6]

The dilemmas posed by these developments cannot be resolved by casual assumptions or superficial guesses. Instead the situation calls for an examination of the fundamental nature and structure of modern war.

Political-Economic Factors

Since the outbreak of World War II in 1939 the problems of national security and of national defense have been of increasing importance to the American people. But during the war itself we were all too occupied with immediate problems of winning the war to think deeply about either the past or the distant future. With the surrender of Japan in September 1945 we as a nation sought the earliest possible return to what was hoped to be a normal condition of peace. In the first six months thereafter, the sense of recent victory, possession of the secret of atomic energy, and the formation of the United Nations, produced such a feeling of security that headlong demobilization soon wrecked the greatest military force in world history.

However, in 1946 and 1947, in spite of a general atmosphere of doubt and confusion, a better understanding of reality began to develop. The confusion and doubt arose from a variety of emerging factors such as: political contention and economic readjustment in the United States; the evidence of Russian intransigence; the Communist drive in Asia; the development of nationalism in Asia, Africa, and the Middle East; the problems of relief, rehabilitation, and reconstruction in Europe and Asia; the resettlement of refugees; the political reconstruction in Eastern Europe; the readjustment of the French colonial system; the development of aggressive Zionism; and the controversies relative to the reorganization of the U.S. Armed Forces. The beginning of a better understanding was seen in the writings of our more discerning commentators and scholars, in the vision of many of our political leaders, and in the reorganization and revision of our systems of high level military education. The

---

[6] Thomas E. Murray, Member of the Atomic Energy Commission, "Reliance on H-Bomb and Its Dangers," *LIFE*, May 1957, p. 181.

essence of this improved understanding was the increasing recognition that all the aforementioned confusing factors were interrelated. In other words, the political, economic, and military elements of our national security began to be seen as a whole. At the same time it became apparent to some that the relatively obscure subject, "logistics," provided a vital link between economic and military affairs. Duncan Ballantine expressed this when he wrote: "As the link between the war front and the home front the logistic process is at once the military element in the nation's economy and the economic element in its military operations." [7]

As a result of this post-war thinking, the subject of logistics became an important part of military education.

In and after 1947 world affairs began to move more rapidly and as the nature of the world conflict became more evident we saw the Truman Doctrine, the Marshall Plan, the seizure of Czechoslovakia, the Berlin blockade, the Communist conquest of China, the North Atlantic Treaty, and the Mutual Defense Assistance Act.

With the unfolding of the full nature and extent of Communist expansion and infiltration, the Korean War, and the subsequent development of the NATO defense organization and forces; the development of the hydrogen bomb; and the great increase of speed, range, and destructiveness of modern weapons; the public became very much aware of the vital importance of our military policy, organization, and commitments.

Under a military reorganization of 1953 the civilian influence in the Department of Defense was heightened by increasing the number of subordinate secretaries. At the same time President Eisenhower increased the use of the National Security Council. This, in turn, emphasized the need for a greater civilian preparation for these responsible duties; and, as a result, various universities established special courses and conferences on national security and defense.

All this while it became more and more apparent that defense

---

[7] Duncan S. Ballantine, *U. S. Naval Logistics in the Second World War.* Princeton University Press, Princeton, N.J. 1947, p. 3.

costs were the major factor in determining national taxes. Over the years as the relations between security and economics became increasingly apparent, sharp differences of opinion as to organization, strategy, and weapons control and employment developed. In particular, in 1956 and 1957 the Symington senatorial hearing on airpower [8] with its minority dissent and other articles and discussions, [9, 10] brought out many implications of thermonuclear war and focused public attention on the nature of the dilemmas our defense planners faced.

In the same period the turmoil within the Soviet satellites, the Suez Mid-East crisis, and the successful launchings of "sputnik" satellites, cast doubt on many previous assumptions as to the Soviet situation, as to the position of the United Nations, and as to the effectiveness of our systems of alliances and bases.

The Influence of the Industrial Revolution

The last fifteen years have seen the climax of one revolution in the conduct of war and the rapid development of another. This change in war was a reflection of the changes within our society and in turn the influence of the change in war upon that society. It is a regenerative, dynamic process of change and development.

This principle can be illustrated by certain examples. In the late 18th century the industrial revolution, whose roots lay in the social, political, and economic developments of the 16th and 17th centuries, began to exert its influence on war.[11]

By 1860 the railroad, the steamship, and improved firearms were the most obvious military fruits of the large-scale, organized use of coal, iron, and industrial machinery which characterized the first phase of the revolution. These new products had

---

[8] *Air Power—Report of Sub-Committee on the Air Force,* 85th Congress, 1st Session, Senate Document No. 29, February 20, 1957.

[9] James E. King, Jr., "Nuclear Plenty and Limited War," *Foreign Affairs,* January 1957.

[10] Liddell Hart, "The Defense of Europe," *New York Tribune,* 19-21 March 1957.

[11] A penetrating analysis of these developments is found in a pamphlet, "The Evolution of the Conduct of War and of Strategic Thinking," prepared by Dr. Herbert Rosinski for the Naval War College in 1955. It will be included in a work he is preparing for The Twentieth Century Fund.

a direct effect on the American Civil War and on the Franco-Prussian War. From about 1875 to 1910 the more highly organized scientific exploitation of natural resources brought into being the great electric and chemical industries, and the internal combustion engine. These, with the concurrent growth of large industrial organizations, formed the industrial background for the conduct of World War I. Aeronautics, while receiving its initial tests in this war, had little effect on its outcome.

In World War II we saw a climax to the pre-nuclear phase of the scientific industrial revolution. In this war the mass use of the internal combustion engine, of aeronautics and electronics, and the advancements in chemical explosives provided weapons and equipments of tremendous range, speed, and power. Engineering refinements, while giving improved performance characteristics, also produced equipment of great complexity which could be supported only by a great number and variety of spare parts. Among other results were a great increase in the volume of supply and transportation, an increase in centralization of authority, and an enormous increase in the volume of communications.

An illustration of the magnitude and speed of the changes of the last two thousand years is suggested in the estimate of the cost of producing a fatal enemy casualty: in 54 B.C. Julius Caesar spent about seventy-five cents per man killed, in 1800 Napoleon spent about three thousand dollars, in World War I we spent about twenty-one thousand dollars, and in World War II about two hundred thousand dollars.

Today we are in the electronic nuclear revolution. Nuclear power and electronically guided missiles with thermonuclear warheads are forcing us to make a rigorous reexamination of our national security policies and positions. In this second revolution we can see all the effects of the previous basic industrial revolution and even more. Possible war destruction has passed beyond calculable limits, the civil population of all nations has become a vulnerable target, and the cumulative effects of new weapons on the human race and on civilization are matters of very deep concern,

As a direct result of these two revolutions, nations have found that the entire country, the entire population, and the entire economy are involved in their national security and national defense.

Since 1950 the United States has undertaken extraordinary politico-military commitments to defend our western way of life against Communist aggression. In some instances these involve only economic assistance, in others military aid, and in others the stationing of large American forces on overseas bases; such as Morocco, Germany, and England. For example, in April 1957 the Secretary of State stated that in exercising the inherent right of collective self defense, "the United States has made collective defense treaties with forty-two other nations." [12] The question arises as to how we can meet these overseas commitments and at the same time provide for our own unilateral defense without excessive inflation and ultimate economic disaster.

The 1958 budget as submitted by the President on 16 January 1957 called for budget expenditures in fiscal 1958 of 71.8 billion dollars of which 45.3 billion was for "Protection and Collective Security" including 1.8 billion for military aid for our allies. There seems to be no reason to expect any significant reduction in this budget in the near future. In fact, the need for and the cost of high-performance, automatic, military equipment seems to be growing. Even with this enormous sum allocated to defense, some persons question the adequacy of the security obtained thereby.

In spite of the natural desire to improve our security, however, some economists believe that a higher rate of military spending would jeopardize our economic stability.

The recent action of the British in drastically revising their concepts of national defense because of their economic limitations is another striking illustration of the emergent fact that *economics is the limiting factor in the development of a military defense system.*

This being the case, all responsible officials must seek to im-

---

[12] Secretary Dulles' Address to the Associated Press, 22 April 1957.

prove our national defense by increasing the effectiveness with which the nation's limited resources are used.

The Point of View

In the face of the modern facts of military economics, and with the obvious need for our military forces to be able to deal effectively with a variety of situations, it is important to examine the basic fundamentals which underlie and even determine policy, strategy, and logistics. Such examination is of interest not only to the military but also to the many civilians who in government and privately sponsored research projects are undertaking defense studies.

While many technical problems must be dealt with in logistics, there is a distinction between the logistic point of view and the technical point of view. The logistic point of view deals chiefly with questions which involve or cut across a *variety* of technical specialties whereas the technical point of view tends to concentrate on the perfection of *one* special field. The logistic viewpoint is essentially that of the commander.

In order to emphasize and to clarify both the scope of the direction of logistic affairs, and the approach to a study of logistics, this book stresses the problem of *command*. Correct perspective can be maintained only through viewing the great mass of detail in logistics from the point of view of the man who must coordinate a variety of technical functions in the achievement of a higher purpose. The *command point of view is that logistics itself has no purpose other than to create and to support combat forces which are responsive to the needs of command.*

The fact that in the study of the theory of war a variety of activities and functions are grouped together under the broad title of "logistics" does not necessarily mean that all of these functions should be grouped under "the logistic division" or any similar single title in fleet, army, theater or service organization, or in the administration or operation of military services or forces. There is no magic in the word "logistics." As a matter of fact the word "logistics" can even vanish from the military vocabulary without in any way altering the nature of war or the manner in which the various factors, which in toto make up the "means of war," operate in relation to strategy, to organization and to combat effectiveness. "Logistics" is merely a convenient term used to encompass the problem of controlling all the "means of war" as appropriate at various levels of command.

Throughout this work certain themes recur, for it is only by examination and reexamination from different aspects, that their full implications to warfare can be developed. These themes are—

(1) Modern war covers an entire spectrum of human conflict.

(2) Strategy should be considered as the comprehensive direction of power for the purpose of exercising control of a field of action in order to attain objectives.[13]

(3) Logistics is the bridge between our national economy and the actual operations of our combat forces in the field.

(4) Unless restrained by wise, adequate, and timely planning, logistic installations and operations tend to snowball out of all proportion to the true needs of combat support.

(5) Sound logistics forms the foundation for the development of strategic flexibility and mobility. If such flexibility is to be exercised and exploited, military command must have adequate control of its logistic support.

(6) The understanding of the nature and degree of logistic control which command should exercise is essential to the attainment of combat effectiveness.

This treatment of logistics, stressing the viewpoint of command, is in no sense a substitute for the detailed publications of the armed forces. Instead the attempt is made to stress those

---

[13] This concept of strategy is derived from a brief paper, "New Thoughts on Strategy" written by Dr. Herbert Rosinski for the President of the Naval War College in September 1955.

fundamental relationships and principles which will endure regardless of the administrative decisions, operational procedures, and terminology which are in effect today. These official procedures and terms can be changed by a simple executive order. On the other hand, fundamental cause and effect relations will continue to operate regardless of how executive terminology and procedures change.

And, finally, as Mahan said:

> Whether this opinion of one man is right or wrong, however, is a very small matter compared with the desirability of officers generally considering these subjects on proper lines of thought, and with proper instruments of expression; that is, with correct principles and correct phraseology.[14]

[14] Mahan, *Naval Strategy,* Little, Brown and Company, Boston, 1911, p. 384.

Chapter 2

The Nature and Structure of War

To fasten attention upon one species of war to the exclusion of the great variety of likely conflict situations is to confuse the part with the whole.[1]

—ROBERT STRAUSZ-HUPE

The events of the last decade have forced a reappraisal of those concepts of war which have been commonly held by the majority of our people. A generation ago it was generally considered that war was a specialized form of brutal formal contest in which nations or groups of nations frequently engaged after failing to solve differences by negotiation. It was considered that the usual state of man was that of peace.

The Nature of War

Now we see it somewhat differently. The usual state of man —and of nations—involves competition, and in an expanding world it involves a struggle for existence and hence a conflict of interests. Thus we see a continuing conflict between peoples and between nations, and we see that there is no real peace in our generation because the conflict is unceasing. It is a conflict which at all times involves violence; and the violence may be political, economic, military, or para-military. The conflict is simultaneously formal and informal, it is ideological and physical, and it is within nations as well as among nations. War can be understood only as it is seen in the context of the unending conflict of which it is a part; it can be understood as merely an accentuation or increase in the degree and scope of the violence of the conflict.

---

[1] Robert Strausz-Hupe, "Protracted Conflict: A New Look at Communist Strategy," ORBIS—Vol. II, Spring 1958, Number 1—University of Pennsylvania.

The Spectrum of Conflict

While complex human relations cannot be completely or precisely defined or delimited, figure 1, "The Spectrum of Conflict," roughly illustrates the major factors and features of international relations—including war—in modern times.

CONTROLLABLE — UNCONTROLLABLE

PEACEFUL INTERNATIONAL COMPETITION SWEETNESS & LIGHT	ECONOMIC COMPETITION PLUS TARIFFS	TRADE QUOTAS	CURRENCY RESTRICTIONS & DEVALUATIONS	POLITICAL CONCESSIONS FOR TRADE PRIVILEGES	DUMPING SURPLUS	POLITICAL SABOTAGE PROPAGANDA. BOYCOTTS	SUBVERSIVE INFILTRATION ARRESTS DEPORTATION	SEIZURES OF SHIPS & CARGOES. BLOCKADES. BORDER INCIDENTS VIOLATIONS & REPRISALS MATERIAL SABOTAGE	RIOTS & REVOLUTON FOMENTED FROM OUTSIDE	SEIZURE OF TERRITORY PARTIAL MOBILIZATION	AIR & NAVAL BOMBARDMENT FULL MOBILIZATION	SUBMARINE SINKINGS EXPANSION OF SCOPE & AREA	EXPANSION OF OBJECTIVES	USE OF T.N. WEAPONS GAS & BACTERIA WAR

PEACE — COLD WAR — TECHNICAL ONLY — HOT WAR

MANY LIMITATIONS — NO LIMITS

ECONOMIC WAR

ABSOLUTE PEACE	RELATIVE PEACE	INCREASING TENSION	LIMITED WAR	UNLIMITED TOTAL WAR

AS TENSION INCREASES, MORE WEAPONS AND TOOLS OF CONFLICT ARE USED. IN EACH CASE AS MORE WEAPONS COME INTO PLAY THE USE OF THE OLDER WEAPONS CONTINUES. THUS, THERE IS A CUMULATIVE INVOLVEMENT WHICH EVENTUALLY MAY GET OUT OF CONTROL.

Figure 1. The Spectrum of Conflict

Showing major features, characteristics and areas of overlap

Further, the term "war" itself is subject to various interpretations. "War" is not necessarily nor inevitably "total." Thus, if we are to understand war we must understand the manner in which wars may be limited. Wars can be limited as to:

The objectives sought by the participants;

The scope, both by the geographic area and by the nations involved;

The degree of effort exerted;

The weapons used.

All wars that we have seen in recent generations have been limited wars. Some of these limitations have been those of discretion, others have been limitations of tacit mutual consent, and others have been those of circumstances.

World War I in general was a war of unlimited weapons, but of limited scope, and limited objectives, and for some participants, limited effort.

World War II was almost unlimited in scope and effort but was limited as to weapons used. Its objectives were cloudy but in many respects do not seem to have been consciously limited.

The Korean conflict was a war of limited objectives, limited scope, limited weapons, and except for North and South Korea, limited effort.

The Hungarian revolt of 1956 is an example of a limited violent internal conflict with the one-sided use of external overt armed forces.

The Suez and other Mid-East and Far-East crises of 1956-58 illustrate many aspects of limitations within the spectrum of conflict, particularly the way in which degrees of violence and use of the tools of conflict can change as various forces, both tangible and intangible, come into play.

An examination of this spectrum of conflict in the light of the events of the last ten years makes it become increasingly evident that the United States must be *prepared* to use military force effectively throughout the entire spectrum. Also consideration of the nature and tools of modern conflict makes it further evident that this force must be *used in harmony* with the other elements of power. We must be prepared for all types of conflict including wars, such as brush-fire, conventional, broken-back, or unrestricted thermonuclear wars. The basic problem facing the nation in this era of conflict is to determine how to utilize the various elements of national power to support the national interest and to accomplish the national objectives.

The Elements of Power

From the broadest point of view the elements of power which are used in this conflict can be considered as: political, economic, psychological, and military. Each element is greatly influenced by modern science and technology. All these elements must be interwoven if we are to have a single pattern of action and policy.

The Tools of Conflict

In specific terms the tools of conflict may be considered as being: overt armed forces, covert armed forces, subversion, sabotage, economic action and pressure, political pressure, ideology, propaganda, terrorism, mental torture, and physical torture. There is, also, much intermixing and overlapping in using these tools. Both their actual use and the threat of their use, have been employed deliberately to support the political objectives of various governments, in accordance with the moral values of those governments.

In summary, the nature of war has changed and is still changing. The nature of war is developing to encompass more and more areas of human relations, activities of people, elements of power, and tools of conflict.

The Structure of War and the Nature of Command

The foregoing brief discussion of the nature of war points to the need of an examination of the structure of war in order to increase the nation's capability of success in all phases of the spectrum of conflict. It is obvious that a nation's efforts must be capably directed, and that this control provide timely harmony among the actions of all the nation's elements of power.

Before the industrial revolution national "command" was frequently exercised by one individual or by a very small group.

Such individual exercise of command in war probably reached its peak in the person of Napoleon. He held within the grasp of his own mind and authority the national political decisions, the formation and equipping of his armies, the strategic disposition of his forces, the details of their logistical support and, finally, the exercise of tactical command in battle.

> When Napoleon went to the front, his secretaries went with him, and his habits of work. In the field, wherever he might be, the blue and white tent was pitched, and its two compartments arranged—one, the study, with its folding table and chairs, the other the bedroom. The papers and

books were unpacked, the maps spread out; and, the moment fighting was over, dictation would begin. However far he was from Paris, the leather portfolios marked "Despatches for the Emperor" must come and go every day, outstripping the fastest mail. Again, whether Napoleon travels in the yellow *voiture de poste,* or in the green-upholstered *berline,* Berthier is sure to be there; and as they jolt along, the Emperor goes through his order-books and muster-rolls, makes his decisions, and dictates his commands. At the first stopping-place, day or night, and the first moment of leisure, Berthier writes them out from his notes, and sends them off, with matchless method and accuracy.[2]

But, as the industrial revolution took effect and war became more complex, the exercise of executive authority and responsibility has become more complex. As has been pointed out, it is essential that all elements of national security policy and action be integrated. As recently stated:

The organization for national security which makes and carries out these policies may very well be the key to survival. That organization must include to some extent Congress and the public. But the judgments of place, time, and degree require so much specialized knowledge that the initial formulation of policy and its implementation must be the responsibility of the executive branch.[3]

Thus, at the national level, because of the enormous growth of the executive functions, there has been in effect a transfer of authority from an individual to an organization. This transfer of executive authority or command from an individual to an organization creates many difficult and exasperating problems of authority and responsibility.

Yet in spite of the organizational changes which have taken place, it is still necessary to preserve a concept of "command" as such, even though it cannot always be literally applied in the classic, or "Napoleonic" sense. The concept of command demands a clear view of the situation, of the objective, of the

---

[2] J. M. Thompson, *Napoleon Self-Revealed.* Houghton Mifflin Company, Boston and New York: 1934, p. viii.

[3] Timothy W. Stanley, *American Defense and National Security,* Public Affairs Press, Washington, D.C. pp. 3-7. An excellent statement and discussion of this aspect of political-military relation.

elements of power which are being brought into play and of the distribution and capabilities of forces. Within the national command organization there must be a variety of areas where individuals of special competence are charged with responsibility for specific action.

While in practice there may be departures from the ideal that authority and responsibility must always be joined, the basic actions which must be accomplished will be the same regardless of the organization.

Since both civil and military *action* must be integrated or blended in modern conflict, civil and military *authority* must also be blended in varying degrees throughout the over-all organization. In this blending a certain amount of overlap is both inevitable and desirable for flexibility's sake.

The various general areas of authority and responsibility, or factors, in war are all interrelated and there is so much overlap that exact definitions are not practicable. For the purpose of this discussion it should suffice to describe them simply as political, economic, geographic, military, psychological, scientific, and technological.

If we examine the military factors we find that they can best be described in the following abstract terms as: strategy, logistics, tactics, intelligence, and communications. These military factors grow out of and are related to the general factors in a manner too complex for ready description. However, insofar as it is possible to make a graphic representation of abstractions, the two groups of factors seem to be related as shown in figure 2. Other than to take cognizance of their existence as matters of importance in the detailed study of war, no attempt will be made to establish the relationship of such matters as weather and climate, cultural patterns, sociology, national objectives, and national policy.

To refer again to the interrelationship of the factors going to make up the structure of war, experience has proved that the greatest area of blending and overlap of authority and responsibility lies in the field of logistics. Logistics is the bridge between the national economy and the combat forces, and logistics thus operates as "military economics" in the fullest sense of the word. Therefore, logistics must be seen from two viewpoints.

Logistics has its roots in the national economy. In this area it is dominated by civilian influences and by civilian authority. In this area the major criterion of logistics is production efficiency. On the other hand, the end product of logistics lies in the operations of combat forces. There logistics is dominated by military influence and by military authority. In this area the

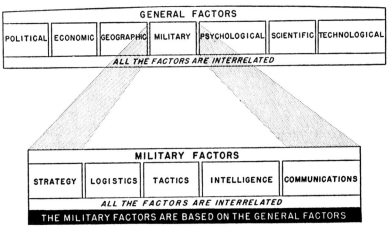

Figure 2. The Structure of War

major criterion of logistics is its effectiveness in creating and sustaining combat forces in action against an enemy. Because logistics is thus under two dominant influences, it is obvious that circumstances may arise under which the civilian criterion and the military criterion are in harmony—or at times, they are opposed.

This is the root of many of the existing differences of opinion as to national defense organization: The criteria of judgment used by civilian executives are frequently different from the criteria used by the military commanders.

If these matters are to be harmoniously managed and adjusted in the interests of improved over-all national security, both the civilian executive and the military commander, whose interests and responsibilities will invariably overlap, must reach mutual understanding. To this end a more detailed discussion of strategic-logistic-tactical relations is appropriate.

The literature of war is vast and many of the books on strategy and tactics are exhaustive. However, while there are many detailed definitions of strategy, logistics, and tactics, none of them shows adequately and briefly the relations that exist among these major military categories of thought and study. Therefore, the following ideas are submitted:

> Strategy deals with the determination of objectives and the broad methods for their attainment;
> Logistics deals with the creation and sustained support of weapons and combat forces;
> Tactics deals with the specific employment of weapons and forces toward the attainment of the objectives of strategy.
> Or, stated somewhat more simply: Strategy and tactics provide the scheme for the conduct of military operations; logistics provides the means therefor.

In considering these major military factors in war we can visualize them as being three intersecting disks (see figure 3).

Intelligence sheds light on the situation which confronts the commander. Communications transmits information to the commander and transmits his decisions to his subordinates.

All problems and situations in war are blends of strategic-logistical and tactical elements and considerations; and they are affected in varying degree by the non-military elements and factors involved. No two problems or situations will have precisely the same blend.

In the field of military planning, for instance, it has been found that at the highest level of military thinking it is not always possible nor desirable to distinguish between what is strategic and what is logistic. The two disks may have merged.

In any event, whenever a commander is faced with a military problem, he should not become so absorbed in one aspect of the problem—whether strategic, logistical, or tactical—that he considers it without reference as to how it affects and how it is affected by other elements. This is true both of the military direction at national headquarters, and equally so of the commander charged with the actual conduct of military action. He should

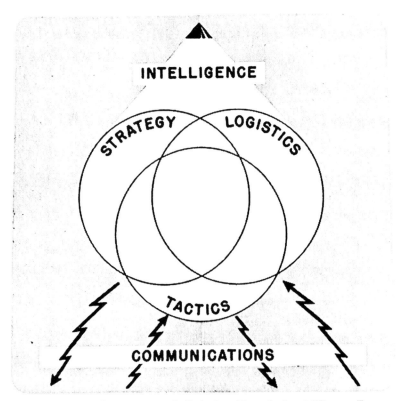

Figure 3. The Structure and Relationship of the Military Factors in War

In all war situations, the actions and decisions of command, whatever the level, are based upon a blend of strategical, logistical, and tactical considerations.

retain cognizance and authority throughout the entire range of his responsibilities. He should avoid the common tendency of some commanders to concern themselves almost entirely with so-called "operational" matters (either strategic or tactical) at the expense of concern over those logistical matters which form the very basis for "operations." In other words, once a commander thinks of the strategic, logistical, and tactical elements as individual or isolated matters he has lost his perspective.

The foregoing brief observations on the structure of war in modern times suggest the complexity of organization required to give successful direction to the nation's effort, and the close-knit interrelations among the elements of the nation's war potential which must be recognized and maintained by the various echelons of command.

Fundamental Concepts

This introduction to the nature and structure of war will now be dealt with in more detail. A statement and further discussion of some fundamental ideas and concepts follow, and there will be presented many of these same general ideas in somewhat different terms.

The *science of war* is the knowledge of the structure and elements of war and the relationships and interacting forces which exist among these elements.

The *art of war* can be considered as the practical application of this knowledge toward the attainment of the objectives of the commander or of the nation.

Strategy may be described as the comprehensive direction of power toward the attainment of broad objectives or aims. This includes the selection and time-phasing of that minimum of specific objectives whose collective attainment will accomplish the broad aim. Dr. Herbert Rosinski says:

> This idea requires the recognition that there is much more to strategy than mere direction of action. It is a type of direction which takes into account the multitude of possible enemy counteractions and thus it becomes a means of control. It is the element of control which is the essence of strategy, control being the element which differentiates true strategic action from a haphazard series of improvisations.[4]

Thus, strategy is primarily concerned with objectives. These

---

[4] Dr. Herbert Rosinski, "New Thoughts on Strategy." This concept was developed in a brief paper on strategy for the President of the Naval War College in September 1955.

objectives provide the ultimate reason or purpose for all other military activity and become the inspiration of command.

Tactics may be considered as the immediate direction of power toward the attainment of the specific objectives of strategy. This entails the employment of specific forces, weapons, and techniques.

Tactical activities involve the coordination and direction of technical or functional activities which deal with the employment of combat forces and weapons.

Logistics is the provision of the physical means by which power is exercised by, organized forces. In military terms, it is the creation and sustained support of combat forces and weapons. Its objective is maximum sustained combat effectiveness.

Logistical activities involve the *direction and coordination* of those technical or functional activities which in summation create or support the military forces.

The study of war, since it includes these related affairs, must of necessity revolve around the study of command. Or, putting it in broader terms, the study of conflict must revolve around the study of the executive organization which manages and directs the action in the conflict.

Admiral R. B. Carney brought these concepts into sharp focus when he said: "Strategy is a plan of action best to employ resources in pursuit of aims . . . In any case great or small strategy is a matter of reconciling desires and capabilities." [5]

The thinking of *command*—that is the command point of view—focuses on the aim, the resources, and the plan of employment.

Command sees strategy in relation to tactical and logistic capabilities. Command sees logistics in its relation to strategy. Therefore, a clear understanding of strategy is essential to an understanding of "command logistics."

---

[5] Admiral R. B. Carney, USN, Address before the Executives Club of Chicago, April 23, 1954.

The Limitation of War

Before the thermonuclear revolution when a nation was contemplating the use of overt force in its conduct of foreign affairs, the range of opposing force which might be used in reaction was calculable. While mistakes in calculation or in judgment frequently led to national disaster, such disasters were usually the result of a series or a group of errors. Even so, in most cases the results while costly were endurable.

Today, in the case of major powers, this range of opposing reaction is exceeded. It extends beyond calculable limits. Thus, the use of force becomes a gamble in which the odds cannot be calculated. This situation places an extraordinary responsibility, both moral and intellectual, on the individuals dealing with national policy and strategy and with high military command.

Under today's conditions any resort to violence in the relationships between nations offers a possibility of the unwitting or unintentional extension of that violence to the extreme limit of a war unlimited in objectives, in scope, in weapons, and in effort. The possibility that any particular resort to violence will bring such a war is beyond calculation. Of course, certain types or degrees of violence will be obviously more likely than others to bring unlimited expansion.

The growth of a general awareness of the necessity for versatility and restraint in the employment of armed forces is indicated by recent authoritative writers.

Sir John Slessor stated:

> But for as far ahead as we need trouble to look we must be able and willing, if necessary, to fight small wars—and fight them with the right weapons. To rely on "massive retaliatory power" as a panacea for all international evils would be to invite not only more wars but even bloodless defeat for the Free World in one outpost action after another.
>
> There is no earthly reason why we should be "nibbled to death" by constant and cumulative encroachments on the periphery of the Free World, but if we are, then we can blame, not our unwillingness to blow up every small local war into World War III, but a refusal to pay the very un-

welcome but relatively inexpensive premium of countering limited aggression by limited means . . .[6]

At the same time Hanson Baldwin wrote:

We must be capable of fighting all-out nuclear war, a limited nuclear war, a major nonnuclear war, small-scale brush wars. But, if we want to survive, we shall avoid, like death, confining our capabilities to any one weapon, one system. We must be able to win without invoking A-weapons; if we cannot our fate is sealed.[7]

In a provocative article in *Foreign Affairs,* James E. King, Jr. points out the difficulty of applying limits to the use of nuclear weapons in that nuclear limits are neither identifiable nor stable. He goes on to conclude that:

The prospect is disturbing, particularly to those who have thought that we could depend upon our nuclear advantages. It was not in the cards that we should owe our security to divine favor. The future counsels prudence, but not faintheartedness. While using every opportunity to reduce international tensions and to extend the reign of order among nations, we must work positively for the limitation of war. To this end we must exert ourselves to the utmost in the technological competition to prevent the balance of advantage from shifting to the other side, and we must make it quite clear that we are prepared to risk annihilation itself to prevent Communist conquest by default, either by threat of nuclear terror or by conventional arms under cover of the nuclear ban. We must, in short, guarantee that only effectively limited hostilities can be rationally undertaken.

Moreover, we must be prepared to fight limited actions ourselves. Otherwise we shall have made no advance beyond "massive retaliation," which tied our hands in conflicts involving less than our survival. And we must be prepared to lose limited actions. No limitations could survive our disposition to elevate every conflict in which our interests are affected to the level of total conflict with survival at stake.

Armed conflict can be limited only if aimed at limited objectives and fought with limited means. If we or our

[6] Sir John Slessor, *The Great Deterrent and Its Limitations.* Bulletin of the Atomic Scientists, Volume XII, Number 5, May 1956.

[7] Hanson W. Baldwin, *The New Face of War.* Bulletin of the Atomic Scientists, Volume XII, Number 5, May 1956.

enemy relax the limits on either objectives or means, survival *will* be at stake, whether the issue is worth it or not. But saying that we must be prepared to lose does not mean that we shall lose, particularly in the long run. Our strengths are many, not least the fact that our revolution offers a better promise to mankind than the Communist alternative.[8]

This, of course, reaches to the heart of strategy—the objective.

Strategy, Objectives, and Control

It is not sufficient merely to state objectives—objectives must be analyzed. An essential element in the analysis of national and military objectives is to describe the situation or situations which will in whole or in part constitute an attainment of the objectives.

In considering the reaction of the enemy to any situation or course of action, not only must one think of how the enemy views the situation as it exists before one takes action, *but one must think of how the enemy thinking will be influenced by the action that one takes.*

Furthermore, it should be emphasized that in no case is one dealing with certainties or with calculable probabilities. For that reason it seems highly unlikely that any machine or formal process, however valuable it may be in assisting the individual to make a decision, will ever be a substitute for soul-searching, rigorous thinking on the part of the responsible individual.

In any event, the one ingredient which above all is essential to a sound decision is a sound and clear objective.

Further, the commander of whatever echelon, having derived his objective, must devise means for attaining that objective. His decision will thus result in a strategy: a plan of action as to how best to employ his means toward his objective. In the development of his strategy he will exercise *comprehensive* (as opposed to specialized) *direction* over the means available to him. Further, his objective will inevitably involve a greater or lesser degree of *control* within a given field of action.

[8] James E. King, Jr., "Nuclear Plenty and Limited War." *Foreign Affairs,* January 1957, pp 255-256.

This concept establishes the primacy of strategy in the conduct of national affairs, as opposed to the emphasis on destruction which is implicit in any weapon strategy. This thought of course leads back to "objectives." The concentration of thought on "control" naturally leads to a re-examination and better understanding of the objectives whose attainment is the purpose of the attempt to exercise control. On the other hand, a weapons strategy tends to equate "control" with "destruction," and tends to obscure the "objective" completely.

Another important aspect is that the concept of continuing control prepares the mind for shifting its emphasis from weapon to weapon or from tool to tool in accordance with a changing situation or with the changing capabilities and use or application of the weapons or weapon systems involved. Thus, the intellectual concept of strategy as involving "comprehensive control" naturally leads to the intellectual concept of flexibility.

Since strategy must be selective in order to achieve economy of force, concentrated attention is required to those minimum key lines of action or key positions from which the entire field can be positively controlled.[9] In this determination the entire spectrum of human conflict must be examined and the various tools and weapons of conflict evaluated as to their suitability and coordination in achieving the necessary control. Thus, "war planning" becomes an essential part, but only a part, of "conflict planning."

We should not expect to attain absolute control in *all* the various areas of action. In other words, we live in a continuing state of risk. The degree of control, the degree of risk, and the degree of balance of forces will never be a single mathematical equation. Nevertheless, mathematical techniques and analyses can be helpful to assist professional judgment in their evaluation.

While in a work primarily devoted to logistics it is not practicable to explore all aspects of control, it is useful to indicate a few specific points for consideration.

---

[9] Dr. Herbert Rosinski, "New Thoughts on Strategy," Naval War College, Newport, R. I. September 1955.

In some areas, we will seek to influence the thinking and attitudes of man; in other areas we will seek to control their actions.

We should be able to distinguish between "control of the sea" or of a specific sea area. We must recognize the need for understanding "utilization" or "exploitation" after "control" has been established. We must think of the negative aspect of "control": that is, "to deny" or "to interdict." We should be able to control or deny either resources, or geographic areas, or both.

Summary

In summary, a series of questions arise—
What is the objective?
What to control or to deny or interdict? Why?
What is the purpose of exercising control?
Where do we wish to exercise control?
What geographic limits?
What degree of control is required?
When and for how long should control be established?
How should control be exercised?
Do we control by destruction? By seizure?
What means or forces or weapons are most suitable for control?

In some instances it will be necessary to use "destruction" as a form of control; for example, in destroying the fuel stored by an enemy force. In other instances it will be necessary to use "protection" as a form of control; for example, to prevent the destruction of one's own or friendly sources of fuel.

In many instances, because our national economy is so largely dependent on the free use of overseas resources, of shipping and of shipping facilities, "protection" will be a major purpose of our actions in war and in peace; in situations of tension, and in situations of open violence.

The many instances of the fallacy of basing one's plans primarily on enemy intentions rather than on a careful evaluation of enemy *capabilities,* supplemented by an estimate of probable intentions, further point up the necessity for flexibility. As previously stated, the train of enemy thought and action stimulated by one's own action anywhere in the spectrum of conflict cannot be predicted. As enemy reaction is noted, the forces being exerted in the various areas of action which one seeks to control must be varied. Thus it is evident that the concept of strategy as involving control requires the ability to use force and weapons with *discrimination,* as well as with precision, mobility, and flexibility.

The degree and nature of the control to be established and maintained will vary greatly according to circumstances.

In all instances the specific military objectives such as "destruction," "protection," "capture," or "interdiction" must be chosen with regard to the further effect desired as related to the objectives of higher command or higher policy.

The requirements of strategy should determine the composition and employment of forces and their associated weapons and weapons systems. That is to say, the forces to be maintained and their roles and missions should be designed to exercise appropriate control in each area in which control is required to carry out the strategy.

In terms of the responsibilities of military command this means that the military commander must be able to use military force in an appropriate manner wherever so directed by higher authority throughout the entire spectrum of conflict. Furthermore, he must be able to recognize where he is in that spectrum, and he must understand the influences which may cause the action to shift from one band of the spectrum to another. He must be able to use his military forces and weapons in such a manner that he will conform to the limitations imposed by higher authority.

In considering how such forces and weapons should be used or countered it is well to remember that so long as the basic causes of any conflict and the objectives of the contestants remain unmodified, the limitation of the use of one tool results in the increased use of the other tools. We cannot place our dependence on an absolute or ultimate weapon, for, if it causes too much destruction, it no longer can serve to attain objectives.

Finally, an examination of the nature and structure of war

must inevitably involve consideration of disarmament as a possible resolution of the causes of conflict. Historically, of course, disarmament has never produced such an effect. For the future, the chances of so doing appear *even more remote;* in fact, we now cannot place our faith in disarmament. As R. L. Meier writing in the May 1956 *Bulletin of the Atomic Scientists* has said:

> When superweapons have been mounted in hidden launching sites up to saturation levels, it appears to be no longer possible to negotiate disarmament at the nuclear level . . .
> This proposition comes as a real shock to many persons of good will. They have had a stubborn faith that somehow, by means beyond their ken, some way of spiking the atomic weapons would be found. But now we enter the irreversible phase where it appears to be even more risky to attempt such disarmament than to leave the situation the way it is . . .
> Yet there is a form of nuclear arms limitation which is due to occur. It derives from the meaning of the word "saturation." There must be a stage, not far in the future, when it no longer pays to produce more material for such weapons . . .
> Because the chances of getting into a stable stalemate were so small, scientists have hitherto concentrated their attention upon disarmament, inspection systems, and the like, which offered brighter hopes of survival, although the chances of realizing them were admittedly small. But a new age has begun. Symmetrical disarmament of nuclear weapons of sovereign powers is due to become technically impossible to supervise. Now attention must be paid to stratagems for preserving a stalemate.[10]

Obviously in such a stalemate of massive destructive power the accomplishment of even limited objectives will be a continuing problem. But, regardless of whether objectives be limited or unlimited, the civilians and military who decide upon the creation and employment of military forces must have an understanding of the interplay of strategic, logistic, and tactical factors.

---

[10] R. L. Meier, "Beyond Atomic Stalemate," *Bulletin of the Atomic Scientists,* Volume XII, No. 5, May 1956.

Chapter 3

Strategic-Logistic-Tactical Relations

But in its relation to strategy, logistics assumes the character of a dynamic force, without which the strategic conception is simply a paper plan.[1]

—COMMANDER C. THEO. VOGELGESANG, USN

The intimate relation between strategy and logistics starts with the fact that much of strategy grows out of the economic situation. Economic factors influence the objectives of strategy and they are intermixed among themselves and with strategic factors in a complex regenerative manner.

The Economic and Logistic Sources of Strategy

Many of the sources of human conflict are economic, such as:

The desire to attain or maintain a high standard of living;

The problem of support of an excess of population;

The desire to control sources of raw materials;

The development of trade routes for sources of materials and for distribution of goods;

The desire to control the focal points of world trade routes, such as Suez.

These and many other elements of economic competition have been stimulated by the industrial revolution. As shown in figure 1, "Spectrum of Conflict," this competition, originally peaceful, may intensify to a point where it becomes economic warfare. It may then combine with social and political competition to produce violent conflict. In this event both the enemy's armed forces and his economy become targets for destruction or control. His logistic system, being the bridge between his economy and his tactical operations, becomes a particularly important target.

---

[1] Commander C. Theo. Vogelgesang, USN, in his lecture at Naval War College on "Logistics—Its Bearing Upon the Art of War," published in *United States Naval Institute Proceedings*, Vol. 39, No. 1, March 1913.

In an equally interwoven manner, economic-logistic factors influence the nature of the strategy to be employed. For example, economic factors can so influence the political stability of a nation or an alliance as to force changes in both policy and strategy. The recent changes in British military policy and the accompanying reexamination of NATO defenses are clear examples of this influence.[2]

In the studies of "war potential" in our War Colleges the intermingling and relationship of these fundamental factors of national security are clearly brought out.

In making a general comment on the dependence of logistics upon strategy an American historian says:

> The major obstacle to effective logistical planning and preparations lay outside the logistical process itself and beyond the jurisdiction of the logistical agencies: specific strategic objectives could not be fixed far in advance . . . Adequate logistical preparations depended on early answers to many questions. Was the deployment of forces to be oriented primarily to one theater, or was it to be more widely dispersed? Would it take the form primarily of ferrying massive and balanced land and air forces to large overseas bases, or would it involve a high incidence of amphibious operations by relatively small, special-purpose task forces? To what extent would strategic bombardment be employed as a substitute for land campaigns against an enemy still greatly preponderant in land power? What specific operations were to be undertaken? What forces would be required? When?[3]

The history of the major high level conferences of World War II, particularly Casablanca (SYMBOL), January 1943, Cairo (SEXTANT) November 1943, and Quebec (QUADRANT and OCTAGON) August 1943 and September 1944, shows how strategy was shaped by economic-logistic capabilities; and, vice versa, how logistic planning was dependent upon strategic decisions.

For example, a British historian says:

[2] The British White Paper of April 4, 1957, as published in abridged form in the *N.Y. Times* of April 5th and subsequent widespread discussions, furnishes an apt illustration.

[3] Richard M. Leighton and Robert W. Coakley, *Global Logistics and Strategy*, 1940-1943. Office of the Chief of Military History, Department of the Army, Washington, D.C. 1955. p. 713-714.

. . . In the middle period of the war, from early in 1941 to the summer of 1943, the limits of strategy had been determined largely by the limits of production, confining the possibilities to a preliminary offensive on the fringe of enemy territory in the West, and to a series of holding operations and limited attacks in the Far East. By the autumn of 1943, that strategy, and production itself, were ready for the fuller offensive designed at Quebec; and on 26th August the Combined Planning Staff submitted a detailed report to the Combined Chiefs of Staff on the relation of means to ends.

Four main shortages threatened to limit the offensive strategy; merchant shipping, assault shipping, transport aircraft, and, in the case of the British, men. The first two were included as specific problems in the Combined Planning Staff's report at Quebec.

. . . As recently as May 1943, the highest British authorities had concentrated specifically on shipping as the most pressing limit on strategy. It was at that time, to the Prime Minister, "the measure of all our operations"; to the C.I.G.S., "the stranglehold on all our operations"; while to the First Lord of the Admiralty, it "will, and does indeed already restrict our whole offensive strategy."[4]

In general these relations between strategy and logistics follow broad patterns. First and foremost is the fundamental relationship whereby the scope and timing of strategic plans are both governed by logistic capabilities. Closely related to this is the converse whereby the composition, the balance, and the deployment of forces and the rate of their build up all are determined by a complex interrelation of strategic, logistic and tactical considerations. The question of the selection of the site for an overseas base and the timing of its build up is again a blend of strategic-logistic considerations.

There is the situation wherein a specific logistic element becomes a critical factor in the formulation of a strategic plan.

There is the situation wherein an important political position is either maintained or lost without recourse to war, by reason of the action of a logistical factor.

---

[4] John Ehrman, *Grand Strategy*. Volume V, August 1943-September 1944. Her Majesty's Stationery Office, London: 1956. pp 25, 26-27.

And, again, there is the age-old strategy of blockade, in which a critical logistic target or an entire economy is subject to the attrition of blockade.

Historical Examples

A few historical examples briefly sketched should suffice to illustrate these patterns.

SCOPE AND TIMING OF STRATEGIC PLANS.

COMPOSITION, BALANCE AND DEPLOYMENT OF FORCES. FORCE BUILD UP.

STRATEGIC OVERSEAS BASE SITE SELECTION AND BUILD UP.

CRITICAL LOGISTIC ELEMENT.

MAINTENANCE OF POLITICAL POSITION WITHOUT WAR.

STRATEGY OF BLOCKADE.

NATIONAL ECONOMICS. CRITICAL LOGISTIC TARGET.

Figure 4. Some Types of Strategic-Logistic Relationships

Logistic-Tactical Illustration

Of all these illustrations, that of Suez 1956 (figure 6) seems most striking and timely. Not only does it represent a typical instance of modern human conflict but it is also a splendid illustration of strategic-logistic interdependence.

Many persons agree that from the political and psychological point of view an immediate powerful military reaction to Nasser's seizure of the Suez Canal in July 1956 might have received strong international support. The fact remains, however, that the British naval and ground forces and their air transport had reached such a state of deterioration by the summer of 1956 that they did not have the capability for concerted fast action.

EVENT:	RESULT:	ILLUSTRATES:
Glorious First of June 1794 Sea Battle Howe vs. Villaret	Chesapeake food convoy arrived. French Revolution survived.	Strategy of blockade. [5, 6] vs. national economics.
U.S. Submarine Campaign vs. Japan	Destroyed Japan's oil transport. Crippled fleet and air force.	Strategy of blockade and critical logistic target.
China Revolution 1947-1949	Nationalist Forces in Mukden surrendered when promised U.S. logistic support did not arrive.	Loss of political position without war—Lack of sound logistic procedure. [7]
U.S. Air Lift Berlin Blockade 1948	Unexpected U.S. capability for airlift sustained Berlin.	Maintenance of political position without war.

Figure 5. Historical Examples of Strategic-Logistic Relationships

[5] Mahan, *The influence of Sea Power*, Little Brown and Company, Boston: 1893. Pages 122 to 160. Describes how Admiral Howe while winning a tactical victory permitted a vital food convoy to reach France in time to enable the French Revolution to survive.

[6] Fred T. Jane, *The British Battle Fleet*. London: S. W. Partridge and Company, Ltd., 1914. pp 94-6.

[7] Admiral Oscar C. Badger, USN, Retired, discussed this in a lecture "The Influence of Logistics on Strategy" at the Naval War College on 23 September 1954. In concluding this talk he said:

Although, I could go on for hours bringing to your attention instances of failure due to abandonment, or even loyal support, of sound logistics principles, I think my point has been made. Our logistics effort in support of the Far East would have lost *any* war, hot or cold, by the manner in which it was conducted rather than by an unwillingness on the part of our Congress or our people to provide adequate funds and authority or effort.

I do not offer these statements as a basis for belief that our situation in World affairs or in the Far East will continue to deteriorate.

On the contrary, I point to these defects in organization

EVENT:	RESULT:	ILLUSTRATES:
CAIRO CONFERENCE 1943 SPECIFIC ITEMS:	MAJOR STRATEGIC DECISIONS	SCOPE AND TIMING OF STRATEGIC PLANS [8, 9, 10]
Normandy Landing 1944	Delay 1 month	Time for buildup of forces and support needed.
Southern France 1944	Delay 2 months	Critical logistic element, availability of landing craft.
Aegean Expedition	Cancel	Critical logistic element, landing craft, oilers.
Moulmeim Landing	Cancel	Critical logistic element, landing craft and steel.

Figure 5. Historical Examples of Strategic-Logistic Relationships
(Continued)

In other words, *their logistic capability was not adequate to support a fast move to establish strategic control at a critical*

Note 7 (Continued)

and in the principles of operation as easily identifiable, and, therefore, correctable. I point to the early difficulties of World War II, and to the action taken to ensure the most effective relationship between our *national objectives and plans* and our logistic support (including qualified personnel). Therefore, I believe that the principal causes of our failures in certain critical areas of the Cold War are correctable by means already fully tested and proven effective.

---

[8] John Ehrman, *Grand Strategy*, Volume V. Her Majesty's Stationery Office, London: 1956. pp 25-52, 113-114, 214-220, 257-258, 464-478, 532-533.
[9] Forrest C. Pogue, *The Supreme Command*. Office of the Chief of Military History, Department of the Army, Washington, D.C. 1954. pp 113-117, 193, 197, 258, 290, 292.
[10] Richard M. Leighton and Robert W. Coakley, *Global Logistics and Strategy 1940-1943*. Office of the Chief of Military History. Department of the Army, Washington, D.C. 1955. pp 200-201, 212.

EVENT:	RESULT:	ILLUSTRATES:
All WW II Pacific amphibious landings.	Successful strategic drive toward enemy homeland and destruction of enemy bases, fleet and air force.	Overseas base site selection and logistic buildup along line of strategic advance.
Normandy Invasion, selection of invasion site and scheme of maneuver.	Established firm base for destruction of German Army and liberation of Europe.	Integration of strategic-logistic-tactical planning. Composition—balance and deployment of combat and logistic forces.

EVENT:	RESULT:	ILLUSTRATES:
Suez Mid-East crisis 1956-1957.	Loss of Franco-British position in Mid-East.	Lack of integrated strategic-logistic plan.
	Facilitated Russian political-economic penetration.	Critical economic-logistic elements, oil and transportation.
	Weakened unity of Western Alliance.	Effect of lack of rapid buildup.
		Effect of lack of sea-air troop and cargo lift.

Figure 6. Other Historical Examples of Strategic-Logistic Relationships

time. [11, 12]

[11] *King-Hall News Letter* #1070: London: January 23, 1957. p. 641-642. Also, *The Economist,* November 24, 1956. "Operation Musketeer." p. 668-669.

[12] General Sir Charles F. Keightley, GCB, GBE, DSO, Commander-in-Chief, Allied Forces, "Operations in Egypt—November to December, 1956" Supplement to *The London Gazette,* Tuesday 10th September, 1957.

Command Merges Strategy, Logistics, and Tactics

While all successful combat operations in history show the relation between tactics and logistics it is worthwhile to consider a specific instance. In the Japanese report of the defense against the American invasion of the Philippines in World War II, Admiral Kurita says:

> However, the difficulties of replenishment of the entire surface force at the time of the activation of the SHO operation (difficulties in deployment of tankers), the shortage of time available if the CinC's plans were to be adhered to and the danger from enemy large type aircraft, resulted in the selection of the route west of PALAWAN although the submarine threat was very great along that route.
>
> Sunrise at 0656
>
> On 23 October at 0634 ATAGO sustained 4 torpedo hits
> TAKAO sustained 2 torpedo hits
> 0653 ATAGO sank
> 0656 MAYA sustained 4 torpedo hits
> 0700 MAYA sank
>
> The above resulted in the loss of three ships in CRUDIV 4, the transfer of fleet flag to YAMATO and the assignment of two destroyers to screen TAKAO enroute ULUGAN (PALAWAN) for repair.

The report goes on to say:

> Also due to the delay in assigning oilers, the First Striking Force was forced to waste a whole day waiting for their arrival at Brunei. This seriously affected our subsequent time schedule, forcing us to transit an area infested with enemy submarines bringing about the loss of two cruisers, and major damage to another.
>
> If the enemy's intentions are deduced, either the necessary oilers should be assigned at least a week before sortie, or they should be spotted ahead of time at a point along the anticipated route of advance.
>
> Oilers assigned to the Fleet should be equipped for fueling at sea. At present, among the oilers attached to the combined Fleet, the only one capable of fueling at sea, is the NICHIEI MARU. The others have supposedly been equipped to some degree for refueling at sea, but not one has had any actual experience and has confidence in its

ability to execute such operations. In the present operations, there was no opportunity to carry out refueling at
sea, but it is absolutely essential that Combined Fleet
tankers be capable of such operations.
As a result of progressive training, all ships of the First
Striking Force had reached a point where they could refuel
at sea, day or night. Under fleet direction, general capability to execute refueling at sea can be achieved by means
of one week's training for tankers equipped for both
tandem and alongside refueling, and five days' training
for tankers equipped only for alongside refueling. Also,
by carrying out such training, deficiencies in equipment
can be discovered and necessary measures promptly taken
to remedy them and reinforce personnel. In this manner,
the tankers can be made into Combined Fleet tankers in
fact as well as in name.[13]

While rigorous analysis of the above reports by historians
has indicated that Admiral Kurita has not mentioned all of the
circumstances and reasons for his decisions, nevertheless certain points are confirmed.

The difficulties involved in his fuel situation were a significant factor in his decision to pass through submarine waters.

The delay attendant upon fueling handicapped his operations.

The failure to provide tankers fitted for fueling at sea made
it necessary to fuel in port.

His relatively slow speed of 16 knots, which made him
vulnerable to submarine attack, was chosen to have fuel.

If higher command had coordinated the logistical and tactical operations more wisely, it should have been possible to
provide the tankers at Palawan rather than Brunei and this in
turn would have enabled Kurita to have taken his force along
the shortest route through "The Dangerous Ground" (which
had been frequently used by the Japanese Navy) directly to
Palawan.

His subsequent passage to San Bernadino Strait could have
been at a higher speed to protect him from submarines and he

---

[13] Japanese report of operations of their First Striking Force in the SHO
Operations, October 16th-28th 1944, WDC 161641 NA 11839. p. 14.

would have had at least 24 hours more oil in his bunkers at the time of engagement.

While at this time the Japanese Navy was suffering from many logistic difficulties imposed by the damage inflicted by the U.S. forces, these particular logistic difficulties, which combined with other factors to cause the loss of three cruisers at a critical time, were not imposed by an enemy. Instead they came from a lack of appreciation of sound logistic fundamentals on the part of the high command, and a lack of integrated planning.

Finally, to show how the three areas of strategy, logistics, and tactics in our theoretical structure merge in the mind of command, it is interesting to read the vivid account of the interrelation of strategy, logistics, and tactics given by General Bedell Smith in discussing the "Normandy Turning Point." He describes how General Eisenhower at General Bradley's field headquarters at a critical time, 10 August 1944, changed the tactical plans to permit Bradley to turn east, away from his original objectives—the Brittany ports—in order to join with the British forces approaching Falaise. In conjunction with Patton's Army at Argentan, this move would cut off the German Seventh Army.

> Out of the pattern of battle had emerged an opportunity for victory in Normandy so decisive that the liberation of all France must follow.
> . . . This one, in the actual making, comprised little more than a nod of the head, a go-ahead sign to his brilliant lieutenant, Bradley, who had already sketched out in his own mind a plan to take advantage of the glowing opportunity then opening before us. But that nod of the head was the personal assumption of a responsibility that could be assumed by no other. It defied obviously grave risks to secure decisive victory.
> . . . When this maneuver was accomplished, General Bradley's forces would be in position to break through to the south and overrun Brittany. General Patton's Third Army was designed for just this purpose.
> Brittany continued to be a major objective throughout most of the campaign until later events canceled its im-

portance to us. We originally intended to use its fine harbors to funnel troops and supplies to the front directly from the United States, as we had in the First World War.

. . . General Bradley was not disturbed about his local situation, particularly in view of the high promise of the new offensive. If the Germans succeeded in cutting through temporarily, the Supreme Commander pointed out that our armor below the break could be supplied with two thousand tons a day by air.

But a hazard greater than the now thoroughly routed Germans was troubling us—supply. It is no great matter to change tactical plans in a hurry and send troops off in new directions. But adjusting supply plans to the altered tactical scheme is far more difficult. It involves relocating vast depots and stores of ammunition which must flow to the fighting troops in an uninterrupted stream. Our bombing of French rail centers, which had contributed so heavily to victory in Normandy, now returned to plague us. The railroads were practically unusable. We laid out two-lane, one-way motor routes across France over which the trucks roared day and night to keep the advance supplied. Even this was not fast enough for the racing armored spearheads. They got their supply almost entirely by air.

Ports were the core of our problem. It was weeks before the destruction caused by German demolitions at Cherbourg could be repaired. Through all our drive eastward, most of the supply continued to flow over the Normandy beaches and through this crippled port. Now a major change was made in our general plan of supply. Enemy garrisons still held the Brittany ports—Brest, St. Nazaire, Lorient. Reckoning on the destruction they would cause before they surrendered, General Eisenhower decided to abandon entirely the project of using Brittany as a base. Instead of a slow advance across France on which the original plans had been made, our troops were already in Belgium. Antwerp had fallen into our hands intact, when the British advance caught its defenders without demolition charges in place. Though the port facilities could not be used until the German garrisons were cleared from the mouth of the Scheldt where they controlled the approaches, Antwerp was now to be our major port of supply.

We had won a colossal victory already. General Eisenhower's quick decision to seize the opportunity offered by the Germans had destroyed all resistance in northwest France. In two weeks our spearheads had raced from Normandy to the Siegfried Line. The invasion of southern France by General Devers' forces on August 15 made such rapid progress up the Rhone Valley that by mid-September our forces were linked from the Channel to the Mediterranean. Hopelessly outflanked, the remaining German forces in France gave up.[14]

Economic Logistic Limitations

The foregoing examples have illustrated the principle previously stated that the practical application of strategic concepts takes the form of tactical operations to establish control, preceded by an economic-logistic buildup.

In terms of general principles it can be said that *economic* capabilities limit the combat forces which can be *created*. At the same time, *logistic* capabilities limit the forces which can be *employed* in combat operations. Thus, it is obvious that economic-logistic factors determine the limits of strategy.

The economic act of industrial mobilization is related to the grand strategy. The operational logistic action is related to specific strategic plans and to specific tactical operations.

In both areas—in mobilization and in logistic buildup and deployment—there must be fully integrated planning and integrated control. This is a type of planning and control where the mind of command is weighing strategic, logistic, and tactical considerations in the light shed on the enemy by intelligence, and is receiving information and transmitting decisions by means of a communications system.

A more detailed discussion of the objectives of logistic effort and of the nature and structure of logistics is necessary and will follow, before taking up the questions of integration in planning and control.

---

[14] Walter Bedell Smith, *Eisenhower's Six Great Decisions.* Longmans, Green, New York: 1956. pp 59-85.

Chapter 4

The Art of Logistics

*Ultimate decisions, the valuations and the choosing of
ends, are beyond the scope of any science. Science
never tells a man how he should act; it merely shows
how a man must act if he wants to attain definite ends.*[1]
—Ludwig Von Mises

While the general scope of logistics has been suggested in
the preceding chapters it is now appropriate to discuss the subject from various points of view in order to bring out its full
meaning. But first there should come a brief statement of the
basic purpose of the tremendous effort which goes into the
elaborate system of modern logistics.

Logistic Objective

*The objective of a logistic effort is the creation and sustained
support of combat forces.* While this statement does not cover
all that needs to be said, it does furnish us with a valuable guide
for the presentation and interpretation of many other descriptions and discussions of logistics. The statement does not deny
the civilian foundation for logistics nor does it belittle the civilian over-all authority in national defense. It does, however, place
the emphasis on the military side of logistics, and it represents
the viewpoint of military command.

In spite of the many great improvements in our logistical
concepts and procedures which have taken place in the last
fifteen years, many of our most important unsolved problems
are logistical. There are still deficiencies and contradictions in
our logistic systems. While some deficiencies are caused by our
failure properly to apply what we already know, there are many
areas where we are limited by our imperfect knowledge of the
art and science of logistics.

---

[1] Ludwig von Mises, *Human Action*, Yale University Press, New Haven,
1949, p. 10.

Among the obstacles to improvement are the existing uncertainties as to the meaning of the word itself and as to the proper place of logistics in military organizations and plans. These uncertainties occur because logistics has several distinct aspects and in each aspect the definitions and descriptions differ. Frequently, therefore, persons talking from diverse points of view may unwittingly ascribe different meanings to the word without realizing the effect caused thereby.

A striking example of the present different usages of the word "logistics" is found in our own Department of Defense. The Joint Chiefs of Staff definition of logistics, which has undergone several revisions in the last eight years, now includes among other matters acquisition, storage and movement of material, and the acquisition and construction of facilities. The staff of the Joint Chiefs of Staff for years was organized to deal with three major categories of activity: strategy, logistics, and intelligence. In 1958 it was reorganized to deal with seven categories: personnel, intelligence, operations, logistics, plans and policy, communications-electronics, and joint military assistance. Thus, the Joint Chiefs of Staff recognize that supply, properties and installations all are sub-categories of the larger subject of logistics.

On the other hand, The Secretary of Defense has an Assistant Secretary for "Supply and Logistics" and another Assistant Secretary for "Properties and Installations." By this organization, The Secretary of Defense implies that logistics does not include supply and that it is quite separate from "Properties and Installations." Thus we have The Secretary of Defense and his subordinates using the word logistics with two distinct and partially contradictory meanings. This discrepancy is probably due to the fact that the practice of logistics has been almost entirely an empiric development with very little thought having been given to theory.

Pure Logistics

In 1917, Lt. Colonel Cyrus Thorpe, USMC, published an excellent little book, *Pure Logistics: The Science of War Prep-*

aration. This initial attempt to develop theory and principle apparently attracted little or no attention until five copies were found in the Naval War College Library in 1945. Some students of war have wondered how many billions could have been saved had the significance of Colonel Thorpe's ideas been fully appreciated before 1941. Unfortunately the book is out of print, the publishing house out of business and only a few copies remain in the hands of individuals.

In his preface Colonel Thorpe says:

> The terms "pure" and "applied" may be used with the same meaning as to logistics as to other sciences. Pure logistics is merely a scientific inquiry into the theory of logistics—its scope and function in the Science of War, with a broad outline of its organization. Applied logistics rests upon the pure, and concerns itself, in accordance with general principles, with the detailed manner of dividing labor in the logistical field in the preparation for war and maintaining war during its duration.[2]

Terminology

In its abstract sense, the word "logistics," like the other abstractions "strategy," "tactics," "economics," and, "politics," is not susceptible to a single, simple, and permanent definition.

In addition to the statement previously made in chapter 2, that "Strategy and tactics provide the scheme for the conduct of military operations; logistics provides the means therefor," there are several other useful and enlightening descriptions of abstract or pure logistics. The previously quoted statement by Ballantine is worth repeating:

> As the link between the war front and the home front the logistic process is at once the military element in the nation's economy and the economic element in its military operations.[3]

Since World War II the term logistics has frequently been used to apply to civilian activities. For the purpose of showing

[2] Colonel Cyrus Thorpe, *Pure Logistics.* Franklin Hudson Publishing Company, Kansas City, Mo. 1917.

[3] Duncan S. Ballantine, *U.S. Naval Logistics in the Second World War.* Princeton University Press: 1947, p. 3.

how this can be related to military usage, a recently developed group of broad descriptions is interesting.

1. *Logistics* is the process of planning for and providing goods and services.

2. *International logistics* is the process of planning for and providing goods, facilities, and services for the support of the military forces and civilian economies, at the international level.

3. *National logistics* is the process of planning for and providing goods and services for the support of a nation's military forces and its operations, a nation's civilian economy, and its international obligations and requirements.

4. *Civilian logistics* is the process of planning for and providing goods and services for the support of the civilian economy.

5. *Military logistics* is the process of planning for and providing goods and services for the support of the military forces.[4]

To illustrate how difficult it is to pin down the term logistics to a single universally accepted definition, two Army historians after a twelve page discussion of the history and meaning of the word say:

> Evidently the term is still in process of rapid and healthy growth. Until it matures and settles down, we must accept it, perforce, in whatever guise it appears—that is to say, with the specific shape, content, and emphases it derives from its concrete environment.[5]

In the face of such uncertainty, if logistics is to be understood it must be approached and described from various points of view. Furthermore, it must be discussed by reference to other intangibles and abstract terms. It is only through the consideration of one abstract term with relation to the other abstract terms with which it is naturally associated, that a true picture can be presented.

---

[4] Captain R. B. Hunt, USN, Retired, "Definitions of Logistics." Prepared under ONR sponsorship for the George Washington University Logistics Research Project, 23 April 1956.

[5] Richard M. Leighton and Robert W. Coakley, *Global Logistics and Strategy 1940-1943*. Office of the Chief of Military History, Department of the Army, Washington, D.C., 1955, p. 13.

Such an approach should give an understanding of the fundamental realities which will endure regardless of the changes which inevitably will take place in the official definitions and administrative terminology and procedures.

Structure, Money, and Financial Management

In spite of the difficulty of agreeing on a single precise definition, it is possible to recognize a definite structure in logistics. While this cannot be represented in a two-dimensional sketch, it becomes clear when expressed in three dimensions. Every logistic problem can be approached in the simple terms of four broad *categories*, three fundamental *elements*, and three basic *aspects*.

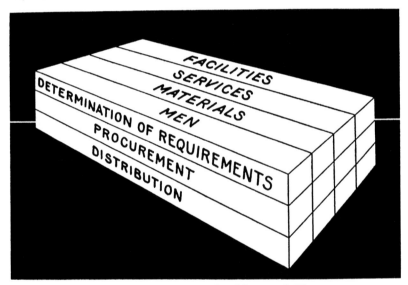

Figure 7. Logistics, the Means of War

Assuming that logistics is "the provision of the means for the conduct of military operations," there are four broad categories of "means." These are men, materials, facilities, services.

In providing these means there are three fundamental elements: Requirements, procurement, and distribution. Regardless of the scale of need or the level of command, a commander must ask:

What logistic resources do I require in order to *create* the combat forces I propose to employ? What resources do I require to *sustain* their operations?

Where, how, and when do I *procure* these logistic resources?

How do I *distribute* these resources among my subordinate commanders in order *to create* and *to sustain* these forces with *maximum combat* effectiveness?

The determination of requirements, procurement, and distribution are processes of management and command which in turn always involve organization, planning, execution, and supervision. These may be considered as the basic aspects of logistics.

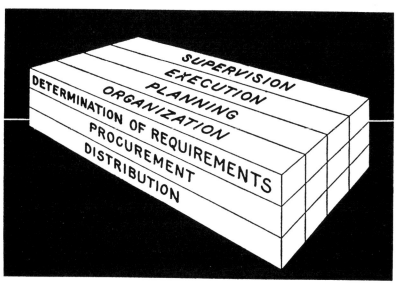

Figure 8. Fundamental Elements and Basic Aspects

These categories, elements, and aspects constitute the heart of logistics regardless of the level or area of command or whether the management and command are civilian or military or a blend of the two. They all are present in every logistic problem and they blend and overlap in accordance with the nature and circumstances of each particular situation.

Each of these fundamentals is the subject of an extensive literature. In the case of *requirements* this consists primarily of the executive directives governing the responsibilities of the National Security Council, the Joint Chiefs of Staff, and the military commanders of the armed services. Furthermore, the histories of World War II deal with the requirements problems in considerable detail.

The literature on *procurement* and *distribution,* much of which is technical in nature, is even more extensive. There are many official directives and historical analyses. In addition, there are extensive Congressional hearings and various reports of the Hoover Commission. To a large degree the recurring controversies relative to the organization of the armed forces revolve around the arguments as to what constitutes the most efficient way of dealing with these fundamental elements of the art of logistics.

While, in this book, no special sections are devoted to these matters, they will be discussed in various ways throughout this work as they relate to specific subjects.

Naturally the question arises as to where money fits into this picture of logistics. From the standpoint of pure logistics, money is fundamental only as it is used to provide men, materials, facilities, and services. From the practical standpoint of applied logistics, money is a very important factor.

Since our economic system is based on the use of money, financial management is a vital element in the national economy and in government. Financial considerations to a large extent govern the relation between the economic, the military, and the political factors. Financial restrictions limit the size of the forces which can be created and maintained in peace. Financial devices are used by management to restrict authority and to control operations in many diverse ways. Methods of strict financial control and accounting form a valuable tool for measuring the relative efficiency of many logistical procedures.

Therefore, good financial management must permeate the entire logistic structure. However, as previously stated, because financial considerations should not override considerations of combat effectiveness to the extent of destroying national security, the criteria by which we judge the quality of a logistic system must include both economic and combat factors.

In general war or at any other time when the survival of the state is clearly at stake, money as such, is of secondary importance. The creation and employment of forces then are limited by the availability of manpower, management, industrial capacity, raw materials, transportation, and TIME.

In either case, peace or war, understanding of basic logistic principles is essential to the task of providing the maximum combat effectiveness within the limitations imposed.

This is true regardless of whether these are limitations imposed by money, or are limitations imposed by the other factors of material, men, facilities, services, and time.

If the principles of logistics were better understood, the budgeteers might be wiser and more discriminating in the manner in which they limit combat forces and at the same time the military secretaries and commanders might more effectively manage the resources allotted by the budgeteers.

Mobilization of War Potential

The degree to which the industrial revolution has involved the whole nation in war is reflected in the fact that modern combat forces and weapons are created and sustained by drawing on every segment of the national resources.

This, in turn, means that the war-making capability of the nation which is frequently called its "war potential," is to a very large extent measured by its ability to mobilize and to employ its economic and industrial resources. This industrial mobilization is a massive logistic process.

Two other descriptions are helpful in understanding this relation of mobilization and logistics:

Civil logistics is the mobilization of the civilian industrial economy to support the armed forces.

Military logistics is the supplying of men and material, and the rendering of services, to the operating military forces.

However, economic industrial resources are not the sole measure of war potential—there are many intangible aspects such as leadership, fortitude, political acumen, administrative ability, strategic insight, and tactical skill. All of these are also vital elements of a nation's war potential. By placing these factors in their proper perspective from the point of view of command we can see how the subjects of economic and industrial mobilization enter into the creation and support of combat forces. It is further evident that in the full development of war potential we have another instance of the interweaving of political, economic, and military factors and another interweaving of strategical, logistical, and tactical factors.

We also find that when we explore these interweavings we are in fact gradually developing not only a theory of war, but also a theory of strategy and a theory of logistics.

Applied Logistics

Abstract speculations, theories, and principles have never prepared a nation to fight and have never won a war. All they have done is to enable man to understand his war problems and to assist him to solve them. In the face of the blending and overlap of the various parts of logistics, it seems obvious that the practical application of the functions of logistics is an art rather than a science.

In order to prepare for war, we must define the practical tasks of the armed forces and we must assign these tasks to specific organizations and individuals. For this purpose we have organized the Department of Defense and the armed forces; for this purpose definitions have been published and specific tasks assigned.

The U.S. Joint Chiefs of Staff have defined logistics as:

> In its most comprehensive sense, those aspects of military operations which deal with: (1) design and development, acquisition, storage, movement, distribution, maintenance, evacuation, and disposition of materiel; (2) movement, evacuation, and hospitalization of personnel; (3) acquisition or construction, maintenance, operation, and disposi-

tion of facilities; and (4) acquisition or furnishing of services. It comprises both planning, including determination of requirements, and implementation.

This definition of applied or practical logistics is in no way out of harmony with the previous broad descriptions of pure logistics. Rather it amplifies them and reduces them to specific functional terms which can be applied throughout the armed forces.

Nowhere are there any orders as to how each Service shall interpret this definition. This is wise, for conditions in each Service vary. In the Navy Department logistics is more decentralized than in the other two Services. The Deputy Chief of Naval Operations (Logistics) has responsibility for coordination and for the determination of material requirements, while the Office of Naval Material and the technical bureaus have the actual operating functions in procurement and in distribution. In the Departments of the Army and the Air Force, the Deputy Chief of Staff for Logistics (Army) and the Deputy Chief of Staff, Materiel (AF) in theory have a much more direct authority.

In practice the definition of applied logistics varies in accordance with the level of the organization being considered. But, always, logistics is concerned with "furnishing the means of war," which are: men, material, facilities, and services.

Functional Activities

If we classify these means in functional categories, they become in general terms: personnel; supply; the building, repair, and salvage of ships; aviation; ordnance; maintenance and repair; construction; transportation; and medical.

In actual practice there are many variations in terminology and organization depending on the Service concerned and the level and area of command. For example, "ship construction and ship repair," and "aircraft construction and repair" in the Navy are categories which cannot be organizationally related to the "maintenance and repair" or the "construction" of conventional Army parlance. "Construction" covers both advanced base development and certain phases of combat engineering.

Petroleum, ammunition, electronics, and certain technical spare parts may be handled separately as special categories.

"Personnel" as a logistic function is unique. While theoretically it is one of the most important logistic functions; and, while it is handled for seagoing naval forces by the commander of the service force and for the combat armies by the logistical command, it is not officially considered wholly a matter of logistic cognizance. This will be seen in the previously quoted Joint Chiefs of Staff definition.

This apparent paradox occurs because the problem of personnel is so important, so big, and so complex that it requires very special management on both the departmental level and the major staff level.

However, this administrative procedure should not obscure the vital fact that personnel is always a major concern of the logistic planner. Ultimately the man is the logistic consumer and, therefore, all logistic plans and forecasts are related to personnel either directly or indirectly. For example, the problem of the relative buildup of combat forces versus logistic forces is largely a problem of personnel; and inefficient personnel is the greatest single source of the "logistic snowball." In practice, the division of cognizance as between the function of planning and administering personnel matters, and the functions of determining the logistic implications of the personnel situation, and providing logistical support for personnel, is a matter for each Service or command to determine.

The great diversity and detail of these functional activities pose a problem of comprehension for the student of logistics unless he is able to distinguish between the technical features and the command features of his task. In each of the functional categories there is an extensive technical literature. In each, the technical staff specialist is essential. However, there is a subtle distinction. The technical specialist is chiefly interested in perfecting the performance of that particular specialty in which he makes his professional career. On the other hand, the commander and the logistic officer must always be thinking of how a variety of specialized functions can be most effectively

LOGISTICS, THE BRIDGE
CHART I

THE LOGISTIC PROCESS USING THE FUNDAMENTAL ELEMENTS OF LOGISTICS: REQUIREMENTS, PROCUREMENT, DISTRIBUTION, AND THE BASIC ASPECTS OF COMMAND: ORGANIZATION, PLANNING EXECUTION AND SUPERVISION, FORMS A BRIDGE BETWEEN THE ECONOMIC SYSTEM OF THE NATION AND THE ACTUAL OPERATIONS OF THE COMBAT FORCES.

THE FOLLOWING CHART PROVIDES AN OVER-SIMPLIFIED DESCRIPTION OF HOW THIS WORKS. IN STUDYING THIS CHART A FEW BASIC THOUGHTS MAY BE HELPFUL.

LOGISTICS IS: AN ART, A SCIENCE, A PROCESS.

THE LOGISTICS PROCESS IS AT ONE AND THE SAME TIME THE ECONOMIC ELEMENT OF OUR MILITARY OPERATIONS AND THE MILITARY ELEMENT OF OUR ECONOMY.

GOOD PROGRAMMING AND FINANCIAL MANAGEMENT SHOULD PERMEATE WHOLE PROCESS. (COMPTROLLER TECHNIQUE IS PART OF THIS.)

THE PROCESS OF FULLY INTEGRATED STRATEGIC-LOGISTIC PLANNING RELATES MEANS TO SPECIFIC STRATEGIC OBJECTIVES. WHEN THIS IS FOLLOWED BY SOUND LOGISTIC PROCESSES AND PROCEDURES THE TIMELY LOGISTIC SUPPORT OF TACTICAL FORCES IS ASSURED.

CRITERIA = {
COMBAT EFFECTIVENESS-ALWAYS.
BUDGET ECONOMY IN PEACE.
TIME-RESOURCES - OBJECTIVES IN WAR.
}

FINALLY, DO NOT THINK THAT THESE DESCRIPTIONS AND CATEGORIES ARE EXACT NOR THAT THEY CAN BE PRECISELY DIFFERENTIATED. IN REALITY THEY ARE INTERTWINED IN WONDROUS MANNER!

Figure 9. Logistics—the Bridge Between the Economic System and the Combat Forces, Chart I

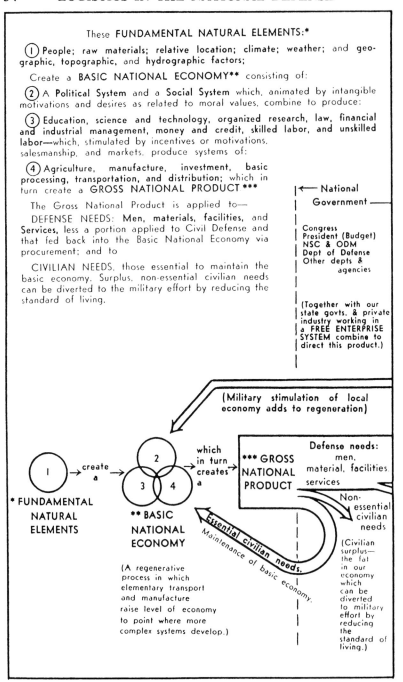

These FUNDAMENTAL NATURAL ELEMENTS:*

(1) People; raw materials; relative location; climate; weather; and geographic, topographic, and hydrographic factors;

Create a BASIC NATIONAL ECONOMY** consisting of:

(2) A Political System and a Social System which, animated by intangible motivations and desires as related to moral values, combine to produce:

(3) Education, science and technology, organized research, law, financial and industrial management, money and credit, skilled labor, and unskilled labor—which, stimulated by incentives or motivations, salesmanship, and markets, produce systems of:

(4) Agriculture, manufacture, investment, basic processing, transportation, and distribution; which in turn create a GROSS NATIONAL PRODUCT ***

The Gross National Product is applied to—

DEFENSE NEEDS: Men, materials, facilities, and Services, less a portion applied to Civil Defense and that fed back into the Basic National Economy via procurement; and to

CIVILIAN NEEDS, those essential to maintain the basic economy. Surplus, non-essential civilian needs can be diverted to the military effort by reducing the standard of living.

|←— National
| Government ——
|
| Congress
| President (Budget)
| NSC & ODM
| Dept of Defense
| Other depts &
| agencies
|
| (Together with our
| state govts. & private
| industry working in
| a FREE ENTERPRISE
| SYSTEM combine to
| direct this product.)

(Military stimulation of local economy adds to regeneration)

which in turn creates a

*** GROSS NATIONAL PRODUCT

Defense needs:
men, material, facilities, services

Non-essential civilian needs

1 → create a → 2 ... 3 4

* FUNDAMENTAL NATURAL ELEMENTS

** BASIC NATIONAL ECONOMY

Essential civilian needs. Maintenance of basic economy.

(A regenerative process in which elementary transport and manufacture raise level of economy to point where more complex systems develop.)

(Civilian surplus—the fat in our economy which can be diverted to military effort by reducing the standard of living.)

Figure 10. Logistics—the Bridge (Cont.), Chart II

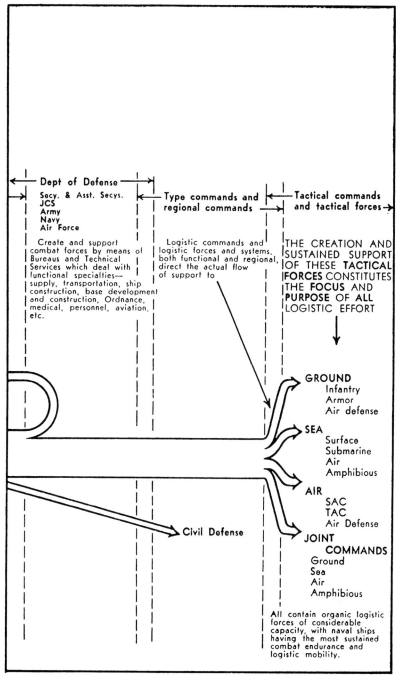

Figure. 10. Logistics—the Bridge (Cont.) Chart II (Cont.)

combined in accomplishing the mission of the command. It is not a question of exclusiveness in thinking, it is rather a question of relative emphasis and primary responsibility.

In continuing this consideration of functional activities from the perspective of command another point is important.

The fact that a certain function is included within the broad definition of logistics does not necessarily mean that this particular function is carried on by an organization which is logistical in name or which is wholly devoted to logistical activity.

Therefore, it is of vital importance to understand that regardless of how the logistic functions are assigned and divided, the functions themselves are the same and must be performed by qualified officers. Furthermore, these functions must be supervised and coordinated by senior officers who not only understand the full implications of their responsibility thereto but also understand the relationships involved therein.

Logistics the Bridge

The above discussion is best summed up by again stating that "logistics is the bridge between our national economy and the operations of our combat forces."

Figures 9 (chart I) and 10 (chart II) present these ideas in diagrammatic form and figure 11, (chart III) shows the general areas of cognizance as command exercises the necessary logistic control.

The basic theme or principle that a commander should control his own logistic support is expressed in many ways and in many parts of this book. This question of the nature and the degree of control of logistics which should be exercised by military commanders in various areas and levels of command is both extremely important and extremely complex.

Regardless of how civilian and military authority may be assigned and blended, command is exercised through planning and through the control and adjustment of the ensuing action. Therefore, it is desirable to discuss the question of planning as applied to logistics.

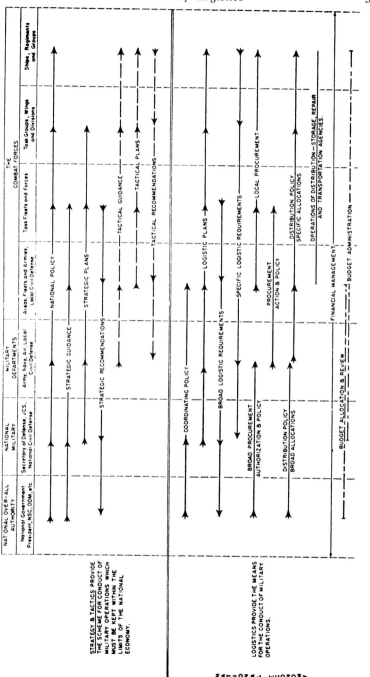

Figure 11. Logistics—the Bridge (Cont.), Chart III
How Various Levels of Command Exercise Logistic Control

Chapter 5

Planning in Logistics

Logistic considerations belong not only in the highest echelons of military planning during the process of preparation for war and for specific wartime operations, but may well become the controlling element with relation to timing and successful operation.[1]
—VICE ADMIRAL OSCAR C. BADGER, USN

In war, as in other competitive activities, success can only follow forethought. At all levels of an organization it is necessary to guide events—and not to let things "just happen" as a result of intuition, lest intuition run out of tools wherewith to accomplish its aims.

Planning in General

Each responsible individual must study the situation which faces him—*and which might face him.* He must weigh possible courses of action open to him, and he must examine these in terms of what his competitor or opponent can do either to thwart him; or, in turn, to gain an advantage. He must consider his courses of action as to:

(1) *Suitability*—that is, will they accomplish the end he seeks?

(2) *Feasibility*—that is, will he be able to provide the right means at the right place at the right time?

(3) *Acceptability or consequences as to cost*—that is, does he stand to use or lose more than he can afford?

Then he must make his decision as to just what he will do, and with what, and when and where. Having made his decision —together with supporting decisions as necessary—he must translate that decision into instructions to his organization in order that action may carry through at the appropriate time.

---

[1] Vice Admiral Oscar C. Badger, USN, "Principles of Command and Logistics," *U.S. Naval War College Information Service for Officers,* Vol. IV, No. 4, December 1951, p. 23.

This is called "planning." It may be "contingency planning" such as for any number or types of possible wars or conflicts; or it may be "operational planning," "strategic planning," or "tactical planning"; etc. In any event, *at all levels of an organization,* there has to be planning which will among other things provide for the means to be in place to carry out the decision.

This planning may concern itself with a national stockpile of raw material; with a mobilization base for industry; with the supply of ships, tanks, or aircraft; or with three meals a day for a man in the trenches. Also, this planning should provide for enough flexibility to permit responsible officials to meet variable situations, within reason, that may arise due to action by the competitor or opponent.

This is "logistic planning" in general. Many of its details will be developed further in this chapter.

Logistic plans are so vital—so ambient—so all-pervasive, that they can be considered to be the common denominator of all plans. If any military plan is to be realistic, logistic considerations and logistic plans must be interwoven with national, strategic, and tactical plans at all levels of command.

In the U.S. armed forces today there are elaborate and detailed planning procedures. These are well designed to meet the needs of the established peacetime legislative and budgetary processes. In general they consist of the orderly development of a group of interdependent plans and programs extending over a period of several years. In some instances the plans themselves project many years into the future with provisions being made for annual modification to bring them into line with the current basic situation.

However, today's peacetime planning procedures have not been tested by major war. Therefore, it is likely that in time of crisis officers in responsible planning positions will be forced to make quick and decisive departures from the normal routines.[2]

---

[2] The manner in which the logistic support of the United Nations Suez Force was accomplished is a representative example of what to expect. This support was planned by one officer who, remaining in his Pentagon office next to the telephone for about four days, disregarded technical legal restrictions, established procedures, and formal channels of communication in order to get the emergency work done.

These departures will require not only individual initiative but also a solid knowledge of the fundamental facts and considerations of wartime needs and pressures which may have been obscured by the formal peacetime procedures.

Classes and Patterns of Planning

In various nations and services the terminology and the procedures may vary considerably but in all cases the planning will be influenced by the same basic factors and in all cases good planning will follow the same general patterns. A knowledge of the patterns and influences should enable one to work effectively with any agreed terminology within any reasonably good organization.

Because the processes of planning are characterized by a variety of methods and nomenclature it may be useful to suggest some general classifications. Thus some of the relations, and overlapping which otherwise might be confusing may be seen in better perspective. See figure 12.

Comment on the various kinds of planning will follow a brief discussion of how the nature of the work changes as the level of the organization or command changes.

Levels of Planning

The creation of armed forces and the preparation of resources for their support can be generally classed as mobilization planning. It may also be called the mobilization level.

The organization of specific combat units for the accomplishment of specific tasks or missions together with the provision of logistic resources—and units—for their sustained support can be generally classed as operational planning.[3] It may also be called the operational level.

---

[3] No attempt is made to conform to current official terminology because this terminology which is frequently classified may be readily changed by administrative order. Furthermore, there is a general tendency to use the word "operational" to apply exclusively to the strategical and tactical aspects of military operations in contra-distinction to the logistic arrangements and movements which are the foundation of all military operations. This not only leads to semantic confusion but in the past it has contributed to the neglect of the logistic provisions which make the strategic dispositions and tactical movements possible. Until a more realistic terminology comes into official use we must recognize and accept this minor hazard to good military planning.

ONE MAY BE ENGAGED:

IN EITHER—		OR IN—
Two general classes:	MOBILIZATION PLANNING	OPERATIONAL PLANNING
	(Both influenced by level of command)	
Two broad approaches:	REQUIREMENTS PLANNING	CAPABILITIES PLANNING
	(May take place at any level of command)	
Two specific types:	LOGISTIC PLANNING	PLANNING FOR LOGISTIC SUPPORT
	(Logistic aspects of the "estimate of the situation")	("The development of the plan")
Two different methods:	LINE ITEM PLANNING	PLANNING BY BROAD AGGREGATIONS
	OTHER TERMS USED: CODE PLANNING; PLANNING FOR CONTINGENCIES	

Figure 12. Planning Categories

The ultimate flow of the mobilization into operations is indicated in figures 9, 10, and 11, "Logistics the Bridge."

The manner in which the nature of the work and the terminology change is sketched in figure 13.

On the international and national levels, logistics deals with the broadest economic and industrial matters. Among these are the sources and availabilities of raw materials, the state of the domestic economy and finances, the availability of manufacturing plants, skilled and unskilled labor, design and production engineers, management, and other similar affairs. Some persons

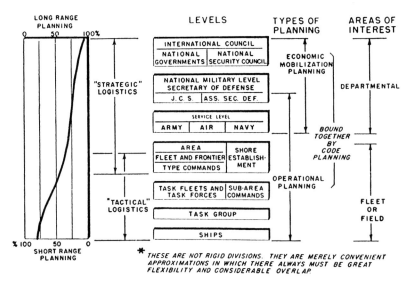

Figure 13. The Levels of Planning in Logistics

may prefer to consider this as a combination of economic mobilization, industrial mobilization, and military planning. The precise labels attached to the process are not as important as understanding the nature and interrelationship of the functions performed.

The international process is exemplified by the military assistance activities and by the mutual security programs. In Europe, for example, these have been placed under the administration of the Commander in Chief, U.S. European Command (U.S. CINCEUR). The process is further illustrated by the work of the Screening and Costing Committee under General McNarney in Paris in 1951, and their immediate superiors, the Temporary Council Committee, the "Three Wise Men." The Lisbon Conference of 1952 was almost wholly a high level logistic conference.

On this highest level the international and national situations and decisions must be continuously interrelated. Therefore, our own governmental organizations must work with their opposite numbers in other nations and with various special or permanent international organizations. It is vital to seek harmony among the national and the international policies, strategic plans, and military programs. While it is naive to expect to achieve complete harmony—particularly in international affairs—it is very important that we avoid contradiction.

In this connection, it is noted that *policies* and *plans* are made by both international and national agencies. On the other hand, *action* is almost always taken by national agencies.

At the top national-international level the activities of the Congress, the National Security Council, the Council of Economic Advisors, the Office of Civil and Defense Mobilization, the Joint Chiefs of Staff, the Assistant Secretaries of Defense, the three military Services, and many other agencies and specially appointed individuals are completely fluid and interwoven. This situation emphasizes the importance of an understanding of the background, and the tensions and fundamental factors which operate in these fields.

Strictly national U.S. action follows a somewhat simpler pattern. The projects authorized and the funds appropriated by the Congress actually determine the logistic capabilities of the armed forces. Within the limits of these practical capabilities and the allocations of the Office of Civil and Defense Mobilization, the Secretary of Defense, the Joint Chiefs of Staff, and the military Services decide as to the specific forces to be built up. At the same time they formulate such broad strategic plans as can be carried out using the forces which are provided.

As a part of this planning the Office of the Secretary of Defense (Assistant Secretary of Defense for Supply and Logistics) makes recommendations as to policies governing the allocation of both raw materials and finished products among the three Services. This office also makes recommendations as to how the productive capacity of certain industrial plants should be allocated.

At this point, the three military Services, through their technical bureaus and services, actually procure and distribute to the operating forces the ships, planes, guns, men, equipment, supplies and services which are the means of war. This is done in terms of specific numbers of specific functional items.

The foregoing comprise the major mobilization processes which constitute, or are associated with the international and national level of logistics.

On this, the mobilization level, the Office of Civil and Defense Mobilization, the three Services, the Joint Chiefs of Staff and the Office of the Secretary of Defense are striving to relate war, mobilization, and budget plans, to the national economy and to political factors. The magnitude of the task, the realities of statutory rules and requirements, and the need to iron out and justify allocations of funds, have resulted in the growth of possibly unwieldy organizations. They also have resulted in a planning process which is, to say the least, long drawn out.

In the lengthy "planning cycle," practically every major activity in the Department of Defense is involved either directly or indirectly. For example, some people are working on budget and finance, some on materiel design and construction, some on raw material, some on transportation. No matter what the division of the work or the terminology used, be it called administration, economic mobilization, industrial mobilization, general planning, or anything else, it still covers the same activities. The men involved are working to "provide the means of war in order to support the national strategy." Regardless of the cut of the cake or the nomenclature used, this effort requires the same basic logistic procedures: first, determine requirements; next, figure out how and where to procure what is wanted, and, finally, distribute it in accordance with the military needs of the situation.

On the highest level we deal in the broadest terms, and as we go down the chain we find ourselves being more specific. At first the emphasis is on civilian control with important military participation. But, as we go down to the operating level, the civilian interest tends to diminish and the military control increases. Civilian control tends to be strongest in the "producer" or business end of the logistic process; military control is strongest in "consumer logistics." The consumers are the military, the producers are essentially civilian.

So far, we have examined the activities of the international and national groups and organizations in planning for war, and we have found that almost every activity of the Department of Defense and of the military Services is concerned with the *means* of war. Accordingly, although not always recognized as such, this process is in fact LOGISTICS—logistics in a very practical sense. If those who do this applied logistic work have an understanding of the purpose, the relationships, and the principles of pure logistics, their efforts will have the coherence which is so essential to the attainment of sound intuition. It is important for them to develop efficiency and effectiveness in harmony, and to avoid operating as compartmented individual groups who see only their own day-to-day crises without relating them to the over-all problems and purpose.

In sum, it is the national top-level planning which provides the basic policies and concepts under which the combat forces will fight; and within that planning level grow the logistic policies and arrangements which will provide and equip those combat forces. It is thus convenient to classify these latter activities as lying in the strategic phase of logistics (see figure 13).

The next level of activity may be described as the operating level or field level. It includes what the Army calls the "Zone of the Interior" and what the Navy calls the "Continental Shore Establishment." It also takes in the theaters of operation, the named fleets, numbered armies, and the numbered air forces. It may be called "operational logistics," and its activities may be said to lie in the fields both of strategy and of tactics.

In considering this division of logistics into various levels, we should always remember that each level overlaps with the other, both above and below. There can never be a sharp cut-off line of interest, although there are various cut-off lines of specific action responsibility. This situation is explored a little more fully below.

Planning on the "operational logistics" level of course does not take place in a vacuum, nor does it commence as an independent or new activity upon receipt of logistic plans prepared by higher authority (such as Departmental plans). Rather, there has been a continual exchange of ideas, concepts, and data between the two levels. Further, the very factors developed by the lower level will be used by the higher level in the latter's determination of gross and over-all requirements. Finally, the strategic plans of the lower level in turn are based on the strategic concepts and plans of the higher level—and, logistically speaking, the higher level strategic plans have been tailored to fit the means available, and *to be* made available, to the lower level of command.

Thus, planning for the actual conduct of this "operational logistics" is based upon the strategic plans and the broad logistic plans and policies of the theater and fleet commanders and upon their estimates of requirements. All of these furnish the necessary guidance to the operational commanders who actually submit the requisitions and operate the basic logistic services afloat.

As we move from the theaters through the fleets to the task forces, we move from strategical logistics to tactical logistics; from the realm of long-range plans and forecasts, to the actual repair and replenishment of combat forces.

The techniques of *tactical* logistics of this nature are under constant scrutiny and improvement in actual practice. On the other hand, the techniques and procedures of so-called theater and fleet *strategical* logistics are frequently imperfect and sometimes neglected in peacetime.

In this connection, anyone can understand the effect of a ship at sea running out of fuel and ammunition. Normally, it does not take complex planning to obviate such a situation. The importance and nature of the long-range concurrent and integrated strategic-operational logistic planning on theater and fleet level, however, are of even greater long-range importance. Accordingly, it is necessary that all these processes be thoroughly understood, so that staffs can produce the planning that will *insure* the readiness of task forces for sustained combat operations in time of emergency.

"Requirements" Planning, and "Capabilities" Planning

The foregoing discussion of the levels of planning in logistics needs to be amplified by looking at the planning process from still another point of view. Earlier it was pointed out that the military departments decide as to the specific forces to be built up—within the practical capabilities of the authorization of projects and the allocation of funds by the Congress, and the allocation of resources by the Office of Civil and Defense Mobilization. Further, it was suggested that much effort and planning had gone into the determination of these limitations.

It is obvious that the highest levels in government and the military Services have to have something to go on, in addition to possible preliminary guide lines, as to the maximum amount of funds which may be made available.

The process here involved is a highly important and complex one which attempts to keep pace with the strategic situation facing the United States. It can be considered as "taking a first cut" at the basic logistic problem of providing the means for the conduct of combat operations. This approach is called "requirements planning."

Here, the process might commence with a tentative strategic concept. For example, a military Service might feel that a situation called for a specific strategic course of action. This course of action would then be examined with a view to determining just what specific combat and logistic forces and resources *must be procured or provided* in order to meet the requirement of the strategic concept.

This process of requirements planning will follow through the sum of courses of action to indicate the tentative requirements of each military Service, and in turn the sum of all military requirements.

At this point there must be made the large strategic decisions as to which courses of action can be retained, or which must be discarded, or which must be reduced in scope—all dependent on considerations of logistic feasibility within the context of national policy at the time.

These decisions having been made, and the allocation of projects, funds, and material having been determined, requirements planning must give way to another approach, that of "capabilities planning."

Capabilities planning consists of the determination of what combat forces you can create, employ, and support *with the means that are or can be made available*. While requirements planning may be the "first cut," capabilities planning is that process which *produces* the "finished goods." Both types of planning take place at the national (and possibly international) level, and they also take place at all the other levels of command. This must be so; it is vital that each commander know what would be needed for him to carry out each of his schemes, and, on the other hand, he must know to what courses of action he is restricted by reason of logistic considerations.

In capabilities planning it is likely that the availability of only a limited number of commodities and services need be examined. Experience will have indicated which are critical to the decision.

Capabilities planning usually moves from a high level *down* toward a lower level (i.e., the higher level is trying to estimate the effect at all levels of certain limitations on the capabilities of subordinates). The use of broad "factors" is sound. The factors and methods used should be susceptible to rapid mathematical manipulation in order that a large number of situations may be readily evaluated.

In requirements planning, it would appear that the planner is on the same street as in capabilities planning, but that he is going in the opposite direction. Here he starts with the objectives and a proposed scheme of maneuver, and works *up* through the levels of command in order to determine what must be produced or budgeted.

"Logistic Planning" vs. "Planning for Logistic Support"

Regardless of the level of command, there are two recognizable broad types of planning in logistics. Both are in use at various levels of command, and each serves a different purpose. Simply for the purposes of identification in this discussion they are labelled "logistic planning" and "planning for logistic support."

The first term, "logistic planning," can be used to indicate the incorporation of logistic considerations into the formulation of strategic and tactical plans. In terms of the formal process of military decision "logistic planning" can be considered as the logistic aspects of the "commander's estimate of the situation." It includes the determination of the basic logistic requirements and the general dispositions necessary to support these plans. All of this can be effectively done only by a constant and intimate relationship between the strategic planners and the logistic planners. In this relationship the former are constantly aware of the logistic capabilities and limitations, and the latter are constantly aware of the dispositions and employment being proposed for the forces and of the estimated nature and strength of enemy opposition.

The second term, "planning for logistic support," can be applied to the detailed planning for the logistic support of the combat forces which are carrying out the decision reached through the estimate of the situation. In terms of formal military decision it corresponds to "the development of the plan." This process of "planning for logistic support" ultimately determines the flexibility of the combat forces; it is the most "practical" type of functional logistics. Among other things it involves the details of supply, the buildup, the cargo lift, and the provision of repair facilities.

It is worth repeating that these two types of planning take place at all levels. The techniques may vary and in many instances they may telescope and become concurrent. Normally, however, the final details of "planning for logistics" follow the basic guide lines laid down in the "logistic planning" stage.

While the details of this "logistic planning" can be complex, the whole system rests on the following simple and straightforward fundamental sequence—

The strategic objectives;

A proposed scheme of deployment and action of combat forces based on an estimate of the enemy situation and capabilities;

Determination of broad logistic requirements and determination as to which of these will be decisive or critical;

Determination of availabilities of these critical items;

Estimate of the effect of shortages upon the strategic and tactical courses of action;

Determination of what can be done logistically, strategically, or tactically to alleviate these shortages or to overcome the handicaps imposed by them.

In this "logistic planning," combat and logistic resources are generally discussed in terms of broad aggregations such as: so many divisions, so many wings, so many carrier groups, so many thousands of tons and thousands of men, of transportation lift, etc.

In "planning for logistic support" the same factors must be taken into consideration. However, since the previous work in "logistic planning" usually assured the soundness of the decision reached, the emphasis is placed on what can be done tactically and logistically to support the strategic decision. This, of course, requires very detailed planning of specific combat units and much more detailed and specific logistic calculations. Line item planning is appropriate in this work.

These processes exemplify the meaning of the expression: "Logistics is a command responsibility."

Excellent illustrations of both "logistic planning" and "planning for logistic support" can be found in the Cairo (1943) and Quebec conferences (1943 and 1944) and the subsequent action by the U.S. military departments and commanders. At these conferences logistic considerations were the determining factors in reaching strategic decisions.

Mobilization Planning vs. Operational Planning

After the strategic decisions were reached, "planning for logistic support" took place at the highest levels. This eventually involved both "mobilization planning" and "operational planning."

However, as the level of planning descended, each of the subordinate commanders had to make his own "estimate of the situation" and reach decisions as to how he would carry out his share of the global strategic plan agreed to at the conferences.

In the case of Admiral Nimitz, Commander in Chief Pacific Ocean Areas, his Assistant Chief of Staff for Operations, Rear Admiral Forrest Sherman, in 1943, prepared the GRANITE Plans. These were the first true "campaign plans" prepared by the United States. They furnished the foundation for CINCPOA's planning for the remainder of the war. Here again, "logistic planning" took place, for the GRANITE Plans dealt with basic logistic availabilities and requirements as related to the projected operations of specific tactical forces.

The orderly development of logistic planning at this stage of the war was in decided contrast to the situation in 1942. In the words of the Army historians:

> But in the most basic realm of logistical planning—the determination of long-range needs and the formulation of programs, schedules, and priorities for meeting them—the absence of a settled and concrete strategy, unavoidable as long as the momentum of the enemy's initial attacks continued, created a virtually insoluble problem.[4]

In due time, satisfactory "logistic planning" went on in each theater and at each level of command in a similar manner. As firm strategic decisions were made, the "planning for logistic support" took place. In Washington specific time-phased functional programs at the mobilization level were prepared to create the necessary forces and provide support. The technical services

---

[4] Richard M. Leighton and Robert W. Coakley, *Global Logistics and Strategy 1940-1943*. Office of the Chief of Military History, Department of the Army, Washington, D.C., 1955, p. 212.

of the Army and the bureaus of the Navy translated these programs into a flow of specific supplies and equipments to the field commanders.

At the level of CINCPOA's subordinate commands, for example, the fleet, force, and type commanders (Army and Navy) prepared specific logistic plans which provided the tactical commanders with the means for the conduct of their combat operations. The ships, the planes, the men, the vehicles, the ammunition, the supplies, the fuel, the food, the medical services and facilities, the repair and salvage services and facilities were focused on the tactical objectives and supporting areas. These supporting plans, in terms of formal military planning, constituted the logistic portions of "the development of the plan."

Methods of Planning

Regardless of the level or the type, the basic problem of planning is to relate the creation and employment of operating military forces to the utilization of logistic resources.

The surest and the most direct method is called "line item planning." This is the calculation of each item of supply and equipment as an individual and specific task. For example, a case of soap, an armature for a generator, a small boat propeller, are all line items. As previously mentioned, for certain situations this is the most reliable and efficient method. However, in high level planning it requires so much time and detail that strategic and logistic planning cannot be concurrent, as they should be.

Another method of planning involves the use of broad aggregations. One example is found in the so-called THREE-FACTOR METHOD. In this, three factors, "activity," "conversion" and "commander's judgment" are manipulated to determine requirements of individual items or certain aggregates or groups of items under a variety of circumstances. In its present state of development this method appears immediately useful in major task forces and area or higher level commands for obtaining approximate requirements in selected categories and for certain kinds of high level "capabilities planning" and in "logistic planning." [5]

As experience is gained in the use of these planning factors, many changes can be expected. New areas of usefulness will be discovered and better statements of so-called "standard conditions" will be made. Certainly the actual figures of the "activity planning factor" will be changed as more usage data are analyzed.

Between these two different methods—one, that of detail, the other, that of broad aggregation—we find a great variety of planning factors and procedures; none of these is static, none is perfect.

---

[5] The following brief explanation of the "Three-Factor Method" will be helpful at this point.

The basic equation of the Three-Factor Method is: Requirements = Activity Factor x Conversion Factor x Judgment Factor.

The *Activity Planning factor* is derived from the significant activity which most influences the determination of a requirement, e.g., personnel complement of a unit is the "activity" most significant in determining a requirement of rations, clothing, or ship store stock; hours of operation is the "activity" most significant in determining fuel requirements, etc. Commodities consumed are expressed in terms of measurable units (barrels, tons, etc.) per unit of time. The activity planning factor reflects the best possible analysis of past and current usage data, which of course, is a continuing job.

The *Conversion factor,* when multiplied by the activity planning factor, provides a consumption rate in workable logistic terms, such as barrels of fuel per day, measurement tons of provisions per day, tons of ammunition per day, etc. When the Activity Planning factor provides such a rate, the Conversion factor is simply one. However, when such commodities as provisions, special clothing and medical and dental stores depend upon complement as the significant activity, the conversion factor for each commodity is necessarily different.

Both of these factors are designed to permit the use of high-speed computing equipment. The planner's job is to select the proper factors and inject them into the machine.

The combination of these two factors gives an estimate of requirements under the assumption of so-called, "standard conditions" or operations, upon which the two factors were arbitrarily based. The basic tables list these conditions for the benefit of the planner. The standard conditions of operations set forth such "standards" as climate, sea, wind, type of employment, degree of enemy opposition, tempo of employment, and percentage of personnel complement on board.

Since, however, so-called standard conditions are almost never met, a *Judgment factor,* also designed for high-speed computers, must be introduced into the computation. This is selected by the planner, based upon his personal professional estimate of how the actual planned operating conditions will vary from "standard."

Planning Factors

All systems, types and levels of logistic planning are based on planning factors of one sort or another. The type used may vary greatly depending on the situation and the level of the planning.

Logistic planning factors have been prepared to simplify and speed up certain parts of the over-all task of "naval logistic planning." If they are to do this, they must be used with discretion and with a clear understanding of their nature, their derivation and their limitations.

Logistic planning factors are numerical values which represent the quantitative relationships which exist between the composition and employment of military forces on the one hand; and the availability, consumption, or utilization of materials, personnel, facilities, and services on the other hand.

These relationships may involve time, distance, volume, weight, area, number of units of a commodity, cost, life expectancy, and other matters. They are used in planning supply, equipment, construction, personnel, transportation, repair, salvage, and hospitalization facilities.

Planning factors may be merely the records of the personal experience of the planner written in a little black book kept in his hip pocket. In other instances, they may be taken directly from some official publication, such as the Navy "Logistics Reference Data" or the Army Field Manual 101-10, "Organization, Technical, and Logistical Data." Again, they may be derived from recent surveys or analyses, the results of which have not yet been officially published. To be most effective, planning factors should be based on the detailed study and evaluation of many types of situations. Such study requires the understanding cooperation of forces on all levels; for example, from fleet and type commanders down through the heads of departments on ships.

All planning factors are based on experience or usage data, some of it good, some of it very poor; some of it obsolete, some of it up-to-date. Therefore, some planning factors are quite accurate and some are hardly better than wild guesses.

Planning factors do not become good planning tools unless the planner knows the circumstances under which the fundamental usage data on which the factors are based were collected and processed.

At first it might appear that for each level of command there would be a prescribed type of planning factor or broad logistical aggregation suitable and sufficient for each situation. While it may be satisfactory to start the preparation of a plan by use of such prescribed data, this constitutes only a beginning of the task.

The exclusive use of broad aggregations is hazardous, because success or failure in war depends on the effective use of specific forces, specific weapons, specific items, and specific persons.

Therefore, even at the highest levels it is essential that the broad aggregation be supplemented by identification, reports, and evaluation of specific critical situations.

These reports and the initial evaluations must come from industry, from each of the Armed Services and from the theater commanders. Incidentally, experience has shown that criticalities can often be expected to occur in raw materials; finished ships, planes, weapons, and equipments; spare parts; petroleum products; ammunition; transportation; and trained personnel.

If we can devise methods and factors that are suitable for various types and levels of planning, we will have done much to simplify the problem. However, we cannot expect too much simplification. Logistic planning will always be a difficult task, a task that challenges our best abilities. Planning factors, regardless of how carefully they may be prepared, can never be a substitute for imagination and good judgment.

Usage Data

The foundation of good planning factors is good usage data. Since this seems self-evident, in the Navy it is interesting to note that the first over-all scientific analysis of fleet usage data was started in 1952 when the Logistics Research Project of The George Washington University undertook the collection and analysis of usage data among ships which had taken part in

Korean operations. Up to that time, while certain individual technical items had been analyzed, no serious attempt had been made to correlate individual studies or to analyze the fundamental nature of the problem.

The result of the general inadequacies of the analyses is that many of our present planning factors are based on usage data that is too broad for accurate planning. We know, for example, how much of certain categories was shipped to the Pacific for a given period during World War II, but we don't know what happened to this material. We don't know for sure how much went for its designed use, how much was lost, or stolen, how much was wasted through deterioration, or how much of the storage inventory aboard ship or in depots was necessary. Unfortunately, therefore some of the planning factors in effect for fleet use today are based on the amount that was shipped during World War II rather than the amount actually used by the ships of the fleet.

Figure 14 illustrates the distortion this can cause.

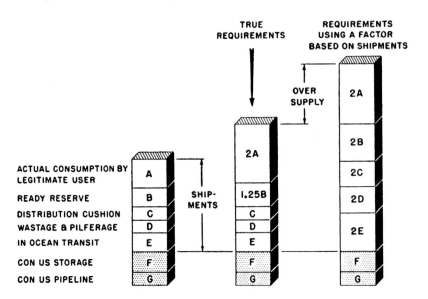

Figure 14. True Requirements vs. Requirements Based on
Total Shipments

If, for example, the number of units in an area is increased by 100% without making any major change in the planned operation, it is likely that *actual consumption* would be doubled, and that *ready reserve* should be increased 25% to handle the situation. However, the *other* requirements would not change.

The true requirement would thus be $2A + 1.25B + C + D + E$.

If, on the other hand, we use a factor based simply on previous over-all shipments we will come up with a false requirement of $2(A + B + C + D + E)$.

In recent years the work of the Navy's Supply Demand Control points in analyzing demand documents has improved this situation in the Navy. Furthermore, it is worthy of note that in the Korean War, although the number of combat ships in the Pacific Fleet was increased by 106%, they were supported by only a 45% increase in logistic support ships.

However, and in spite of this experience, not all our planning factors are built with recognition of the distinction between general averages and analyzed data. Blind use of general averages may result in tremendous oversupply. This explains why so many planners rely largely on the little black note books in their hip pockets.

Influence of Level, Range, and Nature of Situation on Planning Factors

Even given good planning factors and reasonable usage data, logistic planning will vary as to tempo, as to methods used, and as to choice of planning factors and usage data, dependent on the level, range, and nature of the situation.

The *level* of planning has an important bearing on the method and factors used in planning. One of the major problems in high level planning of either the capabilities or requirements type is that of developing planning methods and factors by which many different situations and assumptions can be rapidly evaluated in terms of their logistic implications. At low level, precise factors in relation to very specific items are usually required. At the highest level, however, since the use of detailed factors for each element of the plan causes intolerable delay, very broad factors are used to make general aggregations of commodities and equipments. These broad factors, however, must be accurate enough to give assurance that the lower levels charged with detailed development of plans will receive feasible broad plans.

The time *range* of planning has an important effect on the choice of methods and factors. Normally, short-range planning calls for much more specific methods and exact factors. In long-range planning more room for give and take is permissible, particularly in relation to the time element.

Closely related to the question of range is the question of the *nature of the situation.*

Is it stable? That is to say, is the rate of activity reasonably constant over a long period of time? If so, the problem is similar to the question of "supply management" with its associated elements of "requisition and inventory controls."

Is the situation unstable or fluctuating? Are we fighting a defensive, retreating action with all its unpredictable losses of material? Or, are we fighting an offensive, advancing action, with all its problem of steady expansion of effort and with periodic build-ups to support specific operations? In either of these latter cases, the problem becomes more complex and the maintenance of adequate reserves and flexibility is both important and difficult. Speed of such planning is very important, and important decisions in one logistic category may require quick, if broad, estimates of requirements in another category. *The factors and methods which give great economy in a stable situation may not be adequate for the changing situation.*

Summary

From the foregoing we can see that the way of planning has many pitfalls; it cannot be charted precisely in advance but can be found only through the wisdom of experienced professional judgment. The full development of that judgment requires understanding of the fundamentals of "integrated planning" of "information" and of "programming."

Chapter 6

Integration of Planning, Information, and Programming

. . . An officer may be highly successful and even brilliant, in all grades up to the responsible positions of high command, and then find his mind almost wholly unprepared to perform its vitally important functions in time of war.[1]
—REAR ADMIRAL WM. S. SIMS, USN

If our strategic and logistic plans are to be brought into timely harmony they must be fully "integrated" from their inception through their final execution. This process of integration requires certain formal planning procedures and also the organization of systems of "information" and of "programming." However, these all are of limited value unless they are accompanied by close personal relations among the people involved. And this, in turn, requires an appreciation of the intangible aspects of the situation. This is particularly important because the development of our modern large staff systems sometimes tends to obscure the commander's personal responsibility in the process of fully integrated planning.[2]

Feasibility and Calculated Risk

An example can be found in the common use of the term "feasibility" and "calculated risk." These words have probably been clouded with more ignorance and superstition than any other terms in our war and postwar vocabulary. They are closely related yet each requires careful study and proper qualification

---

[1] Rear Admiral William S. Sims, USN, in an address at the Naval War College, December 1919.

[2] Field Marshal Montgomery, *The Memoirs of Field Marshal Montgomery of Alamein, K.G.*, Cleveland, The World Publishing Company, 1958, pp 74-83. In chapter 6, "My Doctrine of Command," the Field Marshal provides an excellent discussion of this point. In particular on page 75 he emphasizes the importance of the leader creating the "atmosphere" in which his subordinates work.

in use. Final decision in either is a matter of the personal professional judgment of the commander. In each case it is a question of how much risk and how much hardship the commander is willing to impose on his subordinate forces and personnel in order to gain his objective. There are no absolute or arbitrary limits. The decision involves a process of selection of courses of action, and of the development of plans that will make the most effective use of the combat forces and logistic resources which are available. This process is the highest test of military judgment. It requires close personal relationships among the commander and his responsible assistants.

In dealing with the various formulations and representations of the intangibles of war and war planning we should expect to find many differences of opinion and procedure. These should not disturb us—for differences are not necessarily contradictions. Frequently the differences are more apparent than real and usually they merely represent two different but equally good approaches to a problem.

Integrating Strategy, Logistics, and Tactics

An oversimplified graphic representation of that part of the planning process which involves basic logistic considerations is shown in figure 15. This chart is not designed to provide a precise picture of an accepted or standard planning form or procedure, but rather to illustrate a series of important intangible relationships and, in turn, to relate these to the general logistic problem.

The chart is printed in different type faces to indicate the primary responsibilities of different elements of a staff. In the lower echelons a commander has relatively small units and correspondingly limited responsibilities. In most such cases the major thought processes in making estimates and plans must be performed by the commander himself, for his staff assistance is usually very small. However, as we go up the scale of command we find not only that the commander's responsibilities are greatly increased, but also he is given an ever-increasing amount of staff assistance. Finally, at the highest echelons of command there are officers of great experience exercising major area or global responsibilities and assisted by large and highly selected staffs. Regardless of what echelons of command we are discussing the thought processes illustrated in this chart apply. In some instances they may be subconscious reactions reflecting general experience of the commander himself, but in other cases they represent the formal reasoning and the actual planning processes undertaken by the members of the various sections of the commander's staff. The chart does not attempt to illustrate everything that takes place in the estimate of a situation and in the formulation of a plan. Rather, it is drawn from the logistical point of view and illustrates the effect of basic logistic considerations upon strategic planning.

The functions that must be performed entirely by the commander are indicated in light-faced type and a dotted bracket; those functions which are normally performed by the logistic divisions of the staff are shown in bold-faced type and a solid bracket, the functions of the plans and operations divisions of the staff (assisted by the intelligence division) are indicated in italics with a bracket drawn with alternating dashes and dots. Where there is a word in which some of the letters are in one kind of type and some in another, it represents a coordinated effort of several sections of the staff. There follows a discussion of the details of the chart. Numbers in this discussion correspond to the notations thereon.

1. ORGANIZE AND PROVIDE BASIC CONCEPT OF PLAN. This basic allocation of responsibilities and formulation of initial strategic concept constitute the first major step in integrated planning. The commander has a personal responsibility for the organization of his staff and of his forces. In the preparation of specific plans the commander must himself provide the essential foundation of a basic concept.

2. DETERMINATION OF REQUIREMENTS. The second step in this integration of strategic and logistical planning is the determination of logistic requirements. This determination of requirements is made by the logistic division of the staff and

● ● ● ● ● ● ● ● THE COMMANDER

━━━━━━━━━ **THE LOGISTIC DIV OF STAFF**

●━━●━━● *PLANS & OPNS DIV OF STAFF plus INTELL DIV*

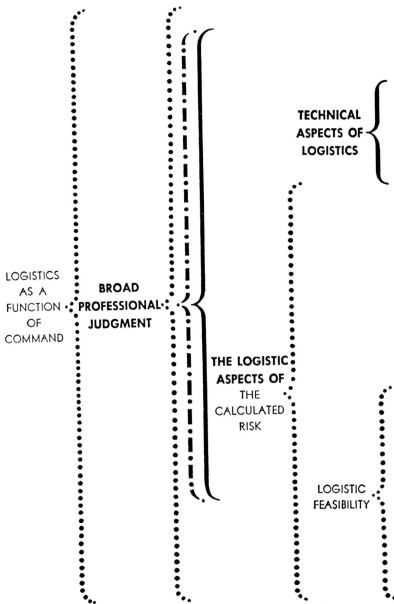

Figure 15. Integration of Strategic and Logistic Planning

1. ORGANIZE AND PROVIDE BASIC CONCEPT OF PLAN

2. **DETERMINATION OF LOGISTIC REQUIREMENTS**
   BASED ON *ESTIMATE OF COMBAT FORCES INVOLVED AND A SPECIFIC SCHEME OF MANEUVER*
   a **PLANNING TECHNIQUES**
      (1) **USE OF FORMS AND PROCEDURES**
   b **PLANNING FACTORS**
      (1) **BASIC USAGE DATA**
      (2) **INITIAL CORRECTION FACTORS CURRENT AREA EXPERIENCE**
   c **OPERATIONAL MODIFICATION**
      (1) **EFFECT OF TIME, SPACE AND WEATHER FACTORS**
      (2) **EFFECT OF** *ENEMY CAPABILITIES AND LIMITATIONS* ✔
   d *DETERMINE CRITICAL ITEMS* **SUMMARIZE**
      POSTPONE CONSIDERATION OF NON CRITICAL ITEMS

3. **DETERMINE AVAILABILITIES OF**
   CRITICAL ITEMS (PROCUREMENT AND DISTRIBUTION)
   a **STATISTICAL DATA AND REPORTS**
   b **EFFECT OF TIME, SPACE FACTORS**
   c **EFFECT OF** *ENEMY CAPABILITIES AND LIMITATIONS*

4. *EVALUATION*
   a *LIMITATIONS ON STRATEGIC AND TACTICAL PLANS*
      i.e. *THE DEGREE OF FREEDOM OF ACTION*
   b *MODIFICATIONS OF STRATEGIC AND TACTICAL PLANS*
      TIME   *SCOPE*
   c *RECOMMENDATIONS*

5. DECISIONS
   a GO AHEAD WITH PLAN
   b MODIFY PLAN
   c ABANDON PLAN AND START A NEW ONE

Figure 15. Integration of Strategic and Logistic Planning (Cont.)

therefore is indicated in bold face. It is based on an estimate of the combat forces involved and on a specific scheme of maneuver both of which are given to the logistic division of a staff by the plans and operations division. These are therefore lettered in italics.

When we come to the initial development of the logistic requirements we find that we can group the process into parts. The first is (A), the development of good planning techniques. These planning techniques normally consist of the provision of sound common forms and standard procedures for planning. In a large area operation, where many task forces and type commanders are involved, if estimates are submitted concerning any one subject on a variety of different forms and with a variety of different procedures, the planning process is greatly delayed.

For example, in planning for the Gilberts and Marshalls campaigns in 1943, the various type commanders submitted their demands for shipping space to CINCPOA using a great variety of forms and terminology. The summarization and evaluation of these individualistic documents wasted many hours of staff work. Early in 1944, hower, CINCPOA Logistic division developed what was known as "Form A" which was a standard form and terminology for the submission and summarization of shipping requirements. The use of this standard form greatly reduced the mechanical aspects of planning, thus making the planning process simpler and hence faster and more accurate.

A second initial element in the determination of logistic requirements is (B) the use of "planning factors." Since all planning factors should stem from basic usage data, we must remember that basic usage data is collected from a variety of sources over a long period of time, and, therefore, merely represents broad general averages. Since no operation is ever "average" it is important that we make corrections to this basic usage data in accordance with the current experience of a particular area.

All of these planning techniques and planning factors are indicated in bold face because normally this portion of the planning process is performed entirely by the logistic division of the staff.

Now, as the next step before the initial determination can be used, we must apply part (C) or "operational modification." In other words, our planning factors and data have been only partly corrected and we need to make additional corrections. These are necessary in the light of: first, the effect of time, space and weather factors on our initial estimate of requirements; and, second, the effect of enemy capabilities and limitations upon these factors.

The effect of time, space and weather is normally estimated by the logistic division of the staff, but when we come to the effect of enemy capabilities and limitations, we find that the members of both the logistic and operations divisions of the staff must sit together around a table and thrash these matters out, each group contributing to the discussions in accordance with its particular knowledge and experience. Therefore, the lettering on the chart is alternately bold face and italics. Good results come only from an intimate integration of thinking at this time.

This process is illustrated by the problem of providing specialized petroleum products for the Okinawa invasion. The general basic usage data available to the planners at this time, based on the general average of previous operations, indicated that there was a relatively small requirement for smoke and fog oil. However, consideration of the latest experience in Leyte, indicated that use of these items was beginning to increase. Certain additions, therefore, were made to the original estimates. However, in November 1944 the author made a trip to Washington and while there was told by Captain Metzel of the Readiness Division of ComInch's staff that we should anticipate a much greater use of smoke and fog oil in the assault on Okinawa. He pointed out that it was the lavish use of this means of concealment that had protected our ships from German aircraft in the invasion of Normandy, and he urged that the author make every effort to impress its value upon the CINCPAC staff. This message was delivered to Captain T. B. Hill of CINCPAC Readiness Division, and on the basis of this evaluation of enemy capabilities, the estimate of requirements for fog oil was greatly increased. In spite of this correction, we found that we did not plan enough. Extraordinary measures had to be taken to expedite the resupply of fog oil after the action was underway. In this case our estimate of enemy capabilities was somewhat deficient because we did not fully appreciate the extent and persistence of the "Kamikaze" attacks.

Having made such operational modification to our initial estimate as appears necessary, we now find we are faced with a tremendous mass of data, in great detail, on the logistic requirements of the plan. For the purpose of reaching sound decisions it is not necessary that all of these detailed requirements be taken into consideration. We must, however, determine which are the critical items: that is, those items which must be present in sufficient quantity at the right time to insure the success of our combat forces, and the lack of which would jeopardize their operations. In this determination of critical requirements again we find the logistic division and the operations division sitting down together at the same table and discussing the situation. Then, when we determine what these critical factors are, the logistic division of the staff evaluates them. Thereafter we consider only the most critical items, postponing the others until the detailed development of final plans.

Thus we complete our determination of logistic requirements. This is the second major step in the process of integrated and concurrent strategic logistic planning.

3. DETERMINE AVAILABILITIES OF CRITICAL ITEMS. Our third step in this planning is to determine the availability of critical items. Here we find ourselves in the fields of procurement and distribution: where and in what quantity can these critical items be obtained? This process requires the use of good statistical data and reports; that is to say, "information

and programming." These latter items will be discussed later in this chapter.

Having studied the basic availability of critical items, we must estimate the effect of time and space factors on their procurement. This process is also the task of the logistic division.

Now just as in (C) of step 2, we have to calculate the effect of enemy action in increasing our use of various elements of logistic support. So, in this determination of availabilities, as well as in the determination of requirements, we must calculate the additional effect of enemy capabilities and limitations on our *sources of supply* and on the *transportation* of these materials to the point where we wish to distribute them to the combat task forces. Again the logistic and operations divisions sit down together, and together arrive at conclusions.

4. EVALUATION. Having determined our requirements, and having determined the procurement and distribution situations, we find that in some cases there will be shortages and in other cases there will probably be excesses. We then undertake the process of evaluation of this situation.

This evaluation is an exacting test of the planner's experience and judgment. For, while we have previously made a selection of critical items, the degree to which any particular item may be deficient before its lack becomes fatally defective is difficult to determine. Frequently we find that certain substitutions may reduce the shortage. In other instances we may find that while no single item is fatally deficient, an accumulation of shortages in certain areas may be serious.

So it is vital that this part of the planning process again finds the logistic and operations divisions sitting together around the table. As a result of these intimate discussions we determine the limitations on the basic strategical and tactical plans that are imposed by the logistic situation. In other words, we estimate the degree of freedom of action that the commander will have in the light of his logistic capabilities. And, if we find that the limitations on freedom of action are too restrictive for his purposes, we consider what modification of the strategical and tactical plans can be made which will permit the execution of the basic concept of the plan. Modifications of this nature may be either in time or in scope.

Time modifications are illustrated by recalling that the invasion of Southern France was originally scheduled to occur simultaneously with the invasion of Normandy. The lack of availability of landing craft and the lack of availability of aircraft for support of that operation, however, were such that the timing of the two operations had to be staggered. In other words, Southern France had to wait until Normandy could release landing craft and planes.

At this point, and when the logistic and operations divisions have completed their evaluation of the effects of logistic shortages or deficiencies, they should be prepared to submit their considered recommendations to the commander as to what actions to take.

5. DECISION. Finally, we come to the last process in this scheme of integrated planning. This step is the one in which the decisions are made. These decisions can be made only by the commander himself. True, he is greatly assisted by the studies, evaluations, and recommendations of his staff assistants; but the decisions are the personal responsibility of the commander, a responsibility which he cannot evade. In general, his decisions can lie in three classifications:

(A) He decides to go ahead with the plan as originally conceived. In other words, he feels that his logistic support is adequate or that he can accept a calculated, an evaluated, or a recognized risk.

(B) On the other hand if he feels that his logistic support is not adequate he may decide to modify the plan. As was said before, while he may modify it either in time or scope or both, such modification is his personal decision. He will, of course, have available to him the advice and recommendations of his staff.

(C) In certain instances the commander may decide to abandon the plan and start afresh.

Where there is an experienced commander with a competent and well trained staff and if he has the initiative or if the situation is relatively stable, the decision is usually either to proceed with the original plan or to modify it. In some instances, however, the situation may have changed radically since the initial concept of the plan, or, other matters outside the power of control of the commander may have intervened in such a fashion as to make the abandonment of the plan necessary. Then again, in some rare instances the quality of the planning may be poor, in which case in addition to throwing the plan overboard, the commander might well cast a very critical eye on his staff and its procedures and methods.

So much for the work itself. Enough discussion has been given to illustrate the general areas in which strategic and logistic planning must take place *within the context of the logistic planning for the operation.* It has been shown how the logistic division of the staff, itself and in collaboration with other appropriate divisions, have come up with basic recommendations as to the strategic and logistic aspects of the concept. And, lastly, there have been indicated those areas in which the commander himself will exercise decision.

These general divisions of cognizance can well be visualized on the chart itself. Thus (turning again to the chart), as we come to the end of this process of integration of strategical and logistical planning, let us summarize what we have found. We find that in 2(A) and (B) we have "the technical aspects of logistics" in which specialists may work effectively in relatively narrow fields. These, therefore, we can bracket in a solid line, and we can call it the technical aspects of logistics.

Responsibility of Commander

When we look at steps 4 and 5, the evaluation and the decisions, the process of *determination* of "logistic feasibility," is the prerogative of the commander himself. While he utilizes the assistance of his staff to help him to make this decision, he cannot evade the burden of decision. These steps—the areas of decision—we therefore bracket in a dotted line.

Next we see the "logistic aspects of a calculated risk." The "calculation" starts with 2(C) and goes down through 5(C). The determination of critical items, and this evaluation, together constitutes the "calculation" which links all the processes. Cognizance over this area of the planning process is clearly that of the commander working with the logistic division of his staff. Accordingly, these words are shown in both light face and bold face type.

It is well at this point to reexamine the phrase "calculated risk." Too often we find the words "calculated risk" used merely as an expression to cloak or conceal sloppy thinking. Of course, in the broad aspects of the calculated risk there are many other aspects to be considered in addition to the logistic aspects. Fleet Admiral Ernest J. King discussed this subject succinctly:

> The ability of a naval commander to make consistently sound military decisions is the result of a combination of attributes. The natural talent of the individual, his temperament, his reactions in emergencies, his courage, and his professional knowledge all contribute to his proficiency and to the accuracy of his judgment. We have spent years training our officers to think clearly and for themselves, to the end that when entrusted with the responsibility of making decisions in time of war they would be fully qualified.
>
> One of the mental processes that has become almost a daily responsibility for all those in command is that of calculating the risks involved in a given course of action. That may mean the risks attendant upon disposition of forces, such as had to be taken before the Battle of Midway, when an erroneous evaluation might have left us in a most unfavorable strategic position; the risks of losses in contemplated engagements, such as the Battle of Guadalcanal on 13-14-15 November 1942; the risks of success or failure dependent upon correct evaluation of political conditions, of which the North African landings are an example, and a host of others.
>
> Calculating risks does not mean taking a gamble. It is

more than figuring the odds. It is not reducible to a formula. It is the analysis of all factors which collectively indicate whether or not the consequences to ourselves will be more than compensated for by the damage to the enemy or interference with his plans. Correct calculation of risks, by orderly reasoning, is the responsibility of every naval officer who participated in combat, and many who do not. It is a pleasure to report that almost universally that responsibility is not only accepted, but sought, and that there have been few cases where it has not been properly discharged.[3]

Next there are the features of the plan which require broad professional judgment. Three brackets, shown in dotted, solid, and broken lines appear. Elements 2 through 4 in general call for the exercise of broad professional judgment on the part of the logistic division of the staff, as opposed to the specialized technical aspects of logistics encompassed in paragraphs 2(A) and 2(B). The steps from 2 to 4 are also bracketed in a broken line as the area in which the broad professional judgment of the operations planners is coordinated with the broad judgment of the logistic planners. And, of course, the over-all dotted brackets indicate the area in which the commander himself exercises his broad professional judgment, that is, in all features of the plan as appropriate.

And, finally the whole chart is encompassed in light face type with the broad description of "Logistics, A Function of Command." Every element in this chart lies in the over-all cognizance of the commander.

In presenting this discussion of integration of strategic and logistical planning, the thought has been carried only through the broad aspects of the estimate of the situation to the point where a decision has been reached. There is no discussion of the further integration that is required in the development of detailed plans (planning for logistic support), nor in the execution of these plans once the decision has been made. Yet, in the development of these plans and in the execution of

---

[3] Admiral Ernest J. King, *U.S. Navy at War 1941-1945,* Washington, U.S. Navy Department, 1946. p. 34.

these plans we require in many instances similar integration of strategic and logistical thinking. Throughout the operation, from inception to completion, will be found time and again illustrations of logistics as a function of command. The commander never can divorce himself from his responsibility for the logistic support of his combat forces.

Supervision of the Planned Action

No matter how brilliantly conceived or carefully prepared any plan may be, it must always be adjusted to the realities of a developing situation.

Consequently all studies of military decision and planning stress the importance of "supervision of the planned action." Among other matters this supervision includes the related topics of "information" and "programming."

Information and Programming

In its military sense a *program* is a plan of procedure phased over time, an administrative course of action specific as to quantities, types, dates, and locations.

Information as used in this discussion is quite different from the information produced by intelligence. In this discussion it is primarily concerned with the vast amount of information as to one's own status which flows in from routine reports. In its ultimate development and evaluation in the mind of command, it is obvious, however, that this general information must be examined in the light of information of an intelligence nature.

Consideration of these subjects highlights one of the many differences between peacetime planning and wartime planning. The emergency or mobilization plans made in peacetime do not come to the fruition or tests of war, if ever, except at long unpredictable intervals. Peacetime planning is primarily a regenerative cycle. Few of the plans are actually carried out as a whole but instead each major part of a plan may be carried out in a series of frequently modified steps. The modifications in one part of the plan induce changes in other parts of the plan. The plans themselves are in a necessary and continual process of responding to changes in strategic concepts, to operational and technological improvements, and to budgetary fluctuations. In any event, the plans are translated into specific programs. Supervision over these programs will necessarily provoke effective response to changing conditions and thus will provide supervision over the planned action.

In wartime the situation is different, particularly when the tactical offensive phase or the strategical offensive phase of a war is involved. Here specific plans are brought to fruition in the execution of campaign plans and their component operations.

These campaign plans are supported by the build-up of combat and logistic resources provided by previously planned programs.

Uncertain theories and untested concepts are replaced by the hard facts of combat losses and by the effects of tactical and strategical successes. Thus, the regenerative process takes place as in peacetime but the motivating influences are somewhat changed.

In a wartime situation, maximum responsiveness to combat situations is essential, otherwise golden opportunities to exploit strategical success may be lost. This latter factor is one of the most important elements in the problem of command.

Both in peace and in war the process of programming has become a vital part of command control. The flow and evaluation of *information* form the foundation of programming.

In later discussions we will see how the proper flow and evaluation of information is necessary to the attainment of both "readiness" and "flexibility." Obviously, accurate information as to the current and prospective readiness of a command is vital to the formulation of operational plans. Furthermore, information is essential to day-to-day operations, both tactical and logistical.

During World War II, in 1944-45 CINCPOA's staff, the operations division kept track of the location and readiness of ships, the ammunition section maintained its own records, the transportation section had its records of merchant shipping, and the statistical section of the logistic division maintained a large volume of records on personnel, storage space, fuel, ammunition, construction progress, general and special supplies, and other matters. While this system worked satisfactorily, it suffered from lack of a central point where all major significant information as to the combat forces and their logistic support was brought together and presented for ready review.

Also during World War II, the Army and Army Air Force commands throughout the world usually had their statistical control officers who collected and evaluated this type of information with varying degrees of effectiveness.

Since 1945 great progress has been made in this area both from the point of view of organization and in the techniques of the reporting and display systems. Each command is faced with its own special situation; and each should organize its "information control" in accordance with its special needs. In some commands this type of work is handled by a "general planning group," in others by a "programming group." In a tactical situation, however, even though the bulk of the information to be handled is logistical in nature, the importance and nature of tactical information and planning and the correlation necessary with intelligence, dictate that the operations war room be the focal point for major over-all information.

Let us now turn to programming. A formal programming organization is, generally speaking, an important tool of command; but it is particularly important in a Joint or Combined area command where diverse forces or units must be brought together in well-timed schedules.

Perhaps the best guide for determining the allocation of the responsibility for programming and for the identification of the areas where the same information should be maintained, both in the control or war room and in the staff divisions detailed files and displays, is to consider the expression "perspective of command." If this be kept in mind while the many details of staff information are reviewed, most of the decisions will be obvious. First, however, it is important to recognize that a moderate amount of duplication and overlap of information is necessary to good planning.

The selection of what data should be available for ready display and of what information should be periodically presented to the commander in person requires discrimination. If too much is presented it may all be ignored; or, if too little is presented, many important considerations may be neglected.

The most intricate and important tasks of programming are those at the Department of Defense and Service Headquarters levels. Here each must adjust its material and personnel plans to the realities and timing of the budget cycle and at the same time be sure that current strategic plans are continuously supported. It is a task that taxes the ingenuity and industry of the staff of the Joint Chiefs of Staff, the general planners, the logistic planners, the comptrollers, and the budget directors. But even when all the plans and budgets have been approved there still remains the necessary task of supervising their execution.

On the highest level, programming is the heart of industrial mobilization. Without it no system of controls can work. As our economy becomes more complex and as our military requirements include more and more of the products of industry, the problem of programming becomes more difficult. More information must be obtained and it must be handled more speedily. This calls for mechanized and electronic reporting and processing systems.

Our economic system is too involved, however, for any system ever to *control* completely. The attempt to control everything causes a rigidity that defeats the purpose of control and actually reduces production. Flexibility is one of the greatest assets of our free economy. We must be wary lest in our enthusiasm for industrial economic controls in time of war, we lose the flexibility produced by individual initiative.

Accordingly, we should limit the scope and degree of our controls to the fewest possible elements of the economy. In many instances indirect controls may be better than direct controls.

The effect of programming control has implications in certain areas of the information problem. For example, in the case of a quick major expansion of naval forces, a vast number of subcontractors have their own interrelations and relations with other procurement agencies that are too subtle and complex to be accurately registered in any formal reporting system. The result is that the Navy cannot accurately gauge and plan its expansion program solely on the basis of a centralized information and control agency which uses only the information that flows through formal official channels. It must supplement this by using the experienced judgment of the production men of both the prime contractors and the subcontractors in the specific problems encountered. It is not likely that this judgment can be quickly obtained by formal questionnaires. It can best be obtained by sending qualified officers into the field to discuss these matters informally and to make on the spot decisions.

A fuller discussion of activities such as the foregoing will be found in the book, *Functions of the Executive* [4] by Chester Barnard, in which he emphasizes the informal aspects of organization.

Programming presents two major problems: that of determining what information is to be acquired and analyzed; and that of devising and using systems and appliances for the analysis and presentation of the selected information. Only when these two tasks are done properly is it possible to evaluate the information. Final evaluation is the task and prerogative of command.

Most of the programming problems of high command, while highly complicated from a production and coordination point of view, are comparatively simple from the point of view of a mathematical theory. Uusually they merely involve a very large number of long problems in simple arithmetic which can be solved by relatively simple electronic machines in a matter of minutes. However, if we attempt to solve some of the over-

---

[4] Chester I. Barnard, *The Functions of the Executive,* Cambridge, Massachusetts, Harvard University Press: 1950. pp 223-227.

all economic problems that are implicit in national programming we may become involved in such advanced mathematics that they can be handled only by the most advanced electronic computers. For example, it would be very valuable if we could determine accurately in advance the complete impact on all phases of our national economy of a major increase or decrease in the production of any one major military item. This problem involves the solution of an "input-output matrix" of such size and complexity that mathematicians and economists are uncertain as to the success that can be expected.

Let us now return to information. One of the most striking illustrations of the "information problem" lay in the development of the Logistic division of the Staff of Commander Western Sea Frontier when that command was reorganized under Admiral Ingersoll in late 1944 and early 1945. Previous to that time critical logistic information had been largely diffused through the offices of the various technical establishments in the San Francisco area and along the whole west coast. Command control was inadequate and it was difficult quickly to obtain accurate information as to the logistic situation in the sea frontier.

In the reorganization, Commander Western Sea Frontier's command responsibilities were both strengthened and clarified. Under the direction of Commodore Paul E. Pihl, USN, *all* important information was channeled through the logistic division of the sea frontier staff where it was evaluated; and selected portions were promptly reported to the Chief of Naval Operations and to The Commander in Chief Pacific Fleet and Pacific Ocean Area.

A great improvement was quickly evident—information that was previously uncertain and hard to get, although important, came in promptly and accurately. The result was that Command could forecast situations and exercise control and plan its operations with certainty. The reduction in avoidable waste that came from improved logistic operations was merely an extra dividend. The important principle involved is: *Command au-*

*thority and information control go hand in hand; one is use-
less without the other.*

The corollary, of course, is: The exercise of the authority
of high command requires an understanding of the principles
of information.

A further point is that when considering such matters as
centralization versus decentralization of command authority and
the question of the location size, protection and mobility of
major headquarters ashore or afloat, the problem of information
is of great importance.[5] Rapid and diverse signal communications are only one part of the problem. Space, facilities and personnel for the filing, sorting, and evaluation of the information
brought into the headquarters by the communication system
must also be provided before command can exercise control.
At the same time, consideration must be given to appropriate
duplication of information and programming data and facilities
in the light of possible enemy bombing, etc.

The Principle of Information

A few examples of the direct significance of information to
the exercise of command have been discussed. Beyond these and
extending into many areas of politics and business there are
many other illustrations to be found. These are numerous
enough to warrant the thought that a basic general principle
applies to all areas of administration and command.

This may be called, "the principle of information." *The exercise of authority gravitates toward the person or agency which
has the most accurate grasp of the significant information.*

This general statement has many implications in many areas.
A strong man insists on having his own direct line to the in-
formation center, be it a comptroller or a programming officer.
He then makes his own decisions with assurance.

A man becomes a "strong man" largely by reason of his
ability to grasp and evaluate the significant elements of a complex situation.

---

[5] Chapter 18 discusses the test of organization as related to readiness.
The question of how information is handled is important to this question.

A weak man loses control partly by reason of his inability to grasp and evaluate the significant elements. He, therefore, must depend on others to make these evaluations and in doing so he tends to lose control of his decisions.

The wise "strong man," however, makes his own determination of what is significant; and, while he will listen to other opinions and evaluations, they merely influence him rather than dominate him. He will recognize the areas of his own competence and the areas in which he should yield to the competence and information of others. In most of our large organizations the "strong man" cannot himself be an expert in all fields. He, therefore, must know how to listen to and how to use experts. The commander must know which "experts" to listen to, and when.

An ignorant man in a position of power will act on partial information, or will make improper evaluations as to the relative importance of significant information and will blunder.

The "strong man" who is unscrupulous, will intentionally distort the significant elements of information and will impose his will by force or by shrewd maneuvers. This in turn may have evil results.[6]

There are many areas of military activity, administration, and command where the general principle of information applies. It can be seen in the functioning of the staff of any command. A staff can largely determine decision by the manner in which they present information. This may occur among the most upright men because of the degree to which complex matters may be oversimplified and distorted when briefed down to the frequently demanded single page. Thus, in effect, "policy" can be made in the lower echelons. A "staff secretary" is a person of great influence, by reason of the information he must possess. There are many illustrations of the "principle of information"

---

[6] B. H. Liddell Hart, *Why Don't We Learn From History?* George Allen & Unwin Ltd., London 1944, pp 13-15. Captain B. H. Liddell Hart cites an example of such deception by Sir Douglas Haig. Haig ordered the removal of healthy prisoners from the cages before an inspection by the British Prime Minister in order to justify his own contention that the German Army was close to exhaustion and that therefore continuation of his Passchendaele offensive of July 1917 was justified.

in the "general staff." Some of these are illustrative of its proper use, others of improper use, such as the "isolation of the commander" by a "palace guard."

The principle of information is intimately related to the organization of any command and to the formulation of major policy and plans. It is particularly important in the logistic aspects of the organization of both a command and a staff because of the tremendous volume of significant information in any major logistic situation. It is well exemplified in the manner in which the comptrollers have been set up in the Department of Defense and in the Navy, where the Comptroller reports directly to the chief executive of his department or bureau.

An understanding of the working of this general principle is necessary to the successful delegation of authority. Finally, we should recognize that the skillful organization and use of information is an essential element in maintaining combat readiness, in developing mobility and flexibility and in controlling the "logistic snowball."

Summary

The foregoing chapters have sketched out the broad elements that go into the business of planning in logistics. That process has been touched upon at the national and supra-national levels, and the levels of planning have been described and explored.

Two general classes of planning—mobilization and operational—have been considered.

Two broad approaches to planning—requirements planning and capabilities planning—have been described. The place of each has been shown in the various levels of command.

Two specific types of planning in logistics—"logistic planning," and "planning for logistic support"—have been discussed. The activities of the former lie in the field of "The estimate of the situation." The latter, part of "the development of the plan," is an activity which deals with the actual determination, procurement, and distribution of logistic means.

The distinction between "line item" planning and planning by broad aggregations has been shown.

The *basis* of all work in the field of planning has been shown to be the judicious use of planning factors and usage data.

There followed an exposition of the steps involved in the process of drawing up logistic plans. Here it became evident that the commander not only is responsible for an operation, but that his personal judgment, knowledge, and decision are necessary at all steps in the planning and conduct both of logistics and of tactical operations.

There was given a discussion of information and programming. These latter are necessary to provide supervision over the action planned—and supervision is necessary to the effective fulfilment of every plan.

And, lastly, the importance of information as a tool of command has been pointed out. The better that information—strategic, tactical, and logistic—is handled, the stronger will be the command.

PART II
OPERATIONAL FACTORS

Chapter 7

The "Logistic Snowball"

The history of ideas is the history of mistakes.[1]
—ALFRED NORTH WHITEHEAD

Having reviewed the structure and interrelationship of war and logistics and having presented several approaches to planning, we can now discuss some of the specific factors and relationships which will affect the working of the operational plans developed.

No commander can predict how his operations will influence the thinking and actions of an opponent. No logistic plan can provide equally well for all possible contingencies. Therefore, there must be continuous active command supervision of the planned action, and continuous command control and adjustment of logistic plans and operations. The most significant elements of this command control lie in a group of related factors.

First, there is the organizational structure of command. Second, there is the basic design of the logistic system, particularly the size and the rate of build up of logistic resources relative to the size and build up of tactical forces. Third, there are the matters of control of supply levels and supply flow, the establishment and administration of priorities and allocations, and the control of movement and transportation. Fourth, there is the attainment of a sense of logistic discipline throughout the whole command. The final step in the exercise of command supervision is to answer the question: What is the command's true state of logistic readiness for sustained combat?

---

[1] Alfred North Whitehead, *Adventures of Ideas,* Macmillan Co., New York, chapter 3, VIII.

In the application of these factors to the formulation of initial plans and in their subsequent supervision, it is important to recognize that all of them are influenced by three interrelated natural forces. Experience shows that logistic activities tend to grow to inordinate size like a snowball, that they tend to become rigid, and that they tend to acquire a very real physical momentum. Therefore, if we are to control and to adjust logistical activities in such a way as to attain the greatest sustained combat effectiveness, we must reduce the "snowball," create flexibility, and control and exploit momentum. These factors and tools of control are so overlapping that they must be repeatedly discussed from many aspects. This is inevitable for they all are interwoven as parts of the same living organism.

The Growth Tendency

The concept that logistic activities naturally tend to "snowball" or to grow out of all proportion to the tactical forces which they support is perhaps the most important single thesis of this book.

The tendency to overgrow has a direct influence on the relative balance and disposition of combat and logistic support forces. It bears directly on the development of strategic flexibility and momentum, and it should be considered in problems of movement control and transportation. Finally, the snowball is a vital factor in the study of logistic discipline. If it is to be controlled it must be taken into account in the development of the command structure.

Influence and Causes

The snowball has its basic causes in three major factors:

First, the effect of the industrial revolution and the consequent ever-increasing ratio of logistic support required to create and sustain a modern tactical unit;

Second, the very high standard of modern living in the U.S.A. coupled with the general lack of logistic discipline;

Third, the failure of many commanders and staff planners to understand the nature of the snowball and its full implications.

Hypothetical Illustration

The logistic snowball has many examples in all services, some of which are cited herein as being representative of how it generally works. For the first example let us examine its working in an advanced naval base.

It has been a widely held opinion that second-rate personnel are suitable for manning advanced naval bases in time of war. How does this affect the situation?

The supply of highly efficient officers, men, and civilian employees is always limited in war. If inefficient personnel are involved, it is likely that many of them will spend their time doing useless tasks, and each administrative unit and staff, accordingly, will expand in order to get the work done. This results from a lowering of quality, which in turn leads to sluggishness in response and to a generally lower quality of planning and administration. This, again, leads to a demand for more personnel with the corollary increases in transportation, housing, messing, medical, and management personnel.

Let us say that "Buck Rogers" denotes a highly selected, well-trained, well-disciplined, and well-equipped officer or enlisted man; and that "Joe Doaks" represents the run-of-the-mill product of the draft and wartime procurement who has not been carefully selected, trained, nor disciplined, and who has only a fair knowledge of his equipment.

Let us further assume that on a newly established advanced base there are one-hundred man days of work to be done each day. The following table is illustrative of what may happen in terms of increased logistic effort resulting from the employment of "Joe Doaks" personnel. (Note: This table, although fictitious, is drawn up from planning factors and usage data compiled from actual World War II conditions by the author).

TABLE SHOWING INCREASE IN LOGISTIC EFFORT RESULTING
FROM POOR PERSONNEL

	"Buck Rogers personnel"	*"Joe Doaks personnel"*	*Increase in effort due to poor personnel*
Man-days work required	100	100	
Extra men required to compensate for personal inefficiency ...	0	100	
Loss due to sickness and accident ..	5	25	
Loss due to punishments, etc..	1	10	
	106	235	129 men
Messing, hospital police and general administration .	27	94	
Officer administration .	7	33	
Total during base operation	140	362	222 men
Amount of housing required	H	2.6H	
Amount of construction man hours ...	C	2.6C	
Amount of initial shipping required @ 6 measurement tons per man..	840	2172	1332 M.T.
Amount of shipping per month to support @ 1½ MT/man/month	210	543	333

Direct Effects

The above estimates are conservative rather than exaggerated, for we know that even in well-established and well-run bases, administrative overhead absorbs somewhat more than 30% of the total base personnel, leaving not more than 70% for actual productive work toward the logistic objective.

In extreme cases, we know that in some instances advanced base units were so ineffective that they actually became a drain on the fleet logistic support rather than a contributor to it.

But even this is not the whole picture because this situation means that 222 more men were procured, equipped, housed, transported, and processed in the United States; that 222 more pay accounts and personnel records had to be maintained than were necessary, and that the tax payers had to pay the salaries and pensions of 222 more men than would otherwise have been required. Furthermore, shipping space for an initial movement of 1332 measurement tons and thereafter a monthly 333 measurement tons of shipping space was unnecessarily used at a time when shipping space was at a premium.

Such an advanced base will be top heavy with personnel and it will use more logistic effort than it is producing. Even though this situation is by itself a significant waste of resources, the over-all snowball effect has only just begun. It will be even further extended if supply systems operate in such a manner as to place excessively large stocks ashore in overseas depots.

A still further expansion is possible in the operations of a fleet freight system, unless such operations are rigorously controlled.

During the war whenever a ship left a continental U.S. naval base there usually were a considerable number of supply requisitions which for one reason or another were unfilled. In many instances, these items were later shipped overseas in miscellaneous cargoes as "fleet freight," with the hope that they would be delivered. In addition, many requisitions for supplies and equipment received from ships overseas were forwarded as fleet freight. This freight system was, of course, inherently slow. On the other hand, the ships being supported were mobile, and strategic and tactical considerations made it necessary that the ships not be tied down to a single freight area. Hence, in the vain pursuit of a cruiser whose operational area had been changed by dispatch, freight might start for Argentia, go on to Iceland, and finally end up in Australia.

Complete records do not exist to show how many hundreds of thousands of tons of fleet freight were shipped. No one knows what percentage was correctly delivered or what percentage was lost, strayed, or stolen. The most optimistic guesses are that not more than fifty percent ever reached its destination in time to fulfill its purpose.

For example, at the end of World War II thousands of measurement tons of undelivered fleet freight accumulated on Guam. At that time it would have served no useful purpose to attempt to deliver it because either the need had passed or it had been supplied from other sources. There is no way of accurately determining the direct cost of procurement of this material or its precise nature.

Post-war studies indicate that fleet freight had an average value of about $1,000.00 per measurement ton. This means that a significant amount of unnecessary procurement existed in one area of a single broad logistic category. While this would seem to be a regrettable waste, it should by itself not cause too much alarm for it is manifestly absurd to expect to kill the last enemy with the last bullet. However, more was involved. This material had been travelling about 15 months and had probably averaged 6,000 miles of travel by land and sea from its original source, through its various paths to Guam. All of this cargo had been loaded and unloaded about three times. This resulted in a further dissipation of logistic effort. A great deal of unnecessary and useless cargo handling had been done by stevedores and cargo handling units, and these were always in short supply. Furthermore, the paper work, dispatches, and other time-consuming administrative functions spent uselessly on this effort slowed down and obstructed the useful work which the people and facilities involved would otherwise have done. Thus the waste and obstruction expanded in an ever-widening circle from the central core of fruitless effort.

This unhappy sequence of cause and effect leads us to the consideration of another important point.

Under-planning—Over-planning Sequence

In all our affairs we see instances of the harmful effects of the human tendency to go to extremes. In logistics this further snowball effect is frequently illustrated by cases in which under-planning is followed by over-planning.

If the logistic aspects of an operation are initially planned and provided on a seriously inadequate scale, experience has shown that the *eventual* commitment of logistic resources to that operation, in an effort to correct the initial deficiencies, will be lavish and wasteful. In other words, *under-planning* produces *over-planning*.

Two major factors enter into the operation of this sequence. Again, as is so often noted, these two factors are interrelated and interacting.

Let us consider the tactical effect. If, in the early stages of an operation, the logistic support is deficient it will not be possible fully to exploit an early or unexpected tactical success. The basic principle here involved is very well expressed by the statement in reference to planning the Normandy invasion:

> . . . as one observer remarked, the faster an army intended to advance and the more violent the blows it intended to strike, the larger must be its administrative tail.[2]

The inability to exploit a tactical success then prolongs the operation or the campaign. The result of this delay inevitably is a great increase in the logistic resources *ultimately* expended to achieve that specific objective. This is a direct effect which is quite simple and obvious.

Indirect Effects

The indirect effects may be less obvious but are also significant. If the planned logistic support is shown to be inadequate in the early days of an operation, the tactical commanders will

---

[2] Ruppenthal, R. G. *Logistical Support of the Armies—The European Theater of Operations.* Office of the Chief of Military History, Department of the Army, Washington, D.C. 1953. p. 332.

naturally exert the greatest pressure to obtain more support. This will in turn produce urgent emergency measures and improvisation. Improvisation, as applied to emergency support for major operations, is always expensive. Furthermore, emergency measures almost always are taken at the expense of the operations of other commanders.

Psychological Factors—Confidence

However, the greatest harm may lie in the psychological effects induced by the original deficiency. Let us assume that the emergency measures were successful and that the tactical situation was saved. The commanders who had too narrow an escape from the disaster of "too little too late" will certainly put great pressure on their own planners and on their own superiors to insure future adequacy of support. All along the chain of command estimates may be arbitrarily increased and extreme oversupply may be provided.

The huge overproduction of 20mm ammunition in World War II and the accumulation of excess fighter aircraft belly tanks on Guam in early 1945 are merely two instances of what may occur from the uncontrolled development of this effect. Additional pertinent illustrations will occur to those who recall the enormous buildup of certain rear area Pacific bases in 1944 and 1945.

At the beginning of the war we were badly handicapped by the lack of bases in the Pacific and Southwest Pacific areas. In a series of early improvisations and a subsequent program of massive proportions, huge bases were built at Noumea, Espiritu Santo, Manus, Guam, and Samar. In the later bases the ideas of the planners were greatly influenced by the deficiencies of the early days. At the same time, commanders of some bases in rear areas were reluctant to reduce the size of their bases as the war moved forward toward Japan. Thus the snowball grew, both near the front and in the rear.

The operation of this phenomenon of "under-planning—over-planning sequence" is one of the more important factors in the growth of the "logistic snowball."

No one supposes that it is possible to plan perfectly in war, nor does anyone pretend that it is possible to eliminate selfish, deliberate overestimates nor to prevent midnight requisitioning by overzealous "can do" personnel. However, if these practices can be controlled and reduced, and if *inadvertent over-planning* can be markedly reduced, tremendous savings can be achieved.

As we see so often, these problems and factors are interwoven with other elements of war. In particular, these matters are related to the development of better logistic planning factors and planning methods, the better training of staff officers, the understanding of the nature of flexibility, the proper provision of logistic reserves, and, above all, the understanding of logistic principles from the perspective of command. All these are necessary to the development of logistic competence and logistic competence is the foundation of logistic confidence.

More than any other factor the development of confidence in the quality and adequacy of one's planned logistic support is essential to breaking the habit of excessive over-planning.

These same elements which create confidence also will act greatly to reduce under-planning.

Modern Supply Concepts

In the last few years the Army, the Navy, and the Air Force all have introduced new supply concepts which recognize and specifically combat some of the snowball effects of the older systems.

On 1 July 1956 the Army began to test Project MASS, the "Modern Army Supply System" designed by The George Washington University Army Logistics Research Group to supply spare parts from the continental United States by air and rapid surface transport directly to the Seventh Army in Europe.

The major feature of the system is that it uses the latest methods of communications, data processing, and rapid transportation to reduce the variety and quantity of items stored in combat and communication zones, thus reducing the size of the depots and the number of personnel in these zones. As yet this system excludes major items and ammunition and so it is still too early to predict its development.

The Air Force concept of supply support for tactical units is developed along the same general line with perhaps an even greater emphasis on rapid communications and airlift for routine logistic support.[3]

---

[3] A discussion of this is found in the January 1957 issue of *Aeronautical Engineering Review* in an article on page 40 entitled "Air Force Logistics" by Allen R. Ferguson of the RAND Corporation, from which the following is quoted:

> In discussing the military situation in the 1960's four salient logistic features were identified—namely, the need for dispersal and other actions to reduce vulnerability, ability to deploy, responsiveness, and economy. This section discusses the role of airlift in attaining these objectives.
>
> In recent years there has been great interest in airlift for routine peacetime transportation. To a considerable extent this interest derives from the fact that, in spite of the great technical advances in transportation, communication, and information processing, it still takes a matter of months on the average from the time that a requisition is submitted by a base in Europe until materiel is delivered.
>
> Aerial resupply used routinely in peacetime, especially if associated with faster communications and paper processing, could greatly increase the responsiveness of the logistics system. Needs at the operating bases could be identified promptly and supplied in a matter of days. Parts shortages could be reduced and the number of aircraft immediately mission-ready increased. As was already mentioned, it may be that only those aircraft which are immediately available will have much military value in a general war.
>
> Thus it appears that routine air movement of parts and components would help achieve one of the essential conditions of the logistics system of the 1960's—namely, increased responsiveness. However, there is also the need for economy, and economical air transportation may be justified in peacetime in terms of dollar savings alone. Let us consider the economies such airlift can provide and the requirements for operating a military air transport force at low cost in peacetime.
>
> *First*, the increased effectiveness mentioned is, itself, a source of economy—and perhaps the most important one. As was pointed out earlier, a given number of combat-ready aircraft can be achieved with a large inventory of aircraft, many of which are out of service part of the time, or with a smaller inventory having a larger percentage mission-ready. If airlift reduces the number of aircraft out of service, this is equivalent to reducing the total number of aircraft required for any given level of combat readiness. *Second*, the investment in inventories of parts tied up in pipe lines can be reduced by reducing the pipeline time. *Lastly*, considerable reductions in the inventories of those high-value parts which are demanded sporadically can be achieved by holding these items in centralized pools and meeting demands by fast resupply.

The Navy through its mobile support concept has recognized that one major aspect of the logistic snowball may be reduced by the greatest practicable utilization of *mobile* facilities in the support of fleet units deployed overseas.

In addition since 1955 a further attack on the snowball has been under test by PROJECT FAST, (Fleet Air Support Test). This is described as "The modern air logistic concept" and it includes a series of tests in both the Atlantic and the Pacific. These tests provide air lift delivery for initial and resupply support for a wide range of supply items, mostly technical.[4]

As with the new Army and Air Force schemes, for effectiveness it depends on improved planning factors, rapid radio communication, and an airlift responsive to the needs of the supply system.

It is hoped that through this system:

(1) Fleet mobility will be increased;

(2) Combat readiness will be improved;

(3) The supply system will be given the means of increasing responsiveness in support of overseas fleets and bases;

(4) Overseas technical inventories, both in range and quantity can be significantly reduced;

(5) Fleets and bases will be provided with less vulnerable sources of supply; and

(6) The over-all cost of technical supply will be reduced.

However, the fact that these new concepts have been translated into specific tests and systems does not mean that the snowball has been defeated. These concepts have been applied only to limited segments of the supply systems. They all demand a higher proportion of radio traffic than tactical commanders are usually willing to allocate. They all require a type of airlift allocation and control which is incompatible with some of the

---

[4] A good brief discussion of FAST is found in "The 'Modern Air Logistic' Concept and Project 'FAST'—Fleet Air Support Test—" by the Planning Division of the Bureau of Supplies and Accounts.

current concepts and directives of the U. S. Department of Defense. Above all, these concepts demand that the tactical forces, who are the ultimate consumers, shall have confidence in the responsiveness and reliability of their supply systems. Then a sense of logistic discipline can develop. The most that can be said is that a promising start has been made in attacking one important feature of the logistic snowball.

Limitation of Resources

If these few selected illustrations of the operation of the snowball meant only that people, money, and material were lavishly wasted it would be bad enough merely from the economic point of view. However, it is more serious, for it implies a disregard of the principle of Economy of Force. From the logistic point of view this principle presupposes an awareness *that our logistic resources are always limited.*[5] The principal limitations are availability of raw materials, industrial facilities, skilled labor, and time. The problem of over-all Command is how to apply these limited resources most effectively in accomplishing the objectives of strategy. An unwise over-expenditure for logistic resources and facilities means that the combat forces have been deprived either of manpower, of equipment, or of training.

Again, the logistic problems of area and force commanders are similarly affected by limitation of resources. There is an additional effect on this level of command, however. Here, if there is an over-all shortage of some resources, and if one commander has an unnecessarily high proportion of available logistic resources, it means either that some other command has been deprived of needed support, or that the whole *scope* or *tempo of all operations has been reduced* to compensate for the excess in one command.

---

[5] The importance of this principle of limitation of resources and its influence on command decision, on flexibility, and on strategic momentum, are vividly illustrated by the differences between Eisenhower and Montgomery in September 1944. Montgomery proposed that all available supply facilities be given him in order to thrust the Twenty-First Army Group directly toward Berlin. Eisenhower felt that a pencil-like thrust into the heart of Germany would fail and refused Montgomery's request. The correctness of this decision is still being debated. See Dwight D. Eisenhower, *Crusade in Europe.* Doubleday and Company, Inc., New York, 1948; and *The Memoirs of Field-Marshal Montgomery,* The World Publishing Company, Cleveland, Ohio, 1958.

The importance of maintaining the maximum tempo in offensive war reemphasizes the factors of flexibility and of combat momentum.

The importance of strategical-tactical-momentum and the difficulty of establishing the proper balance of resources devoted to combat forces as opposed to logistic forces makes it of vital importance that the commander be aware of the way the logistic snowball can grow, and that he control his planning and operations so as to keep in balance.

Chapter 8

Flexibility and Momentum

. . . the flexible employment of forces is the central task in directing a war, a task most difficult to perform well. . . . flexibility in command can be realized only through the discovery of order, light, and certainty amidst such circumstances peculiar to war as confusion, darkness, and uncertainty.[1]

—MAO TSE-TUNG

All students of war have recognized the need for flexibility in the planning and control of military operations. Several examples from recent conflicts serve as illustrations of the benefits of flexibility, particularly when coupled to mobility.

Historical Examples

In September 1950 the amphibious landing at Inchon completely disrupted operations of North Korea forces. It also served to shift the center of gravity of the conflict, and thus transformed its whole course.

In early 1943-45 the American forces in the Central Pacific and in the Southwest Pacific repeatedly changed physical objectives and time tables in order to speed up operations and to bypass powerful enemy forces.

In these, among other instances, the qualities of mobility and flexibility of forces, plus the flexibility of the mind of the commander (and the correct evaluation of good intelligence), permitted strategic exploitation of tactical success and circumstances.

Conversely, the inflexibility of Hitler's mind, illustrated by his forbidding his field commanders to make tactical retreats, was a major contributing factor in the great disasters suffered by the Germans in the Russian campaigns.

However, it is not enough merely to say "Keep flexible!" If

---

[1] Mao Tse-Tung, *On the Protracted War,* Foreign Language Press, Peking, 1954, p. 101.

we are to render more than lip service to this worthy ideal we should recognize and understand those factors which contribute to or detract from the flexibility of military organizations, plans, and dispositions. It takes many factors to provide flexibility, but it takes only one major inflexible characteristic to destroy the usefulness of all the good factors and make the plan or force rigid. Flexibility is achieved only by a recognition of the factors which are involved and the manner in which these factors act. After this there must be continued follow-up. No one should deceive himself by believing that he has achieved flexibility when by reason of budgetary, organizational, or intellectual limitations, he cannot in fact act with flexibility.

The evacuation of the Tachens Islands in January-February of 1955 is a striking example of logistic and tactical flexibility. Without advance preparation the U. S. Seventh Fleet evacuated about 25,000 Chinese troops and 17,000 civilians. At the same time the same force was able to provide from within itself strong surface and air defense for the operation. The command organization, the logistic support doctrine, and command control of logistics were the fundamental bases for this accomplishment. In terms of size this was a small operation. In terms of political-strategic-logistic-tactical relationship and in terms of evidence of military flexibility in the force, it was a very significant operation.

More recently the redeployment of our forces in the Formosa area in 1958, brought these same elements into play.

In another area of conflict, the evacuation of Americans from Suez in 1956 and the landing and reinforcement of forces during the Lebanon crisis of 1958 demonstrated these factors.

It is obvious that flexibility and mobility are closely related and that each is essential to the development of the other. While the two terms are not synonymous their interrelations will suggest further trains of thought.

Flexibility Is Rooted in Command

As with other important factors in war, flexibility has its

roots in the concept of command and in other aspects of the intellectual preparation of the commander.

There are two basic concepts of the exercise of high military command. At one extreme are the British who believe that unity of effort in field operations is adequately attained by "cooperation."[2] They feel that at almost all levels, the units of each separate military service should be independently commanded. At the other extreme is the German concept of the "Feldherr" where exclusive authority is delegated by the sovereign to a single over-all commander at the .national level.[3]

In between these extremes the current American concept of command seems fairly well stabilized in a general position. The American doctrine of "Unified Command" provides that in joint operations various units of all services will be provided to a single officer who will command and coordinate their operations. In the exercise of this command he usually acts through the commanders of the units of the various services. The unity of effort at the top of the military structure is accomplished by a civilian Secretary of Defense advised by or acting through the Joint Chiefs of Staff. The present concept clearly excludes the idea that the chairman of the Joint Chiefs of Staff ever becomes *the* commander, or chief of staff of the Armed Forces.

This American doctrine is taken on the grounds that: (1) unity by cooperation only will lack clear, decisive authority in critical combat situations; and (2) the single chief of staff or "Feldherr" will almost inevitably become the slave to an inflexible and dogmatic strategy.

As mentioned in chapter 2, one of the excellent features of the concept of strategy as the exercise of comprehensive control is the ability to shift from one weapon to another in accordance with the needs of the situation rather than to commit oneself to the exclusive employment of a single weapon. To be effective, a strategy must be flexible. A strategy based upon the use of a

---

[2] Creswell, *Generals and Admirals*. New York, Longmans, Green 1952, pp. 184-188.

[3] Rosinski, *The German Army*. The Infantry Journal Press 1944. pp. 181-196.

single weapon, that is, a "weapon strategy," is so rigid that it may be readily circumvented by an enemy who is flexible.

The perspective of command (outlined earlier in this work) is essential to flexibility for only from this perspective can the various alternative courses of action be evaluated. Flexibility in the mind of the commander does not imply indecision or lack of firmness. It does mean that the commander refrains from making unnecessary commitments in the early stages of an operation.

Two further points are in order: (1) It is not sufficient for the staff and subordinate commanders to have a mere statement of the objectives and mission of the commander in their mind. If full flexibility is to be achieved they must have the type of intuitive understanding that results from a thorough analysis of the objective and the mission of the command. (2) Finally, if the commander does not have a clear personal knowledge of his logistic capabilities the full play of his mind will be either seriously hampered or grounded on fiction.

Flexibility and Organization

Under the American doctrine of unified command, it is usual to organize the forces under the "task force" principle. (Note: It is always done in the case of the Navy). Under that principle, a commander is chosen to accomplish a task, forces are provided to him of appropriate types or services in sufficient quantity, and the execution and responsibility of the task are delegated to him. This task force method of organizing combat forces is inherently flexible.

In peacetime it is equally desirable that authority be delegated and exercised. In that way commanders will be trained and ready for wartime tasks. In that way the wartime needs for flexibility will be based upon, and will exploit, peacetime organization.

While factors of economy may make it necessary to modify the wartime organization somewhat for peacetime operation, these modifications should not be such as to require a major shift in command structure on the outbreak of war.

Furthermore, peacetime centralization of administrative authority for reasons of economy rapidly approaches the point of diminishing returns. Peacetime economy apparently gained by great centralization should not be sought at the cost of sacrificing wartime flexibility; nor should it be sought in such a way as to inhibit the growth of decision and initiative in field and fleet commanders. Those qualities of decision and initiative are achieved by the exercise of delegated authority. They are vital to the development of flexibility in our command organizations.[4]

Again, the desire for peacetime economy may bring about the assignment to one commander of several tasks which would make conflicting demands upon his time and resources in war. If that condition arises, the command structure should be such that his subordinates may readily move up to positions of greater responsibility in time of need. For example, if it should be necessary to assign to an overseas naval Service Force Commander major tasks both ashore and in mobile support of a fleet, he should be provided with several subordinates to whom he can delegate major operating tasks while he exercises general supervision.

It naturally follows that the whole staff itself in peacetime should be capable of being split up to meet a wartime situation. Among other things, this points up the need for providing selected Intelligence and Information to each subordinate.

Only when the command, the staff, the headquarters and the intelligence and communications systems are designed to meet wartime rather than peacetime needs, can the speedy readjustments characteristic of a flexible command be made.

---

[4] Commander J. H. Garrett, Jr., SC, USN, *Characteristics of Usage of Supply Items Aboard Naval Ships and the Significance to Supply Management.* Article in the Naval Research Logistics Quarterly, Vol. 5, No. 4 December 1958, published by the Office of Naval Research, Washington, D. C. This article shows how recent Department of Defense policies have resulted in greater centralization of authority, particularly in transportation. It points out how these policies have made the logistic system less responsive to the needs of the combat commanders and have reduced the area of their decision and initiative.

The Composition of Forces

The composition and disposition of military forces and of logistic reserves are important considerations in the development of flexibility. Thus, if a force is designed to do one task only, great effectiveness in that particular task may be achieved. The flexibility of the force, however, will be small. On the other hand, a force whose combat elements are so balanced as to be able to fight a variety of types of action gains greatly in its tactical flexibility.

When such a force also includes a built-in or attached logistic support element, great strategic and tactical flexibility are attained. This is particularly true if there be uncommitted reserves of combat and logistic resources available for selective augmentation of the operating forces as the situation develops.

In addition, it is important to recognize the distinction between "strategic" or functional forces and "area" forces. (This will be discussed more fully in chapter 14). For example, large "heavy striking" naval forces should not be committed purely to a regional or an area command, for this tends to counteract the flexibility that is inherent in their mobility and capacity for self-support. On the other hand, light naval units of less mobility and less endurance very appropriately may be assigned to area commanders as "sea frontier forces."

Finally in connection with the composition of forces, it should be noted that homogeneity within task forces contributes to their flexibility in that it simplifies supply and facilitates planning and tactical control.

Flexibility in Planning

While the analysis of objectives, command relations, the composition and disposition of forces, and planning are all intimately related, there are certain aspects of the planning process that specially contribute to flexibility.

The integration of strategic, logistic, and tactical planning by officers working in close physical proximity to each other is an essential factor in increasing the flexibility of a command. If either the strategic or logistic group has to guess at the requirements of the other, or delay decision until facts can be ascertained, flexibility is reduced.

The importance of the element of physical proximity has sometimes been disregarded by high command both during and after World War II. For example, when CinCPac moved from Pearl Harbor to Guam in 1945, his principal naval logistic agent, Commander Service Force Pacific Fleet, was left at Pearl Harbor.

The fact that we were able to make significant changes in our plans in spite of this handicap was due largely to two other causes. The first was a combination of logistic factors—such as the large supply buildup that already had taken place ashore and afloat, and the strength of the trans-Pacific pipeline. The second factor (sometimes neglected in analyses) was the fact that having by this time gained the strategical offensive, we were working on our own timetable. The enemy had lost his power seriously to disrupt it other than by stubborn defense at some of the points we attacked.

The maximum development of doctrine and the use of standing operating procedures will reduce the volume and complexity of major plans and will thus facilitate comprehension of the essentials. A clear understanding of objectives and of principles rather than of rules, permits the senior commander to delegate authority with assurance. He can give his subordinates that freedom of action which is so necessary to the swift exploitation of favorable situations. This is the potentially great reward of a flexible approach.

Perhaps the most important contribution to flexibility in planning lies in the understanding of the correct use of assumptions and alternate plans.

Too often the word "assumptions" has been used to cover a multitude of facts which, while of interest to the planner, may not necessarily be vital to the execution of the plan. On the other hand, if the "assumptions" are restricted to those elements which are so vital that the plan must be abandoned or radically changed should they not be true as assumed, and if for each of these assumptions an alternate plan be prepared, flexibility will be improved, and the plan will in any event be more sound.

Sometimes, in the name of flexibility, plans may be written in a vague rather than a general manner. This particularly and frequently applies to command relations. There is no excuse for vagueness other than the inability to reconcile a positive difference of opinion between strong and conflicting political or service interests. When this is inevitable it should be recognized and adequate compensating alternatives prepared in advance.[5]

A plan should not go into any more detail than is necessary; otherwise it tends to lose flexibility. However, this again is no excuse for writing plans in a vague or ambiguous manner. Instead it means that in some parts of a plan, final decision may be deferred or left to the discretion of subordinates. In either case deferral or delegation should be explicitly stated.

Even though a plan may be general rather than detailed, it still should be tested for soundness by analyzing in detail one or more of the various interpretations or alternatives. This can and should be done on the staff level during the preparation and development of the basic general plans without interfering with the duties or prerogatives of subordinate commanders. In fact the staffs of the subordinate commanders can well assist in this analysis. If restrictive detail can be avoided, the plan as finally issued can then be general enough to provide for discretion and initiative on the part of subordinate commanders, and still be a solid rather than an indecisive foundation for action.

A sound *logistic* disposition and plan, will support several *strategic* plans and a large number of tactical plans. Therefore, the logistic plans should be carefully scrutinized to determine which aspects contribute to flexibility and which may detract from it.

The Effect of Command Control

The degree to which a commander controls his logistic support has a profound effect on the flexibility of his position. The

---

[5] An interesting example of vague command relations is to be found in the plans for the invasion of Japan in 1945. Neither Admiral Nimitz nor General MacArthur was given clear responsibility because of the strength of the political and Service interests involved.

principle that a commander should control his own logistic support—while in general fundamental to the attainment of combat effectiveness—should not be interpreted in a rigid manner. In general it means that in planning an operation, the commander of the force involved, upon submission of his logistic requirements, will be allocated specific resources for his immediate control, and he will be assured by higher command of a time-phased availability of resupply of a predetermined nature. It then becomes his duty to redistribute these allocated resources among his forces as he sees fit in accordance with the unfolding situation.

In the exercise of this control the logistic characteristics of the forces involved must be carefully considered.

For example, in an organization or situation similar to the Third and Fifth Fleets of the U.S. Pacific Fleet in World War II, it may not be practicable to split the control of the mobile logistic unit below the level of the command responsible for the whole operation. However, it should be recognized that the individual task forces of such a fleet had a large built-in logistic capability and that they had the assurance that scheduled replenishments would be met according to plan.

The movement control system is an inherent part of the exercise of command control. Such a concept of movement control carries with it, of course, the control of sufficient transportation, either organic or attached, to support fast unexpected moves.

Coupled with the foregoing elements of command, there is the requirement for information, and sufficient headquarters facilities and communications both to process and transmit this information, and to transmit the will of command.

Finally, in reviewing the attribute of flexibility we can see how its creation starts in the mind and concepts of the commander and in the availability of both intelligence and information. It has its physical foundation in the adequacy and distribution of combat forces and logistic resources. It depends on mobility which in turn depends on logistics by way of transportation and movement control. Lastly, all of these attributes are also part of flexibility's first cousin—momentum.

Momentum and Mobility

Momentum can be considered both from the strategic-tactical point of view and from the logistical point of view.

From the strategic-tactical point of view, exploitation of momentum is similar to the "killer instinct" of the boxing ring. It means that once a decisive opening has been obtained every resource is concentrated to obtain overwhelming victory by the most rapid succession of powerful blows. It aims at the complete destruction of enemy fighting power in the area concerned. The enemy is permitted no respite to regroup his forces and to recover his strength. It is the basic principle of the "Blitzkrieg," a principle as old as war itself. It was the guiding spirit of Nelson, Stonewall Jackson, Rommel, and Patton.

Nothing does more to decrease one's losses than to develop this strategic-tactical momentum. For example, during the 1940 campaign in France, Rommel's 7th Panzer Division lost 682 killed, 1,646 wounded, 296 missing, and 42 tanks totally destroyed. In turn, it captured 97,648 prisoners, 277 field guns, 64 anti-tank guns, 458 tanks, 4,000 lorries, 1,500 cars and over 1,500 horse drawn vehicles.[6]

The development of momentum is a matter of three points: creation and recognition of opportunity, fighting spirit, and logistics.

The logistic aspect of strategic-tactical momentum is, as in physics, a function of mass and mobility, and, as in physics, momentum varies with the speed. Mass can be provided, not by sheer bulk of supply, but by the hard core of bare essentials represented by "true economy" of supply. *By "true economy" of supply is meant the careful planning and build up of supply levels to provide those supplies and facilities which are essential to firepower and movement; and the concomitant ruthless elimination of non-essentials.*

---

[6] B. H. Liddell Hart, *The Rommel Papers*. New York, Harcourt, Brace and Company, 1953. p. 84.

Admiral Halsey's sweep into the China Sea, 9 to 21 January 1945, is an interesting example of such exploitation based on minimum but determined and resourceful logistic support provided by Captain J. T. Acuff, CTG 30.8, who gave Halsey's forces at sea 1,559,000 barrels of oil and 3,416,000 gallons of aviation gas.[7]

The *mobility* aspect is found in the availability of transportation and in the manner in which the plans are prepared and the command organized. These factors were partly covered in the previous discussions of "flexibility" and of "planning."

In addition, the commanders of logistic forces must be fully represented on the planning team in order that they may have a complete understanding of the purposes and problems of the tactical commanders. In order to provide the maximum of mobility, plans should be prepared in such a way that adequate reserves of the critical elements are made available to the commands involved. *These reserves must not be prematurely committed nor committed to secondary purposes.* A reporting system should be established in such a way that those who are responsible for the conduct of the operation and its logistic support know the precise state of supply availabilities.

Finally, the commands must be so organized that the tactical commander has unquestioned control over his own logistical support allocated to his use.

The foregoing points are not technical problems. They are problems of command. Only if the commander understands the nature of the technical problems that his subordinate and the technical officers must solve, and only if he has confidence in them and provides them with freedom and authority, will he develop the mobility and flexibility to exploit his potential and to acquire strategic-tactical momentum.

Logistic Momentum

Logistic momentum, as such, is somewhat different. It becomes of importance in the roots of our logistical system, it

---

[7] Carter, W. R. RADM, Ret'd. *Beans, Bullets and Black Oil,* Government Printing Office: 1953. pp. 272, 276.

spreads all through the broad fields of procurement and distribution, and it reaches its most critical point in the operation of large forces in combat. In a major operation, the logistical preparations develop an actual physical momentum of the "means" of combat; a momentum which must be recognized in the planning and conduct of such operations.

Initially, on the national level we must recognize how difficult it is for the operating forces and the industrial plant of the nation to acquire momentum at the start of a war. It takes time and great effort to build up the advanced area stockpiles necessary to support sustained offensives. It takes even more time and effort to achieve the industrial momentum which is the foundation for this buildup.

Another interesting aspect of logistic momentum should be noted. It can be found in the areas of procurement and distribution. Here the purchase and flow of supplies sometimes continue long after the need for the supplies has diminished or entirely stopped.

This is sometimes due to the fact that the supply of those particular items has been put on an automatic basis (which sometimes is an excellent move). In other instances the continued excess flow has been due to "lead time." In these cases, the process of changing the rate of production is so long that it may not be possible for the supply system to respond quickly to the change in demand even when recognized. (The establishment of "Supply Demand Control Depots" in the Navy supply system has done much to improve this situation in the Navy.)

However, we cannot expect perfect responsiveness. A point of danger is that a supply system may be geared too closely to peacetime operations; and that it may not be either technically or organizationally prepared for the very great changes that war brings. The problem of responsiveness is intimately related to the study of usage data, planning factors, the "logistic snowball," to "flexibility," and to "readiness." It is significant that the larger, or more centralized, our over-all system becomes the greater the need for responsiveness, and the greater the difficulty of attaining it. One question arises: When do the economic advantages of greater centralization disappear, and when does it turn into a handicap?

Another example of momentum is found in the manner in which an inadequate system of planning and controlling the allocation and movement of shipping in relation to overseas port capacity results in a pile-up of shipping in the overseas ports. This snowballs because there is an immediate resort to "selective unloading." This in turn reduces the efficiency of the unloading process; and this in turn causes further congestion. In the meantime, ships on the high seas must continue their voyages to these congested ports because they are carrying urgently needed material; and loading plans in the continental U.S. ports become upset and confused and their operation becomes less efficient.

Thus, uncontrolled logistic momentum reacts to reduce combat effectiveness and to increase waste.

Control of Momentum

Sustained operations always require a specific buildup. This holds in all operations, Army, Navy, or Air Force.

For example, even with their large storage capacity, modern ships cannot sustain offensive major operations without replenishment from stocks prepositioned in the whole logistic chain running from the underway replenishment groups through the mobile support forces, back to the advanced and continental naval bases. Similarly, regardless of whatever dispersion of supplies may be in effect, major joint offensives will require an even greater buildup.

The buildup constitutes in effect a pipeline with major storage tanks and with surge tanks to take care of fluctuations. Material is moving through this system with such real momentum that it is impossible to reverse the flow. It is very difficult to change its rate or direction except by providing ample vacant space in the surge tanks and by setting up a positive, accurate, and rapid system of logistic controls and communication.

If these controls do not work, the momentum of the personnel and material in the pipeline is such that it continues to flow regardless of need or of high command orders. The excess spills out the end of the pipe in the combat zone and creates confusion, trouble and waste (the snowball). But, a still more adverse consequence is that this excess becomes a burden to the combat forces by reducing their mobility and flexibility, for the unwanted material clogs access to the wanted material all through the system of transportation and depots.

From the foregoing, and from other illustrations, we can see how the forces which produce and control momentum may come into play. Just how these can best be handled is a matter of command judgment.

We can be sure that the future will show many differences of opinion. In the Navy these will probably center around the proper relation of movement control to requisition control and in the division of responsibility and authority among the Navy Department, the sea frontier, the supply center, the service force, the fleet, and the area.

While various considerations may preclude complete clarification in peacetime we must not delude ourselves that we won't pay dearly for any fogginess or undue complexity in war.

Relation to Movement Control

The key to the control of this great physical force lies in the prosaic term "MOVEMENT CONTROL." Not all commands nor all services approach this in the same way. It is quite distinct from the operation of a transportation system although, in some instances, both functions may be performed by one command. After command has determined what shall be moved, when, and where; Movement Control determines how and by what routes and systems of transportation it shall be moved. The transportation system responds to the directives of movement control. *While movement control has many technical features it is not a technical function. Since it is the key to tactical exploitation, it must be understood and exercised as a command function and viewed from the perspective of command. Once command control over logistic movement is diminished, combat effectiveness is directly reduced.*

A further discussion of the details of movement control will be preceded by a discussion of the buildup of logistic forces and the manner in which this buildup is controlled by the use of a system of priorities and allocations.

Summary

In this chapter the factors of flexibility and momentum have been examined. Flexibility is a great and vital military asset. It flows from the mind of the commander, and it is through his art that his forces in combat are ready and able to exploit changing situations or to make or meet new situations. This quality of strategic flexibility is largely dependent upon both the organization of the command, and upon the soundness of the logistics of the command.

All types of flexibility require:

(1) A clear understanding of objectives;

(2) Real delegation of authority in peace;

(3) Adequate information and intelligence;

(4) Provision for adequate reserve forces, reserve supplies and support facilities;

(5) Alternate strategic and tactical plans all based on a sound basic logistic plan; and

(6) Command control of logistics.

A sound basic area logistic plan with a well-balanced logistic support force, a good area movement control system and a modest, area controlled, land, sea, and air transport capability, provide the fundamental logistic foundation of strategic and tactical flexibility. This foundation permits rapid and perhaps decisive movement in the early stages of an emergency before the more massive national facilities can come into full play. Later these same intra-area transportation capabilities are essential to continued efficient logistic support.

Momentum has been shown to affect strategy, tactics, and logistics. In the former it is an essential requirement to produce a "kill"; it, also, is related to mobility and is largely dependent on logistic planning. However momentum in the logistic organization itself, and in the flow of supplies, has both its good points and its hazards. The potentially bad effects of the momentum of logistics can be overcome by appropriate command control at the various levels of command.

Chapter 9

Buildup and Disposition of Logistic Forces and Supplies

It is no great matter to change tactical plans in a hurry and to send troops off in new directions. But adjusting supply plans to the altered tactical scheme is far more difficult.[1]

—GENERAL WALTER BEDELL SMITH

As mentioned previously, command has powerful tools to control the forces of inordinate growth, of rigidity, and of momentum which characterize the logistic process.

Tools of Control

The basic pattern of logistics and control will be established by the manner in which the logistic forces are built up and disposed relative to the combat forces. The next tool of control lies in the control of requirements and in the establishment and administration of priorities and allocations. These matters are intimately concerned with movement control and transportation. The final control is found in *discipline*. For these tools to be effective they must operate within an organization which is designed with the interplay of the forces and the controls in mind.

The use of these tools of control by any particular commander is limited by the degree to which he has authority over the composition of his own force and over his logistic support. In some instances he may merely submit recommendations to his superior commanders and trust that their decisions will be based on an understanding of principles. In those situations where he has authority, however, his personal judgment will be severely tested by the manner in which he combines these tools of control to increase his combat effectiveness.

In all nations whenever the threat of enemy aggression dimin-

---

[1] General Walter Bedell Smith, *Eisenhower's Six Great Decisions,* Longmans Green, New York, 1956, p. 82.

ishes or becomes less obvious, economic factors exert an increasing pressure on the political leaders to decrease the armed forces. However, as the government yields to pressures for shorter terms of conscript service, for instance, and for reduced military expenditures, they are reluctant to admit that their actions have decreased the military security. Two arguments are frequently used to substantiate these military cuts. The first is that advanced technology provides greater defense for less money. The second, which is the more pertinent to this discussion, is that the cuts have been made chiefly in the logistic forces and that the combat power remains the same.

A colorful comment on such an incident was made by Sir Stephen King-Hall when he referred to the British defense cuts of March 1957:

> We have just listened to BBC news in which Lord Home, Minister for Commonwealth Relations, has explained "that the defence cuts are designed to reduce the tail of our defence effort and give it more teeth so that we shall be a first class power." Surely it must occur to his Lordship that a statement of this character is a most damning indictment of the Cabinet's behaviour in defence matters over the past few years. Why has the existence of the superfluous and expensive tail only been discovered when for economic reasons we have to spend less on defence? Has all the money spent on what is now called "the tail" been wasted? If in due course we reduce the size of our armed forces in Europe what immense humbug it is to pretend that it not only makes no difference to the physical defence of the West but may even make it stronger!

> Behaviour of this kind in the conduct of a private company would put the directors in the dock at the Old Bailey. That Ministers can make the kind of statement we are now discussing shows the contempt in which they hold public opinion and since very few people either in the press or Parliament ever seem to get up and say, "You impudent rascals, how dare you insult our intelligence with this arrant nonsense," we must regretfully admit that the contempt referred to above is well founded.[2]

---

[2] King-Hall *News-Letter* No. 1079, 27 March 1957, London. p. 719-720.

Both the Army and the Navy started World War II with inadequate concept of the magnitude of their logistic tasks; and they consequently grossly underestimated the proportion of resources which should be devoted to logistic forces. The subsequent readjustments frequently took the form of the under-planning—over-planning snowball sequence previously described. While deploring this sequence we still should recognize that the determination of the proper ratio of logistic forces to combat forces is in fact one of the most perplexing problems which high command must decide.

Inadequate Army Concepts

For the Army the problem occurred just as clearly in the Pacific as it did in the European theater. For example, speaking of the Southwest Pacific Campaign Plans of 1942 and 1943, the Army historians say:

> There was no real attempt to work out the logistical implications of these outline plans. While MacArthur stressed the fact that additional resources would be necessary, OPD planners were blandly optimistic, . . . For the most part, however, OPD planners glossed over the welter of logistical difficulties standing in the way of an early resumption of the offensive, and paid little heed to the clear warnings of Nimitz and MacArthur that the reduction of Rabaul would require large additional air and ground forces. Logistical difficulties and insufficient air power had been primarily responsible for the failure to complete Task One and launch Tasks Two and Three in 1942, and the remedy for the logistical shortcomings revealed at each stage of operations had been late in coming and usually inadequate.[3]

The excellent documentation of the Normandy invasion and its immediate aftermath furnishes us with many illustrations of the factors which must be considered in laying the logistical foundation which is essential to the strategic exploitation of tactical success.

The question was acute in the build up of United States Forces in the United Kingdom in 1942 where in the early stages

[3] Richard M. Leighton and Robert W. Coakley, *Global Logistics and Strategy 1940-1943*. Office of the Chief of Military History, Department of the Army, Washington, D.C., 1955. p. 414-415.

of the planning both the magnitude and the timing of the logistic build up were grossly misjudged in spite of the lessons of World War I.

> In determining what constituted a "balanced force" there was much opportunity for disagreement. Ground, air, and service branches inevitably competed for what each regarded as its rightful portion of the troop basis. . . . *Only 11.8 percent of the 1942 Army troop basis had been allotted for service troops,* . . . of the total AEF force of nearly two million men in France at the end of World War I, 34 percent were service troops exclusive of the service elements with the ground combat and air force units . . .[4]
>
> But in the spring of 1942 few trained service troops were available for duty in overseas theaters, and *service troops beyond all others* were required first in the United Kingdom. It was imperative that they *precede combat units* in order to receive equipment and supplies, prepare depots and other accommodations, and provide essential services for the units which followed.[5]

While uncertainties in buildup plans occurred because strategic decisions were shifting, nevertheless there was a continued effort to cut down on the service buildup. Throughout the Normandy planning and operations there was a continuing see-saw argument as to the service buildup. This is illustrated by the following:

> In allocating the available lift there arose the ever-recurring argument as to the proper ratios of combat and service troops. One facet of this eternal conflict has already been seen in the competition between ground and service forces for larger shares of the theater troop basis.[6]

Not only did growing mechanization require larger numbers of technicians and multiply the tonnages and number of supply items; the growing destructiveness of modern warfare, toward which the heavy bomber had made a large contribution, made it necessary to rebuild a country's lines of communications as

---

[4] R. G. Ruppenthal, *Logistical Support of the Armies,* Volume I Office of the Chief of Military History, Department of the Army. p. 56.

[5] *Ibid,* p. 57.

[6] *Ibid,* p. 299.

armies moved along. This further increased the logistic burden.

> The competition between combat and service troops for available lift was pointedly illustrated in January 1944 when supreme command was considering a major alteration . . . that provided for enlargement in both assault area and size of attacking forces. One officer . . . expressed apprehension lest . . . service forces would also request increase of strength in the early stages. He believed such demands should be resisted.[7]

However, General Eisenhower, recognizing that a wider bridgehead would give a wider road for supply, decided that:

> Whatever force was placed on the continent has to be a balanced one and any attempt to introduce excessive combat forces without adequate buildup of service forces and an increase in supply buildup capacity would reduce the division slice and lessen the support capabilities of the communication zone.[8]

Nevertheless, Mr. Churchill after the successful landing held the opinion, in reference to the planned movement of troops from the United States, that "the administrative tails were too long and he desired that there be more 'fighting divisions' at the expense of service units."[9]

In referring to this, Major General Harold R. Bull noted that it had "become 'a favorite pastime . . . to compare the excessive American tonnage required per divisional slice to that required by the British.' He . . . pointed out the difference in the respective tactical missions of the American and British army groups. The U.S. . . . lines of communications . . . which would add immeasurably to their logistical problems."[10]

Thus, it seems that some opinions were based on preconceived ideas rather than on an analysis of the problem of logistic support of an army on the offensive. The concern for the buildup of logistic forces was justified by events; for in spite of the urgent pleas of the logistic commanders for the timely buildup of transportation units, in the planning stage their estimates were cut back or only belatedly and grudgingly granted by the

---

[7, 8] Ruppenthal, *op cit,* p. 300.

[9] *Ibid,* p. 451.

[10] *Ibid,* p. 452.

army, the theater, and War Department. Thus, when the break-out from Normandy finally came and a major tactical success was scored, full strategic exploitation could not be achieved for lack of sufficient transportation. The heroic improvisations of the "Red Ball Express" and the conversions of bomber air-craft to fuel carriers were not sufficient to maintain the logistic support.[11] In September 1944 the Allied armies halted their ad-vance toward Germany because of lack of logistic support at the front, although there were ample supplies ashore in the Normandy Base Area, 300 miles away.

> The crippling impact which logistic difficulties were to have on plans for future operations was only gradually realized, but it was fully comprehended by the end of Sep-tember, when the 12th Army Group began to dole out supplies to the armies through a strict rationing system based on assigned missions. The shortages experienced during the pursuit had provided only a foretaste of the real difficulties to come. For the next two months supply limitations were to dominate operational plans, and the Allies were now to learn the real meaning of the tyranny of logistics.[12]

Thus, the Army historian sums it up in terms previously quoted in the first chapter.

Inadequate Naval Concepts

Rear Admiral Worrall Carter, USN, Retired, the Commander of the famous Service Squadron Ten of the U.S. Pacific Fleet in 1944-45, provides an excellent statement of the Navy's prob-lem in the first two chapters of his book, *Beans, Bullets, and Black Oil.*[13]

He discusses how the Navy had always recognized the need for overseas bases but before World War II had been uncer-tain as to the degree to which floating facilities could take the place of shore installations. While many naval commanders had long recognized the need for floating mobile naval facilities, local political and business influences, among others, had suc-

---

[11] Ruppenthal, *op cit,* pp. 553-583.

[12] *Ibid,* p. 583.

[13] W. R. Carter, RADM., Ret'd. *Beans, Bullets, and Black Oil.* Govern-ment Printing Office 1953. pp. 1-10.

cessfully opposed this development. Even though the work of the destroyer tenders at Queenstown in World War I furnished confirmation of the idea of floating support and new concepts for future development, the Navy Department was somewhat skeptical. Thus, the base force (the predecessor to the service force) which had been gradually developed into an efficient *supplement* to the shore logistic establishment, at the outbreak of war was in no way equal to the task of supporting sustained offensive operations.

The basic idea of the Navy had been that since construction effort was limited first by budget, second by building facilities, this limited construction effort should be concentrated upon combat ships. Accordingly, only a small number of auxiliary ships were built. The conversion of merchant ships was thought to be the most practicable source of additional auxiliary ships.[14]

The most significant implication of this basic *decision to improvise* logistic support was that we had no real idea of the amount of logistic support that would be necessary to maintain the combat effectiveness of the fleet.

As Carter says:

> The Base Force war plans for an overseas movement visualized two somewhat vague schemes. One was that the fleet would fight at once upon arrival in distant or advanced waters and gain a quick victory (or be completely defeated), and the base would be hardly more than a fueling rendezvous before the battle. Afterward (if victorious), with the enemy defeated there would be plenty of time to provide everything. The other idea was that the advanced location would be seized, the few available repair and supply vessels would be based there, and the remaining necessary facilities would be constructed ashore. The trouble with this thinking lay in the fact that if the enemy refused early action there was no assurance that the base could be held with the fleet not present. On the other hand, the fleet if present could not be serviced without adequate floating facilities while necessary construction was being accomplished ashore. So the idea of fleet logistics afloat was becoming more and more firmly rooted; only time was

---

[14] Carter, *op cit*, pp. 1-10.

needed to make it practical, as our knowledge and experience were still so meager that we had little detailed conception of our logistic needs. Even when someone with a vivid imagination hatched an idea, he frequently was unable to substantiate it to the planning experts and it was likely to be set down as wild exaggeration. How little we really knew in 1940 as compared with 1945 shows in a comparison of the service forces active at both times.[16]

The versatility of naval forces is so great that it is difficult to make a sharp distinction between combat and logistic service. In World War II many vessels of the amphibious types served in both capacities. The table of growth shown below lists naval vessels in three categories so as to provide a realistic picture of what happened as our Navy expanded. The relative growth of these categories is shown in figure 16.

Type of Vessel:	1940	1943	1945	Final Relative Growth:
Combat	267	753	2167	8 to 1
Combat and Logistic	14	241	3187	228 to 1
Logistic	77	323	2167	28 to 1

Figure 16. Table of Growth in World War II

Regardless of the niceties of definition, it is obvious that the proportionate amount of logistic effort required in a major war had been grossly underestimated.

In the Navy the failure to forecast the magnitude of the over-all logistic requirements of modern offensive naval warfare was accompanied by a similar lack of understanding of the capabilities of mobile fleet support. The two factors combined to produce a paradox.

Merchant hulls were not made available for conversion in adequate numbers to provide sufficient mobile support. *There-*

---

[16] Carter, *op cit*, pp. 4-5.

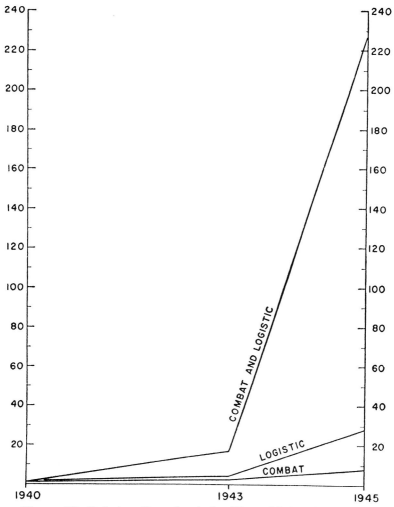

Figure 17. Relative Growth of the Three Major Categories of Naval Vessels

fore, even more merchant ships had to be employed to create and to support the bases which were made necessary by the supposed scarcity of merchant hulls. It was a vicious cycle— a logistic snowball!

As has been indicated, in 1942 our available auxiliary ships were grossly inadequate in number. As a result of this deficiency in fleet logistic support the Navy initiated a huge program of advanced base development. This base program reached a high point in the Leyte Samar area where Carter describes the situation in 1945 as follows:

> At Naval Station Samar, . . . during June 88,977 long tons of cargo were discharged from War Shipping Administration vessels and 24,672 tons from Navy ships, a total of 113,649 long tons, . . .
>
> When June ended there were 3,783 officers and 67,793 enlisted men at shore-based activities in the area, of which 2,831 officers and 58,604 men, including Seabees, were at the Naval Station, Samar. . . . The number of men ashore was not, however, a factor of usefulness. The Leyte Gulf development, most of which, as planned, was to be at Samar, on Manicani, and Calicoan islands and vicinity, was never of great usefulness to the fleet, which depended principally on floating facilities. In all fairness it should be said that this great shore development might have been worth its cost many times over if the war had continued and the Japanese had fought the invasion of their homeland foot by foot for another year or more. Might have been! If enemy action, typhoons, and other unforeseen disasters had been great and the floating facilities suffered from them, the huge base and repair facilities might have developed to high worth. . . .
>
> Of all these facilities, involving so many men and so much effort and money, perhaps the one most necessary— or to put it more positively, the only one positively necessary except the air fields—was the great ABSD, the floating drydock for our biggest ships.[16]

The course of events thus proved that initially the over-all logistic concepts of both the Army and the Navy were grossly inadequate.

The Causes of Underestimates

These few examples serve to illustrate how in both the Army and in the Navy there were serious and prolonged underestimates of the logistic tasks and differences of opinion as to the best balance of forces.

---

[16] Carter, *op cit,* pp. 378-379.

The root of the differences seemed to lie in two basically different concepts of the conduct of campaigns. One was that all strategic planning should be based upon the development of a solid, flexible, logistical base and that the development and operation of such a base required the same degree of skill and access to high command thinking as did the tactical planning. The other concept has never been clearly and openly expressed but in effect it seemed to imply that logistic planning and operations were secondary military activities which ambitious technical specialists were trying to inflate for purposes of "empire building."

In the Army this difference in concept seemed to induce jealousy, struggles for power, and frequent personal conflicts between the staffs of tactical and logistical commanders.

> A noticeable tension developed in the various headquarters and permeated even the lower echelons. Some staff officers at SHAEF and 1st Army Group showed open hostility toward the SOS. This lack of confidence inevitably lessened administrative efficiency.[17]

That similar situations are not frequently found in Navy *histories* may reflect more of a difference in its historical writing than a difference in the concepts of its officers.

In describing this constant struggle in the Army, Ruppenthal points out how the logistic snowball was increased by uncertainties in decisions, and by the psychology of the continual battle for concessions which should have been made without question.[18] This type of inter-staff conflict creates suspicion, which in turn breeds on suspicion, to increase waste.

However, these philosophic differences are only part of the story. Other important factors are involved.

The basic reason for the increasing ratio of service troops to combat troops is the ever-greater mechanization of our combat forces. This started with the Industrial Revolution and has

---

[17] R. G. Ruppenthal, *Logistical Support of the Armies,* Volume I Office of the Chief of Military History, Department of the Army. Government Printing Office, Washington, D.C. p. 264. Others comments pertinent to this problem can be found on pages 159, 160, 167, 205, 208, 211, 264-66, 424.

[18] *Ibid,* pp. 160, 169, 191, 201, 209-11, 264, 299, 300, 553-83 all contain material pertinent to this struggle and its ultimate effect.

continued ever since;[19] in the age of missiles and satellites it will probably grow even more.

In the light of this known trend it is difficult to understand some of the frequently expressed claims that the armed forces can be reduced in manpower without being reduced in fighting power, merely by the expedient of reducing the service forces.

It is, however, true that improved fighting power with reduced manpower can be obtained *if* the term of peacetime enlistment is increased and *if* both peacetime and war training are increased to improve the efficiency and versatility of the individual officer and man. Furthermore, the development of high morale in both combat and service forces is essential to this improved efficiency. *These factors contain the key to preventing the "logistic snowball."*

If for political reasons these common-sense measures are not possible, then we must learn to accept the unpleasant reality of an increasingly ponderous "administrative tail" for our Army, Navy, and Air Force.

Part of the solution, however, lies in the hands of the military Services. Recognizing the inevitable effects of the need for increased logistic support resulting from advanced military technology, we must establish such command controls as will minimize the growth of logistics for its own sake.

The basis for effective control is the fundamental principle that *mere size is no suitable object; rather, the efficacy of the logistic support rendered is the true aim.* In other words, the objective is to attain the maximum sustained combat effectiveness.

The Disposition and Control of Resources

It is just as important that logistic resources be properly disposed as that they be of adequate size. The solution of these questions can be considered as the basic logistic "design" of an area or theater of war.

---

[19] For a commentary from the history of the Korean War which provides further substantiation see Doctor James A. Huston's article, "Korea and Logistics" in *Military Review* of February 1957, Issue Number II. The pertinent passage is quoted in full later in Chapter 18.

It is in fact a problem in system design: The design of a system for the distribution of the means of war. It is somewhat similar to the design of a dynamic liquid flow with reservoirs, surge tanks, manifolds, and valves. Rather than a single liquid, however, it must handle many thousands of items with different characteristics.

The design of the system must take into account the levels or capacity to supply at each point of storage and issue. The Army logistic problem centers about the fact that the maintenance of the firepower and mobility of a combat unit requires daily resupply of almost all essential items. Naval ships, on the other hand, have the built-in capacity to support themselves in combat for 30 to 90 days providing that resupply of fuel and ammunition be assured every three to five days. And, aircraft, whether shore based or ship based, must land at a base after each combat or logistic mission.

Thus, the term "level of supply" sometimes can be deceptive. In certain categories it can be usefully expressed in terms of days of usage. In other categories days of usage has no meaning and instead specific quantities must be prescribed. For example, the consumption of food is regular and can be expressed in terms of days. On the other hand, fuel oil or aviation gas cannot be reduced to days of supply on the same basis as food. Instead they must be thought of and provided in terms of specific quantities for specific uses. Ammunition also must be considered as a special category.

In a similar manner, each functional activity of the base or logistic system must be described in terms of its capability to support combat forces.

Another basic question in the logistic design of a theater lies in the determination of the relative size of the combat and logistic forces.

Logistic Objective and Planning

To settle these problems we should go back to our fundamentals as related to the never ceasing conflict of requirements desires versus capabilities realities. What are the logistic needs which will support those combat forces we should like to employ in the time, manner, and place that will achieve our strategic objectives? And, contrarily, what strategic objectives can be attained by the combat forces which can be created and supported by the logistic resources which are available within the time limitations of the situation?

Obviously, the first need is for good logistic planning factors, i.e., "The quantitative-time relationship between the employment of military forces and the expenditure of military resources."

These are not problems for solution merely by intuition nor, at the other scale of thinking, can they be solved solely by mathematical formulas. There must be both skilled professional judgment and good logistic planning factors, with the final answer emerging as a decision of command.

We can never expect to plan so accurately as always to avoid imbalances between combat and logistic forces. However, we should be able to plan much better than we have in the past. When we reexamine the history of World War II it appears that most of the past failures to achieve an even approximately correct balance are due to a combination of several causes, such as:

Lack of good logistic planning factors;

Unwillingness to devote adequate talent and effort to the analysis of the logistical implications of strategical and tactical concepts;

A fear lest the logistic snowball get out of hand;

Failure to understand logistic principles, particularly how our advancing technology inevitably makes greater and greater logistic demands.

One of the best discussions of the situation is found in John Ehrman's *Grand Strategy*.

But this strategy, borne simultaneously with heavy commitments in the Far East, was expensive in men and material. As we have seen, the British could not fully support their commitments. The question therefore arises, how was the ratio established between supply and effective strength, and could it have been modified?

This was not a large proportion of the numerical strength, even allowing for the high numbers allowed by the planners for a British division, including all arms and support, in the different theaters—38,000 in the Mediterranean, 56,000 in south-east Asia, and 40,000 for "Overlord." The demands on equipment and transport were also high. In the first two days of "Overlord," an armada of over 4,000 assault ships and craft carried seven divisions and their supplies across the Channel; two months later, over 1,500 assault ships and craft enabled three divisions to land in southern France. Such figures pose an obvious question. Was the Western Allies' strength in battle disproportionately low in relation to the effort that went to produce it?

The question of the proportion of "teeth" to "tail" was one which constantly troubled the Prime Minister, not least in the last two years of the war. But he never received a satisfactory reply, and perhaps he never could. For while the question was plain, it raised implications whose complexity made a single answer difficult if not impossible. It is indeed often hard to find not only an answer, but the data on which an answer could be based. For such data derive from accepted standards of calculation, whose validity in turn depends on the relations between planning and material. When these are uncertain—and they were sometimes uncertain during our period—it is perhaps as useful to examine the reasons, and to see the results for the calculations, as to discuss the calculations themselves. . . . The increase of mechanization and of armour since the First World War, and the growing complication of weapons, had already swollen the size of the "tail" behind the lines. It now tended to grow further as new offensives set new problems for technique.[20]

Two major principles previously mentioned are reemphasized by this experience. First, the objective of all logistic effort is the creation and sustained support of the most effective combat forces. In some instances a reduction of the size of the combat force, in order to increase the size of the logistic support force, will result in a significant increase in the total combat effective-

---

[20] John Ehrman, *Grand Strategy*, Volume V, August 1943-September 1944, Her Majesty's Stationery Office, London: 1956. pp. 49-50.

ness of the whole force. Second, if the logistic aspects of an operation are planned and initially provided on a seriously inadequate scale, it is quite likely that the eventual commitment of logistic resources to that operation will be lavish and wasteful. In other words, *under-planning* produces *over-planning*.

Perhaps the best answer to the over-all question of the pattern and level of logistic suport is summed up by Field Marshal Rommel:

> The best thing is for the commander himself to have a clear picture of the real potentialities of his supply organization and to base all his demands on his own estimate. This will force the supply staffs to develop their initiative, and though they may grumble, they will as a result produce many times what they would have done left to themselves.[21]

The necessary corollary to this statement is, however, that the picture will be clear only when the commander understands both the weaknesses and the strength of his support and recognizes the forces which serve to create the strength and to cause the weakness. Some of the more important of these forces will be found in the succeeding chapter on the control of priorities and allocations.

---

[21] B. H. Liddell Hart, *The Rommel Papers.* New York, Harcourt, Brace and Company, 1953. p. 97.

Chapter 10

Control As Applied to Priorities and Allocations

*Actually the issue, as is usual, was not in the realm
of "yes or no" but in that of "more or less."*[1]
—WINSTON CHURCHILL

The determination of what logistic resources are required
in order to create and to support the combat forces, is obviously a basic command decision. It is equally obvious that
not everything can be done at once and that not every commander can have all the forces and resources which he would
like to have.

Importance and Early History

Therefore, we can be sure that in any future war, just as
in the past, the establishment of effective systems of determining and administering priorities and allocations in many logistic and economic areas will be imperative. It will be particularly
important in transportation, in personnel, and in critical equipment and materials. These problems will be urgent both in the
effective mobilization and employment of our industrial power
and in the command and coordination of our combat operations.

The experience of the Quartermaster Corps of the U.S, Army
illustrates the difficulties caused by what can be called "the
inflation of priorities." This arose from the use of a system of
priorities without associated allocations.

In 1940 a priorities system was established by joint action
of the Army, the Navy, and the National Defense Advisory
Commission to insure preferential treatment of defense production. However, within a few months it was proven inadequate
for more and more military projects were placed in top priority
category, thus inflating it.

---

[1] Winston Churchill, Closing the Ring, The Second World War, Vol. V,
A Churchill Reader, Edited by Colin R. Coote, Houghton Mifflin, Boston,
1954, p. 212.

Although the priorities system determined the order of preference, it controlled neither the quantity of material distributed nor the time of delivery. It was therefore unable to insure orderly and integrated procurement by all the supply services. Orders with low priority ratings could be continually deferred while successive higher rated orders were processed and shipped. A balanced production of all items needed in the Army supply program became impossible.

Not infrequently, supplies on order by the Corps were "lifted" by other services by the simple method of placing higher ratings on them.

Experience in the administration of the defense effort had early indicated the need for other types of controls to supplement the priorities system. Of these the most important were allocations which would gear the entire defense program to the available supply of critical materials. Only by allocating these materials to the end use could a balanced production program be realized and competition between the services to complete their requirements be eliminated.[2]

The "Controlled Materials Plan" established in July 1943, which allocated to a procuring service all the materials required to make a given set of end items with the service in turn reallocating materials to specific contracts, is an illustration of this principle.

On a more general theme another history says:

On the dangers of imbalance, as on those of sin, almost everyone could agree. But "balance" meant something different to each of the claimants. The result was bitter contention within the Military Establishment, and between the military and civilian authorities, over the priorities structure that would govern the division of the national product.

Long before Pearl Harbor, the lack of a firm policy and of effective machinery to decide among the competing claimants had resulted in over-loading the top-priority ratings and depreciating the lower ones. In the flood of orders and new programs of early 1942 the situation

---

[2] Erna Risch, *The Quartermaster Corps: Organization, Supply, and Services,* Volume I, Government Printing Office 1953, p. 290-295.

quickly got out of hand. The Army and Navy Munitions Board reported late in February that, out of a total scheduled or in prospect for 1942 (about $56 billion at this juncture), over $31 billion, or almost 56 per cent, was in the top-priority band.[3]

One solution, illustrated by an example in the Navy, is as follows. In 1942 and early 1943 The Office of The Vice Chief of Naval Operations established a priority system for the shipment of naval cargoes to the Pacific. While this was beneficial it did not solve the problem caused by the various commands which were competing for the same transportation "lift." However, in 1944 as the volume of cargoes rose with the build up of the offensive, an allocations system was established by which each theater was granted a *periodic* shipping allocation. The Commander in Chief Pacific Ocean Area reallocated his share of the available lift to his component and type commanders; they, in turn, determined the priorities of the various units which were scheduled for shipment to them. The operation of this system of allocations and priorities was ultimately delegated to and administered by the Commander Western Sea Frontier. It produced a markedly more efficient handling of shipping and cargoes.

The attempt to use priorities to regulate the flow of personnel and material by air transport resulted in many difficulties. It was not unusual for material to wait months at an air depot in spite of the fact that it could have moved in weeks by sea transport.

In the light of the increasing need for air transportation to support modern overseas supply systems and to control the logistic snowball, it is interesting to note the comments of the British historian, John Ehrman:

> The provision of transport aircraft was not a strategic factor of the same magnitude or persistence as that of assault shipping; but occasionally in Europe, and constantly in Asia, it had a similar effect. Air transport was not funda-

---

[3] Richard M. Leighton and Robert W. Coakley, *Global Logistics and Strategy 1940-1943*, Office of the Chief of Military History, Department of the Army, Washington, D.C., 1955, p. 199.

mental to the Allies' tasks in 1944, as sea transport was fundamental. But it was a potent adjunct to both land and seaborne operations, proving vital to the first stage of "Overlord," to the whole course of the campaign in Burma, and to the support of China; and its distribution at times aroused discussion of strategic priorities as sharp, though not as serious, as that aroused by the landing ships and craft.

These in turn depended first on the domestic allocation of priorities, and secondly on the subsequent allocation of production between the two allies.[4]

Experience in building advanced bases in World War II showed clearly that priorities of construction had little meaning unless they were supplemented by specific dates for the completion of minimum operating facilities and for final completion. Otherwise the absurd situation arose in which a unit was forced to live in the mud with no facilities whatever until the final finishing touches were applied to a unit which held an arbitrary and uncontrolled higher priority.

In the light of various experiences in the control of procurement, of transportation and of base construction, it seems proper, therefore, to explore some of the history and basic factors and principles that concern this area of the logistic problem.

An illustration of the basic problems and considerations involved is found in the differences of opinion in mid-September 1944 between General Eisenhower and Field Marshal Montgomery as to the best plan for the final drive on Germany.[5]

Eisenhower advocated a "broad front" strategy utilizing all forces in one coordinated drive; and he invited his Army Group commanders to comment.

Montgomery in reply suggested a "narrow front" concept, saying in part:

---

[4] John Ehrman, *Grand Strategy*, Volume V, August 1943-September 1944, Her Majesty's Stationery Office, London, 1956, p. 38-39.

[5] This situation is thoroughly analyzed in *The Supreme Command* by Forrest C. Pogue, p. 290 to 298; published by the Office of the Chief of Military History, Department of the Army, Washington, D.C., and in *Eisenhower's Six Great Decisions* (Europe 1944-1945) by General Walter Bedell Smith, published by Longmans Green, New York, 1956, p. 215-216.

1. I suggest that the whole matter as to what is possible, and what is NOT possible, is very closely linked up with the administrative situation. The vital factor is time; what we have to do, we must do quickly.

2. In view of para. 1, it is my opinion that a concerted operation in which all the available land armies move forward into Germany is not possible; the maintenance resources, and the general administrative situation, will not allow of this being done *quickly*.

3. But forces adequate in strength for the job in hand could be supplied and maintained, provided the general axis of advance was suitable and provided these forces had complete priority in all respects as regards maintenance. . . .[6]

While Eisenhower finally decided to adhere to the "broad front" concept, the merits of the two schemes are still being debated by historians. The point here is that the strategic concepts were inextricably involved in the question of the allocation of logistic resources, and in the concomitant request for an "overriding priority" for a particular operation under one strategic concept. Both of these questions involved high level command decisions.

General Walter Bedell Smith said in his comments:

Following our swift progress across France and Belgium, the Field Marshal became convinced that if all supply were directed to his 21st Army Group, he could drive forward on a relatively narrow front with an attack which would carry him all the way to Berlin. He was sure that our offensive drive had demoralized the enemy forces. He now felt that the operation he proposed would cause the collapse of Germany and so end the war.
Even had the success of the Field Marshal's proposed operation seemed more probable, to concentrate all our supply and transport for his support would have completely halted operations on every other part of the front. This would not have been important if Montgomery's victory was rapid and complete. In any other alternative our other

[6] Forrest C. Pogue, *The Supreme Command,* Office of the Chief of Military History, Department of the Army, Washington, D.C., p. 290-291.

armies would have been almost immobilized through lack of both supply and transport. Thus they would have been unable to furnish reinforcements if the Berlin drive found itself in trouble.

The same would have been true if all supply had been given to any other part of the line. I believe there was disappointment in this country when General Patton's Third Army was halted that September because his rapidly advancing columns had outrun their supply lines. If our advance had been less swift, so that supply could have paced it, he could have penetrated further. But even if his narrow thrust had not been stopped by German concentration, it would have brought him to an area where it would have been practically impossible to supply him across the Rhine. Thus, at worst, we would have risked a serious military defeat.[7]

The importance of command control of logistics as it relates to priorities and allocations is also clearly brought out by General Smith in the following words:

On September 1, General Eisenhower had taken tactical command of all ground forces in the battle zone. This arrangement was always part of the strategic plan. Field Marshal Montgomery was to have tactical command of ground troops until we were firmly established on the Continent and the American 12th Army Group was in being, at which time General Eisenhower would assume tactical command. In late August, the Field Marshal proposed that he continue to exercise tactical control of all ground forces in addition to commanding the 21st Army Group. In practical fact, this would have meant that General Eisenhower was abandoning his authority as supreme commander, for it was his responsibility to exercise general tactical control over the huge area of the entire front. With the needs and assigned missions of the various forces familiar to him, he alone could have the knowledge to allocate supplies and divisions for the separate operations. Had Montgomery, too, been in a position to reassign units and allocate supplies for forces other than his own, serious confusion could have resulted. General Eisen-

---

[7] General Walter Bedell Smith, *Eisenhower's Six Great Decisions (Europe 1944-1945)* Longmans Green, New York, 1956, p. 215-216.

hower rightly refused to consider the Field Marshal's proposal as workable.[8]

Factors in Command Control

When we examine this situation and its implications we can see some valuable general principles.

For the purpose of this discussion the following descriptions are used:

Priorities: constitute the *relative* order of need for a commodity or service.

Allocations: constitute an absolute, rather than a relative, grant of a commodity or service.

It is a basic principle of military command that higher authority assigns missions or tasks to various subordinates and allocates to them the forces necessary to their accomplishment. Thereafter he exercises general coordination, gives general directives and exercises general control. To the greatest practicable degree he delegates to various subordinates the details of execution. Higher authority must give freedom of action to its subordinates. Within the limits of this freedom as prescribed by higher authority, the subordinate has both the right and the duty to exercise initiative. One of the most important areas of his decision is that of determining the relative order or the relative importance of all the individual acts that collectively make up the task assigned to him, unless this order has been specifically determined by the superior as an essential part of the plan.

Nature of Priorities and Allocations

The amount of available material or services allocated to a subordinate constitute the practical limits of his freedom of action. This allocation is the proper function of the superior. It is the prerogative of the subordinate to utilize this freedom within the prescribed allocations to the extent that it does not violate the expressed intent of the superior.

For illustration let us assume a situation where a commander

---

[8] Smith, *op cit*, p. 220.

is directing and coordinating the operations of five subordinate commanders called, A, B, C, D, and E (figure 18).

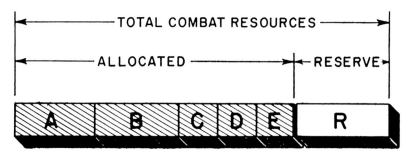

Figure 18. Allocated Resources

In a system where priorities alone are used, subordinates A, B, C, D, and E, all have equal right to assign values to their needs for materials or services. These values are assigned, not in relation to the whole task as determined by the common superior, but only in relation to a supposed relative need. Relative to what? Are the values assigned relative to the *other tasks of the particular subordinate* requesting the priority? Or, are the values relative to *all the tasks of all the subordinates?*

If it be the first, then in designating priorities among his own projects the subordinate is discharging his proper duties within proper limits.

If the second condition obtains, the subordinate is attempting to make a relative evaluation between his own projects and those of his associated commanders. This is beyond the area of his competence and authority.

If, on the other hand, a third situation exists and without broad allocations the superior establishes detailed priorities among and between the material requirements of his subordinates, he in turn is interfering in the executive management of their affairs which he, supposedly, delegated to them by assigning tasks.

Neither of the systems described in the second or third situations will work satisfactorily. In one case all of the subordinates at once engage in an inflation of their demands for priorities to such a degree that the relative terms or values become meaningless. In the other case the superior becomes so hopelessly involved in detail that efficient administration is impossible.

In the rare exceptions which can be cited where priorities *without* allocations worked well, a closer examination will probably show that there was no scarcity of the commodity at all and therefore controls or priorities never had been necessary.

Relation to Command Control

When making allocations it is well to remember another point of theory and principle: In logistical operations, just as in tactical operations, it is necessary to establish reserves of resources which can be committed only by the commander.

If in the course of a campaign or an operation a tactical commander observes that the combat resources allocated to one of his subordinates are inadequate to the task assigned, he is faced with a normal command decision. He either commits part of all of his reserve, or he reallocates a part of his resources, taking from one to give to another. In some cases he may reduce the task assigned or else tell the subordinate, "So sorry, you will have to do the best you can with what you have at hand." In any case, he still leaves to his subordinate the details of how to conduct his assigned tasks.

Let us return from this tactical analogy to logistics. The task of the commander is to assign tasks and to allocate resources. When the relative importance of the missions of the various subordinates has been decided by the common superior, he confirms this decision by the degree to which his allocations fulfill their needs for resources. The task of each subordinate is to accomplish his own task using the allocated resources in accordance with his professional judgment.

In some instances the commander may administer the priorities system himself—in other cases he may delegate this administration to a particular operating subordinate commander. In all cases the priorities within the allocated resources will be determined by each of the subordinates, not by the administrator.

In the operation of the system it is quite likely that inequalities, excesses, or shortages will develop. In this case the administrator should make recommendations. Better still, the basic plan should provide procedures whereby the administrator can make certain *temporary, emergency* allocations together with a prompt report of his action to the superior authority.

The question of priorities and allocations is closely related to the problem of the degree of centralization of authority in the operation of logistic services. In areas such as construction and transportation some persons advocate complete centralization at the highest level of command. Others advocate the greatest possible degree of decentralization. Too much centralization ultimately produces rigidity and sluggish response. Too little centralization may cause waste through inadequate use of critical resources. The wisest policy is to find that balance between these two extremes which will meet the needs of a particular situation. While it is extremely difficult to state general rules it appears that it is best to centralize the control of major work which requires mass movement or mass production techniques, and to decentralize control of the lesser volume of local activity. For example, mass point-to-point or inter-theater transportation should be centralized at a higher level than should local or intra-theater transportation.

In other words, each commander should have enough capability in each logistic category to handle those small but vital day-to-day tasks on which his flexibility depends. The capability for such decentralized operation can be achieved either through an organic unit already available to the commander, or by the allocation to that commander of a logistic unit provided from a larger more centralized resource.

And finally, in its exercise of logistic control it is necessary for command to understand the relation of movement control, and of transportation, to the operations of systems of priorities and allocation. In this connection John Ehrman in his story of the major strategic decision of World War II, shows how at the highest levels of strategic and operational planning the whole relation between strategic objectives, logistic planning factors, the size and balance of combat and logistic forces, priorities and allocations, frequently has revolved around problems of transportation.[9]

Overriding Priorities

An important aspect of the priorities situation is that of "overriding priorities." The use of overriding priorities comes as a direct result of the inflation of priorities as previously mentioned. While in some cases, as for example the preparation of landing craft for an amphibious invasion, overriding priorities *may be* justified, normally they should be avoided. *An overriding priority by its careless or improper use may create havoc in the orderly preparation for battle.*[10]

If, for example, claimants A and B have equal importance in the performance of their missions and each has a claim for commodity X, which is in short supply, and claimants C, D, and E, have a somewhat less urgency in their tasks, the initial *allocation* of X on the basis of estimated requirements might be one or the other of the two following cases of possible hypothetical allocations:

Case I:		*Case II:*	
A	100% of requirements	A	90% of requirements
B	100% of requirements	B	90% of requirements
C	80% of requirements	C	70% of requirements
D	70% of requirements	D	70% of requirements
E	25% (Task reduced)	E	10% (Task delayed)

Now, if an overriding priority system is in operation, *and if more of the commodity X is received:* In Case I, A might claim the right to a reserve of 10% or 25% additional X *before* C, D, and E, are increased.

This action might very easily be harmful and the wiser course of action might be to increase C, D, and E, before providing reserve for A and B, even though the A and B jobs have "priority."

---

[9] John Ehrman, *Grand Strategy*, Volume V, August 1943-September 1944, Her Majesty's Stationery Office, London, 1956, p. 27-32, 477-478.

[10] Richard M. Leighton and Robert W. Coakley, *Global Logistics and Strategy 1940-1943*, Office of the Chief of Military History, Department of the Army, Washington, D.C., 1955, p. 270-271.

In Case II, A might claim the right to get 100% before E got the necessary increase for him to start his job. The overriding priority makes no allowance for judgment but provides an arbitrary system which encourages waste and inflation of need.

Actually, in either Case I or Case II, if additional resources of X are received, *a reappraisal of the entire situation should be made* before reallocating these new resources.

Forethought

When we review the detailed histories of the development of working systems of priorities and allocations during World War II, we find that in every level and area in order for command to exercise this control it is necessary to establish a flow of information, a means of discriminating selection of what information is pertinent, and a means of evaluation from the perspective of command.

This means that the nature of the problems must be thought out in advance and staffs and facilities to handle the problems trained and planned. Experience has shown that: "Planning *after* a shortage exists can never be fully effective and is always wasteful of resources . . . This would have established the control at the beginning of the operation rather than midway."[11] This conclusion, reached by three historians in their analysis of wartime production controls, is equally applicable to the control of operations in a theater of war.

Summary

In this chapter the factors of priorities and allocations of resources have been considered. In any war, shortages of various items are bound to appear. Such shortages may be general—that is on the mobilization level—or they may appear at almost any level of command as local shortages of various resources. At any level, such shortages work to restrict the combat operations of the commander, and, consequently, priorities and allocations automatically become problems for resolution by command.

---

[11] David Novick, Melvin Anshen, and W. C. Truppner, *Wartime Production Controls,* New York, Columbia University Press, 1949, p. 387.

Chapter 11

Movement Control and Overseas Transportation

*The strategy of the free nations is inextricably tied to
their ability to move freely on the sea and in the air.*[1]
—ADMIRAL ROBERT B. CARNEY, USN

Transportation is so involved with all the other factors and
elements of war that frequently the fundamentals get lost in a
welter of detail and of conflicting opinions. The differences
center around: first, the command of transportation facilities;
and second, the allocation of transportation lift.[2]

Claimants for Control

The arguments both for administrative authority and for the
allocation of lift include the following competing claimants and
conflicting interests:

(1) The civil versus the military;

(2) The functional command versus the regional
command;

(3) The inter-theater lift versus the intra-theater lift;

(4) The tactical versus the logistical;

(5) The organic versus the non-organic transportation agencies;

(6) The staff function versus the operating function;
and

(7) Centralization versus decentralization.

---

[1] Admiral Robert B. Carney, USN, in an address delivered at the Naval
War College on 7 June 1955 entitled "Principles of Sea Power."

[2] Excellent discussions of our World War II experience in these matters are
found in Duncan S. Ballantine's *U.S. Naval Logistics in the Second World
War*, Princeton University Press, 1947, pp. 76-93 and 117-131. Also in Chester
Wardlow's *The Transportation Corps: Responsibilities, Organization, and
Operations*, Chapter 1, pp. 1-23, published by the Office of the Chief of
Military History, U.S. Army, Washington, D.C., 1951; and Chester Wardlow's
The Transportation Corps: Movements, Training, and Supply, Chapter 8,
pp. 517-525, published by the Office of the Chief of Military History, De-
partment of the Army, Washington, D. C., 1956.

The proponents of one cause sometimes tend to take an all-or-nothing attitude. A commander seldom has either as much authority as he desires or as much transportation as he thinks necessary. All of the above claimants can present plausible justification for their views. Therefore, compromises and adjustments are inevitable in all of these areas of contention. If we are to make these compromises wisely we must seek to understand the relation and the distinction between transportation efficiency and logistic efficiency. Leighton and Coakley have commented:

> But whereas efficient transportation, under wartime conditions, thus emphasized the movement of freight and personnel in the mass, efficient supply demanded the delivery of specific items to specific destinations at specific times. A shipload of war material delivered safely overseas was half wasted if half the cargo consisted of filler items not needed immediately, while urgently needed tanks and signal equipment (bulky in relation to weight) had been loaded, in the interests of saving cargo space, on a later vessel. As General Lutes wrathfully protested in February 1943, "this business of just pushing on subsistence and ammunition and stuff that [is] not needed overseas as filler cargo, as has been done in the last eight months, [has got] to stop. . . ." From the point of view of supply, efficiency in transportation was not an end in itself, but had to be measured in terms of effective supply.[3]

Critera of Judgment

Here we have the crux of the arguments: What are the criteria by which we should judge the excellence of a military transportation system? To what degree are the normal criteria of the business world applicable to the judgment of military transportation?

In the business world profit and loss are the criteria of judgment. Furthermore, in civil life the consumer usually has the choice of which means of transportation he will patronize. Therefore, in the interest of his own efficiency he evaluates the relative cost of all means of transport in relation to his over-all

---

[3] Richard M. Leighton and Robert W. Coakley, *Global Logistics and Strategy 1940-1943*, Office of the Chief of Military History, Department of the Army, Washington, D.C., 1955, p. 329.

costs. Frequently in a particular instance he may choose to use premium transportation.

In normal business situations there is a definite relation between the demand for and the supply of premium transportation. Therefore there is usually competition among the suppliers of premium transportation and between premium and low-cost transportation.

The consumer's demand for transportation services responsive to his need induces transport companies to supply him with it.

The military world is quite different.

Under our present organization and system the availability and responsiveness of transportation both high- and low-cost is determined by the decisions, policy, and organizational and budgetary decisions of higher authority. The ultimate consumer, that is the tactical commander, has little choice.

In the military world the criteria by which we judge the excellence of a transportation system are quite different and much more complex. It is not possible to place a monetary value on combat effectiveness; nor is it possible to use a profit and loss criterion for logistic efficiency. Instead three different sets of criteria and three different points of view should be used in evaluating the operation of a transportation system:

(1) The maximum efficiency and effectiveness of "carrier operation";

(2) The maximum efficiency and effectiveness of a supply distribution system; and

(3) The maximum economy and combat effectiveness of the consumer (the tactical commander).

Carrier efficiency and supply efficiency are frequently but not always in harmony. However, in some instances they may be contradictory.

Carrier efficiency and consumer economy and combat effectiveness are frequently but not always in harmony. In many instances such as in "combat loading" they are contradictory.

Supply efficiency and consumer economy and combat effectiveness are nearly always in harmony. Rarely are they contradictory.

Carrier efficiency is easy to judge.

Supply system efficiency is somewhat more difficult to judge.

Consumer economy and combat effectiveness are extremely difficult to judge, so much so that many persons feel we can only guess at them and therefore the question of evaluation is hopeless. For that reason they may not receive adequate consideration in the design of logistic systems.

There is not the slightest doubt that in a major conflict it is necessary to attain a high degree of efficiency in the use of all forms of transportation. However, the law of diminishing returns operates here as elsewhere. When the logistic snowball begins to grow, and the overloaded transportation system is not responsive to the needs of the tactical commander, the over-all transportation requirements are also greatly increased. *Under such conditions, statistical evidence of high transportation efficiency has little meaning if it is not related to over-all logistic and combat effectiveness.*

Interrelationships

In previous discussions it was pointed out that in their modern *supply* concepts the three Services are attacking one important aspect of the logistic snowball. It was further pointed out that these new supply concepts required that the area commander have sufficient control of intra-theater transportation to make rapid delivery or redistribution of critical stocks within his own area.

We also see an interrelationship of transportation, the snowball, priorities and allocations, logistic efficiency, and combat effectiveness. We can also see how the subject of command control of logistics is related to these questions and to the matters of centralization versus decentralization; organic versus non-organic; inter-theater versus intra-theater; and tactical versus logistical. These questions can be sorted out and properly related; and this can take place only by means of a thorough analysis of objectives from the perspective of command.[4]

In addition we should be able to distinguish between movement control and carrier operation.

With these relations and distinctions clearly in mind we can emerge from the forest of detail and make wise command decisions as to organization and as to priorities and allocations of transportation resources via land, sea and air.

The Nature of Movement Control

While the principles of priorities and allocations apply to all areas of logistic effort, they are particularly important in transportation. Here the vital link between high command logistical decision and the practical operation of our transportation systems lies in "movement control"—the same movement control which was previously mentioned as a key to the exploitation of flexibility and momentum.

Movement control may be described as the planning, coordination, and control of the movement of men, equipment, and supplies in accordance with the directives of command planning. It is based on the strategic and tactical plans of command. The movement control staff acting as the agent of command specifies what is to be moved, where it is to be moved, when it is to be moved, and by which type of transportation it is to be moved. It views all forms of transportation equally; but it has no responsibility for the *operation* of transportation systems.

---

[4] A discussion of current disadvantages of this situation is found in the paragraphs on transportation in an article by CDR. J. H. Garrett, SC, USN, entitled "Characteristics of Usage of Supply Items Aboard Naval Ships and the Significance to Supply Management," in the December 1958 issue of the *Naval Research Logistics Quarterly*, Vol. 5, No. 4, particularly pages 292-297. Three parts of his conclusions on page 303 are most significant:

> Growing technology is expanding the range of unpredictable demands for repair parts and at the same time making their ready availability even more essential to Fleet readiness.

> A distribution system for delivery of items not included in either allowance or load list to naval ships "at sea in distant areas" is essential for Fleet readiness.

> The prevailing philosophy of centralization in organization in the Department of Defense precludes the essential degree of responsiveness in the transportation aspects of the Navy distribution system to supply the items of unpredictable demand within a satisfactory time period.

Movement control and carrier operation may be considered as two sides of the same broad coin of transportation. One directs the movement, the other carries it out. Both are interested in the same basic problems and information but each places its own special emphasis on different aspects of these matters. Since movement control is a vital link between the logistical decision of command and the practical operation of the transportation systems, *movement control* is interested in the following specific facts which are essential to transportation planning:

(1) What material and personnel are to be moved in the support of military establishments and operations;

(2) The times and places this material and personnel will be available for lifting;

(3) Advance notice of the arrival of ships and precise knowledge of their cargo;

(4) The means of identification of material and personnel and its relative urgency. This is important in planning movements wherein both routine maintenance shipments and shipments for special operations are involved.

(5) The availability, whereabouts, and schedules of carriers suitable for lifting the various units and equipments involved.

(6) The port and port clearance capacity at the destination.

(7) The port loading capacity, the backlog, and the inflow at each port of embarkation.

(8) The program of arrival of shipments from other areas or from external movement control systems.

In routine resupply operations both in peace or in war, good movement control is necessary both to logistic and to transportation efficiency. In times of crisis its importance and its complication both increase. One critical movement control failure in time of crisis can wipe out the transportation economies of months or years. Our problem, therefore, is primarily that of devising control systems suitable for war conditions.

While the nature and organization of movement control systems will vary with the level of command, its basic concepts and principles apply at all levels. It is in essence a function that is properly performed by a staff agency or by a subordinate command and is one of the chief means by which command controls its own logistics. In its strictest organizational sense it is primarily logistical in nature, but in many instances, as in amphibious operations and in the army combat zone, it merges with tactical operations.

In an assault, for example, where the movement of the tactical units is closely controlled, movement control is the essential element of the initial assault itself. It is the key to the resupply and follow-up of the assault echelons. It determines what units and materials will be brought into the combat zone; and it programs the whole flow of materials and units to and through the ports and airfields which are supporting the operation.

Historical Examples

A review of some of the movement aspects of the Normandy invasion provides good background.

In order to provide a movement control system to marshal and embark the Normandy invasion forces, to make the best use of shipping and to avoid clogging the ports a "Buildup Control Organization" (BUCO) was established. BUCO, a staff group under a British Brigadier, and which included British and American ground, sea, and air representatives, was under the joint direction of the allied Army, Naval, and Air Commanders-in-Chief. It was not an agency of the Supreme Commander but operated directly under the tactical commanders.

Two subordinate executive agencies were established, "Movement Control" (MOVCO) and "Turn Around Control" (TURCO). MOVCO's task was to prepare a daily force movement table and an allocation of ships to units. This was issued to the Headquarters Southern Base Section for accomplishment. TURCO's task was to assist naval commanders in controlling the movement of ships and landing craft. It was responsible for bringing these units to embarkation points as designated by BUCO.

The commander European Theater of Operations Service of Supply (ETOUSA-SOS) was assigned the task of mounting the invasion forces. His subordinate in command of the Southern Base Section set up an EMBARKATION CONTROL organization (EMBARCO) to exercise detailed control over every movement from troop concentration area to embarkation point. In the first days of the invasion the movement of men—and particularly of supplies—was thrown off schedule by the failure of the shipping to complete the round trip within the expected time. This was due to difficulties in unloading and particularly to selective unloading. Furthermore the lack of manifests on the beaches tied up shipping. Ruppenthal cites an example:

> . . . Many vessels arrived at the far shore with their contents unknown to shore personnel. One example of the results is seen in the search for 81-mm mortar shells, which were urgently needed in the Normandy hedgerow fighting. Because the troops on shore did not know where this type of ammunition was located in ships lying offshore, they called forward a large part of the ammunition in U. K. waters. Even then they had to conduct a ship-by-ship search to find the desired items. Late in June, after hearing many complaints on the subject of manifest, General Eisenhower became impatient with the poor performance and promised that heads would roll if no improvement was shown.[5]

In the outloading ports men and supplies piled up, thus aggravating the problems caused by the 24-hour delay of D-Day. The ports became so crowded that on 12 June the units were so badly scrambled that troops could not be sorted into craft loads at all. The situation became so complicated that even the available ships could not be loaded. Only extraordinary measures such as the indiscriminate shipment of troops without regard to craft-loading plans, *coupled with the absence of*

---

[5] R. G. Ruppenthal, *Logistical Support of the Armies,* Office of the Chief of Military History, Department of the Army, Government Printing Office, Washington, D.C., p. 422.

effective enemy interference resulted in the cleaning up of the chaos.

The development and the ill effects of some forms of logistic momentum are best described in the words of Ruppenthal:

> The entire movements machinery was under constant compulsion to accommodate itself to changes in the build-up schedule or to the unpredictable shipping situation. Build-up priority tables were closely followed only in the first few days, after which BUCO issued frequent changes in priorities. Despite the fact that. such changes were anticipated they caused great confusion. There was no reversing the marshaling process. Once a unit moved forward, its place was immediately taken by another, and every change in the priority for embarkation necessitated holding other units in the marshaling areas like a train on a siding, while higher priority units were processed past them. Even so, much of the congestion could have been prevented. Southern Base Section had been advised to hold 25 percent of the marshaling camp capacities free for such contingencies, and had failed to do so. The result was that the lines of communications became choked, and elasticity of control was nullified. To aggravate matters, units were occasionally called forward on short notice and without regard for their "readiness date," and were found to lack most of their equipment.[6]

In the British zone where the control of movements under BUCO was simpler and more decentralized, less difficulty was experienced. The fundamental causes of the American difficulties seem to rest in the failure of high command to establish clear lines of responsibility and authority as between BUCO, MOVCO, TURCO, the high command staff agencies, and the subordinate command operating agency, ETOUSA Service of Supply. EMBARCO, the staff agency of the SOS, encroached directly on the authority of MOVCO, the executive agent of BUCO. This in turn caused a lack of balance as between the movements in and out of the marshaling areas and the failure to match movements with port capacity.

---

[6] Ruppenthal, *op cit,* p. 425.

While the details may have varied greatly, essentially these same faults occurred in the early Pacific campaigns and even in the Korean war. Since large joint operations such as these are always complex, and since staff and command relations are always likely to become complex, it is important to seek the general principles applicable to such large operations.

Organization for Movement Control

Movement control begins to operate in those planning stages of any operation wherein the assault and follow-up programs are developed. However, since no single agency can operate effectively all the way from the beach or air head all the way back to the original sources of power in the continental base, there must be orderly shifts of control from the combat tactical commander at the scene of action to the rear area and zone of interior logistical commanders and authorities who act under the directives of the strategical commanders.

On the highest levels the broad policies which govern shipments between areas, and the volume of movements into each major area, should be controlled by an international or national agency or system. The control of volume should be exercised by allocating transportation capacity or lift. This top movement control should have authority over both the movement of military and non-military cargo.

The over-all movement control agency should work in harmony with the movement control systems on the lower levels. Each area and each sub-area should have its own movement control agency. Each area commander within the limits of his space allocation should control what moves and its relative priority. He normally would have no movement authority in cases where higher authority controls movements of non-military cargo into or through his area. In these movements his authority extends only to routing and protection. (This restriction also applies, incidentally, to military cargo destined for other commands which passes through his area.)

A movement control agency should have cognizance of movement by all means and methods. If control over sea and overseas air movements is not brought together in one control agency, serious deficiencies may develop. For example, at the outbreak of the Korean War, sea transportation movements and air transportation movements were handled separately. Every Far Eastern command wanted men and equipment by "highest priority." Even though the Military Air Transport System rapidly increased its airlift capacity, it could not begin to meet the demand. Within three weeks a two-months backlog was built up at its airport of embarkation at Travis Air Force Base in California.

Naturally, a priority system alone is ineffective in resolving such a problem. If, on the other hand, the backlog could have been shifted readily to surface transportation, delivery of the entire flow could have been greatly expedited. What is more important, the vital and very expensive air transport could have been reserved for shipments of the greatest urgency.

In the organization of a movement control system, it is important to take into account the problems of area organizations, of logistical coordination and the logistic staff organization.

In the case of the movement control organization of an area commander or a sea frontier commander, it should have a very close relation to the requirements control group. Some persons, in fact, believe that the two should be combined in one staff agency or at least under the same direction.

There is always a basic dilemma in setting up movement control: it is the sea frontier or the port of embarkation commander who knows what material and units are ready for shipment; but it is the area commander who knows what is needed. A satisfactory resolution of this dilemma can be found only if the "movement" people are continually aware of changing requirements. It is fundamental that to be effective, a movement control system must be based upon a prescribed combined system of priorities and allocations which, in turn, is administered by an agency responsive to the needs of the commander in the field.

In some commands the function of movement control is handled by the operations division. As the level of the command goes up, however, the problem of movement control becomes too big for it to be so established. Movement control problems tend to shift from a tactical matter in a low level command to a logistical matter as the level rises. Furthermore, as the size increases there is more and more of a tendency for the movement control agency to become autonomous in its practical action.

Movement control can be so vast in its scope that its decentralization may become very important. It requires such a large amount of information, and it may exercise so much influence that frequently it should operate as an individual staff agency or subordinate command rather than simply as a staff division. Movement control is intimately related to transportation, and thus is often considered as an integral part of the transportation problem and organization. It must also be always sensitive to command requirements and priorities. In the scheme of military fundamentals, an efficient movement control system is essential to the attainment of flexibility, to the development and exploitation of strategical and tactical momentum and to the control of logistical momentum.

Movement control programming varies with the level of the agency or command. A national agency may program many months in advance, an area agency may program several months in advance and a sub-area or local agency may find it inadvisable to program more than several weeks in advance. National agencies deal in aggregated volume or space while operating agencies deal in specific shipments.

Each program must take into consideration the program of its superior agency, and each agency must send its program to its subordinate agencies. *The rapid and wide dissemination of program information and allocations is essential to smooth movement control.*

The Controlled Buildup of Forces

As was previously discussed, one of the most controversial problems in logistics is to decide the best ratio of combat forces and logistic forces. In actual war operations the same problem has a great influence on the movement control.

In the Central Pacific in World War II, this aspect of the over-all problem was handled in the CINCPOA Echelon Conferences held under the direction of the Logistic Division of Admiral Nimitz' Joint Staff. In these conferences the amount of shipping space available beyond the immediate assault amphibious lift was allocated to the various claimants who were supporting and following up the assault. These included the reinforcement of combat troops, resupply and maintenance shipments for combat troops, and the buildup and support of the garrison forces who built and manned the complex of advanced bases for whose establishment the amphibious operations were undertaken.

The decision and space allocations made at this conference were called the "garrison shipping plan." Together with the "amphibious force assembly movement" and "assault plans" this formed the basis for the movement control of each operation in the campaign. Throughout 1944 and 1945 this system improved steadily. The system worked splendidly when it was adequately manned and equipped and when its lower level control agencies moved forward with the combat commander. Such smooth forward movement of shipping and movement control was finally achieved in the invasion of Okinawa. Here a specially modified LCI (Landing Craft Infantry) was assigned to the port director as a headquarters ship. By anchoring this LCI near the flagship of the Commander Attack Force and by maintaining close contact with the Commander Landing Force and the similarly improvised LCI headquarters ship of the prospective Commander of the Naval Operating Base, a high degree of order in the control of movement was established.[7]

Perhaps the chief significance of this example is to demonstrate that by anticipating the need for special facilities, for clear command and staff relations, and for well organized information, logistical and transportation efficiency could be vastly improved. On the other hand, in many earlier operations

---

[7] The pile up of shipping which took place in Okinawa in the late summer of 1945 was due to the changes in the build-up plans for Okinawa rather than to the basic design of the movement control system.

the control agencies had been inadequately manned or lacked equipment or information, or the staffs of combat commanders had made hasty or arbitrary decisions without a clear knowledge of the requirements and shipping system and situation. Confusion and waste had been the inevitable result.

Movement Control and Overseas Transportation

When we read of the successes and difficulties of the past we can see certain fundamentals of movement control which apply all through the structure of war planning and operations. Yet we seem slow to learn certain lessons.

In the last few years there have been many discussions and analyses of the problems of overseas transportation. Both air transportation and sea transportation operate in accordance with the same basic principles of transportation, the understanding and application of which are necessary to the efficient operation of our logistic systems. Much attention is properly being paid to the development of more efficient transportation systems. Steady improvement is being made in the related fields of organization, ship and plane design, control of ocean shipping, cargo handling techniques, port design and operation, port equipment, personnel training, and materials handling and packaging. However, there is evidence to show that deficiencies in command planning that took place during World War II, were repeated in the Korean War. Lieutenant General Palmer say:

> Repeatedly in World War II, supplies were landed in such an excess of tonnage over the capabilities of the local logistic organization to cope with it, that pretty soon many things could not be found at all. The next thing, the Zone of the Interior had to rush out a special shipload of something which was right there in the theater—and always at a time when ships were worth their weight in gold. Soon the war moved on and supplies were left behind, which are still being gathered up and sorted out to this day. Two years after the Korean War started, I visited Pusan. They had been working hard, and by that time they had sorted out probably 75 percent of the supply tonnage there. Twentyfive percent of the tonnage on hand was not

yet on stock record and locator cards; they did not know what it was or where it was.[8]

These facts and tendencies have their implications from the point of view of the commander.

In the first place no command which has major strategic or major logistical responsibilities can function effectively in war without special and positive provision for movement control. Movement control is one of the necessary mechanisms through which combat command exercises control of logistics.

In the second place, the selection of the officer to head up the movement control of any major command is a matter of importance. It requires a combination of specialized technical knowledge combined with the command point of view. It is an area where a broad understanding of the blending of logistics and tactics is of the greatest importance.

Two decisions must be made: At what time, during a large sustained offensive operation should movement control pass from the tactical commander to the logistical commander? At what place should this command cut-off line be located[9]?

These are questions in which informed opinions can be expected to differ. The best answers will vary as conditions vary. But unless the importance of these points is recognized and positive provision is made for making and disseminating the decisions, very serious confusion will probably occur.

In the immediate area of combat the tactical commander must have unquestioned control over movements. In the rear areas the logistical agencies, either staff or command, must

---

[8] W. B. Palmer, Lieutenant General, *The Quartermaster Review,* July-August 1953 (Reprinted from April 1953 issue of the Army Information Digest).

[9] R. G. Ruppenthal, *Logistical Support of the Armies,* Office of the Chief of Military History, Department of the Army, Government Printing Office, Washington, D.C., pp. 207-210, 433-438. Ruppenthal discusses the broadest aspects of this describing the differences between Generals Bradley and Lee as to the development of the communications zone on the continent after the invasion of Normandy. Among other things he says:
> One of the key features of the logistic structure was the question of when the army rear boundary should be drawn. . . . Both steps were of direct concern to the tactical command for they involved the progressive surrender of its control over supply operations and the rear areas.

have control. Where and when the shifts shall be made is a major problem of command. *The major aid in solving this problem is to develop in the tactical commander a sense of confidence in the logistical commanders and their staffs.* This can be expected only when the logistic officers have demonstrated their capability and their understanding of tactical situations and their needs.

The recognition on the part of tactical commanders of the desirability of an early and deep shift of the cutoff line comes only when they understand the nature and scope of the logistical problem that must be solved to provide for the exploitation of a tactical success.

The foregoing principles apply to land warfare and to sea war, and they apply to amphibious and to airborne operations. But, most particularly, they apply to joint and combined operations which involve the combination of amphibious and airborne operations. They will apply in even more force as the new weapons of our age come into use. They apply in defensive situations as well as in offensive situations. They will apply in a global atomic war or in a localized brush fire.

In applying the principles of control to movements, each command and each staff agency should limit its action and directives to those elements of the problem which can be managed at its level only. That is to say, an "area movement control agency" should not attempt to control all movements within each sub-area. The principles of exercising unified control by means of policy determination, by general planning, by allocation, and by delegation, should be adhered to as far as possible. Detailed control should be exercised only where necessary. *Appropriate restraint in the exercise of power is fundamental to good management.*

Objectives and Efficiency

Since we seem prone to ignore some of the lessons of the past, it may be useful to again examine fundamental objectives and relationships.

The objective of all logistic effort is: The creation and sustained support of effective combat forces.

Thus, the effectiveness of combat forces is the chief criteria by which to judge logistic effort.

This distinction is an illustration of why command perspective rather than technical or purely functional perspective should dominate logistic thinking.

Functional or technical efficiency is important but it should always be subordinate to combat effectiveness.

In the vast majority of cases functional efficiency will contribute to combat effectiveness but in some instances it should be knowingly and deliberately sacrificed to the greater aim.

Furthermore, in transportation the broader, longer range point of view will show that improved transportation efficiency can be achieved once the concept of maximum combat effectiveness is recognized in all its implications.

In other words, much of the difficulties and past inefficiency of our national *transportation* in wartime can be traced to:

(1) A lack of understanding on the part of transportion authorities of the problem of command; and

(2) A lack of understanding on the part of command as to the problems of transportation.

Such lack of understanding may well lead to the establishment of faulty concepts and procedures. For instance, it is frequently assumed that the maximum loading of ships and the shortest turn around of all ships are, in fact, the criteria by which logistic efficiency can be measured. This is true only when the objective of logistic effort is attained. Thus, while transportation efficiency may be improved by maximum loading and minimum turn arounds, when these are attained at the expense of reduced effectiveness of the combat forces, true logistic efficiency is diminished rather than enhanced.

For example, during World War II there were many instances of huge quantities of supplies being unloaded from ships and piled up in sea ports in such a way that they could not be identified nor issued to the combat forces which required them.

Furthermore, in many instances they cluttered the ports to such a degree that identifiable supplies in the holds of other ships could not readily be moved ashore. Noumea and Oran are two ports where this occurred in 1942 and 1943. As General Palmer pointed out, essentially the same troubles recurred in Korea in 1950-52.

If a smaller number of ships had been allocated and loaded for selective unloading, it appears probable that the logistic support of the combat forces would have been better *and the over-all requirement for shipping would have been reduced.*

Even if port facilities and overseas storage systems may be developed to handle and issue large quantities of supplies efficiently without apparent waste of shipping, if too much dependence is placed on overseas shore depots, shipping will, in fact, be wasted even though the statistical picture may show the opposite. This results, of course, from the enormous amount of shipping which must be assigned to the building and operation of the base facilities *whose sole purpose is to support the combat forces.*

In other words, sometimes there may be a difference between real and apparent logistic and transportation efficiency and there may be a difference between effectiveness and efficiency. A hypothetical situation in which the overseas operation of a fleet is supported by a combination of underway replenishment, shore and floating bases, is useful to illustrate this.

One of the major factors in the build up of large overseas shore establishments is the necessity for handling and rehandling cargo ashore when it is ultimately to go aboard ship in the same port. If the over-all cargo operation can be designed so that cargo can be unloaded direct from a point-to-point cargo ship to a using combat ship or to a fleet issue ship, a great saving in cargo handling facilities, equipment and personnel obviously can be effected. Several steps must be taken within the over-all operation to achieve this saving. Not only must the cargo ship be routed to arrive at the right place at the right time, but also the initial loading of that ship must be such as to permit the rapid movement of cargo *direct to the receiving ship.* Loading plans which will permit rapid unloading direct to the consignee *require selective unloading and thus partial loading.*

The question then arises as to when and to what degree is the partial loading (60%—80% capacity) of point-to-point shipping justified by any savings in the construction and operation of a fleet replenishment base made possible as a result of increased speed and effectiveness of cargo handling resulting from partial loading of certain ships.

Let us assume as situation "A," that the cargo operation is designed to make full use of the tonnage of each vessel; and that replenishment is to be done through a fleet replenishment base. Under these circumstances all the cargoes will be unloaded and placed in store at the base. Supplies will be re-handled on a partial basis for issue to the using ship. Let us further assume that this cargo operation will take 100 ships sailed each calendar quarter from the continental U. S. to support the overall hypothetical fleet effort. Each of these ships would be loaded to capacity on each outgoing voyage.

Let us now suppose hypothetical situation "B" where the same combat effort is being supported; let us further assume that the basic logistic plans of the fleet include making use of the "mobile support concept." Under this concept, the construction of a fleet replenishment base ashore is held to a minimum; the shore installation is supplemented by fleet issue ships which can, and do, move into areas wherever the fleet to be supported may find itself; where the issue of supplies from such ships is a rapid and simple matter, with a minimum of repeat movement or transhipment of cargo; and where in many instances the issue ships which receive the cargo from the point-to-point vessels are themselves "underway replenishment" vessels: scheduled for meetings with the fleet at sea. Under these circumstances, it is likely that as many as 20 ships per quarter should be specially loaded for rapid and selective transmission of cargo —that is, be partially loaded so as to simplify *delivery,* and thus get the maximum of efficiency in cargo handling. Such partial loading—resulting in about only 60% of maximum capacity—

would appear to be a waste of otherwise valuable shipping space.

On the other hand speed and ease of cargo handling at destination, coupled with delivery of a large volume of supplies direct to the consignees and with little or no transhipment through a shore base, would result in compounding savings. Thus, full exploitation of a concept such as this would in fact bring an *over-all* saving. The complete supply of the fleet could be accomplished by the 20 ships in partial load, plus only about 55 ships fully loaded whose cargoes would have to be handled through the facilities of the advanced shore base.

In situation "A" the over-all shipping demand would be 100 ships per quarter. In situation "B" the over-all demand would be 75 ships a quarter. In other words, *it is good shipping economy to apparently waste shipping space if by so doing the "logistic snowball" ashore can be materially reduced.*

The precise historical data and the equations which would prove these assertions are not available. Our study and research in the field of logistics have not come up with the figures. On the other hand, the Navy's general experience, and recognition of the general truth behind this hypothetical example justify its use.

Responsiveness to Command

The basic problem of sea transportation is closely related to two fundamental and difficult logistic problems. These are: the need for accurate determination of the over-all time phased logistic requirements of the combat forces, and the need to keep the build up of storage levels in overseas depots a minimum.

An important element in the development of a plan for overseas transportation is found in the exercise of the authority and responsibility of command at the theater level. This requires the integration of area strategic and logistic planning and the exercise of logistic coordination by the area commander. It also emphasizes the importance of "information and programming." If these features of area command are neglected, the accurate determination of combat requirements, and of what is the minimum requirement of logistic build-up, are impossible. Furthermore, the key to the efficient operation of overseas ports in time of war lies in these same features.

The organization of the transportation and movements systems is closely related to the mobility and flexibility of the combat forces. In peacetime, movements are of less volume and more predictable than they are in wartime. The major movements and transportation systems can thus operate effectively with a high degree of centralization. However, in wartime with greater volume, greater urgency and less predictability, the centralized routine inter-theater systems cannot handle all the necessary work. There is an urgent need for an intra-theater system more directly responsible to the theater commander.

A practical illustration of effective intra-theater transportation which was fully responsive to the needs of the tactical command is to be found in "Service Squadron Eight of World War II." This squadron which at one time included over 400 vessels had the general function of "the supply, transportation, and distribution of fuel . . . provisions, general stores, and ammunition to the fleet and bases."[10]

While we should not expect to repeat the situations and conditions of the WW II Pacific Fleet, nevertheless the need for control of the distribution of supplies to moving naval combat units will remain. Furthermore, the basic principles of organization and of transportation developed to meet this fundamental need in WW II will hold.

Carter's resume of these operations is very instructive:

> When the war suddenly ended, Squadron Eight was of size never contemplated when it was created and commissioned 4 years before. In July 1945 the commissioned ships under its administrative command, and often partially or wholly under its operational control, numbered 365, ranging through every type from big troop-carrying cargo ships down to barges. . . . The growth of the squadron also is indicated by its personnel: 5,000 men in March 1943; more than 65,000 in August 1945. To all these ships and

---

[10] RADM. W. R. Carter, Ret'd. *Beans, Bullets, and Black Oil,* Government Printing Office, 1953, pp. 97-104.

men must be added the merchant vessels, allocated by the War Shipping Administration for transportation of dry provisions, whose schedules had to be coordinated carefully with those of Navy ships in Squadron Eight in loading at such ports as San Francisco, Oakland, San Pedro, and Seattle and in arriving at half a dozen major bases and anchorages in the Eastern Pacific. On many of these vessels there were Squadron Eight storekeepers and an issuing supply officer.

It is stating only the obvious to say that naval ships cannot fight properly without adequate ammunition, and that speed cannot be made without fuel. For these necessities ships are entirely dependent upon the supply lines. The function of Squadron Eight in the Service Force was to schedule, load, and transport logistic support vital to the forward Squadron or by the shore bases concerned. In performing this function Squadron Eight was perhaps the most important factor in the whole supply line. It carried out its duties unfailingly, under many difficulties and shortages of all sorts, including shortages of vessels and men. There never was a raid, attack, or full-scale operation which was delayed or handicapped by any failure of Service Squadron Eight, probably the only supply train in the history of warfare with such a record. Thus it can be seen why Service Squadron Ten was so dependent upon Service Squadron Eight, why it was in a sense a distributing outpost of Eight.[11]

Effect of Faulty Concepts

Faulty concepts lead to waste even under the best of administration. When such concepts are aggravated by poor coordination the bad results are greatly increased.

It may be useful to illustrate this point by generalizing some of the lessons of the past and contrasting them with a hypothetical ideal.

In many war or emergency situations it has been the practice to submit requisitions for material, to order the shipment of units and supplies, and even to sail ships, without reference to the port capacity of the overseas area. When this situation is

---

[11] Carter, op cit, pp. 103, 104.

allowed to occur in any area of major operations there follows a natural sequence of events.

To meet the urgent demand for supplies created by the emergency, there is an immediate increase in demand for ship bottoms. This is usually met by the requisition of vessels, by recommissioning of vessels, and by the diversion of vessels from other operations. The outgoing flow of cargo increases rapidly, and heretofore in major crises this has always overloaded the receiving and distributing capacity of the overseas ports.

A series of reactions to the overloading of ports has been immediate and inevitable:

(1) The combat forces are handicapped by the difficulty of obtaining their most urgent requirements and are exasperated by the flow of nonessentials to the combat area ports.

(2) There is an accumulation of ships waiting to unload in these ports.

(3) The combat commander orders selective unloading in order to meet his immediate needs. This selective unloading aggravates the situation in the ports.

(4) There is an urgent demand for the priority shipment of cargo handling equipment and for the expansion of ports, facilities, and personnel.

(5) Investigators are sent overseas and on their recommendation emergency, and hence very expensive, measures to increase overseas port capacity are taken.

Major congestion may then develop at ports of embarkation. If this happens even the national land transportation system may become disrupted and the adverse effects may spread back to basic industry in spite of the operation of holding and reconsignment facilities.

From this point the sequence of events is not so predictable, but rather is determined by the ability of the enemy to exploit the situation which has arisen. If the enemy has the ability to exploit our logistic weakness in the affected area or in some other combat zone, the adverse effects may be very serious.

If the combat situation stabilizes, the emergency measures eventually become effective and, as in Korea, a modus vivendi is established. If, as in Korea, the logistic demand levels off and becomes reasonably predictable, it does not make too much difference who controls the shipments from the ports of embarkation. Almost any system will work reasonably well if competent officers are in key positions.

If, however, the combat situation does not stabilize, if the area of war spreads, if we wish to exploit a success, or if we must execute a prolonged withdrawal, we may find a serious situation. Our capabilities have been reduced. This is the case because the ports of embarkation, rather than the area commander, control the latter's logistic support to a degree greater than is consonant with the sound principle that the combat commander must control his own logistics. Logistics is no longer fully responsive to the voice of command and command is commensurately hampered.

Need for Integrated Planning

When there is complete integration of strategic and logistic planning at the theater level, and if the area commander does, in fact, exercise logistic coordinating authority, the story can be quite different. As a part of its normal work, before a crisis has developed, the area staff has available for quick reference an analysis of the actual port capacity of all ports in its theater. It also has an estimate as to how the major ports can be expanded. But, most important of all, the theater staff by its studies and integrated planning has learned to recognize the vital importance of port capacity to strategic plans and to tactical operations.

The operations division of the staff realizes that it is never possible to give combat commanders all the material that they would like to have in order to fight. Cooperation between the operations and logistic divisions of the staff makes it possible to discriminate between vital and merely desirable elements of logistic support.

The result of this understanding cooperation can be that the orders and requests for material and equipment which go from the area commander to the continental United States bear a definite planned relation to the area's ability to unload and distribute cargo. Furthermore, in the early stages of the situation, requests for the men and equipment necessary for planned port expansion are submitted.

The area may request that a moderate amount of shipping be specially loaded for selective unloading, and be maintained as a floating reserve in the combat area.

It can be shown that the allocation of a few ships for retention and planned selective unloading will greatly reduce both the over-all requirement for sea transportation and for procurement of supplies.

Therefore it is better to make a modest allotment of ships for this purpose than to insist that: "There will be no retentions, and there will be no selective unloading." In the face of combat necessity these are inevitable. If acknowledged, they can be controlled; if unrealistically resisted, however, they will get out of control.

If we look now at the port of embarkation we can see a picture of order as opposed to the near chaos which can frequently ensue. Because the allocated shipping is adequate for essential combat needs and is flowing smoothly and turning around in a reasonable manner, the number of contradictory and countermanding orders received by the ports of embarkation is diminished. The area commander has established *his* priorities within the allocated shipping space and the administration of those priorities by the designated agencies is relatively easy.

What has been done by this recognition of the full implications of integrated planning and logistic coordination on the area level? All of the slices of the pie that were cut in the functional division of the transportation problem have been put together in a fundamentally sound structure. The people working at the improvement and fitting together of these slices can do their vitally important work with the assurance that it is intelligently related in a coherent over-all strategic-logistic concept. The combat support is more adequate, the combat operations more effective, the violent swings of crisis planning have been moderated, the logistic snowball has been reduced.

Summary

In summation, movement control and transportation are two aspects of the same vital and all pervading element of logistics, and hence of combat power. While transportation efficiency is of great importance it must always be subordinate to logistical efficiency. This is so because logistical efficiency has sustained combat effectiveness as its chief criterion.

The efficient use of overseas transportation, both sea and air, is dependent upon many factors. First comes sound national and area organization and command relations, whereby the top service and government organizations, the operating agencies in the continental U.S., and the areas work in harmony for common objectives.

The basis for this harmony is the integration of strategic-logistic planning. An essential part of this integration is "information and programming." Command action is made possible by "movement control" at all levels. Movement control is guided by a system of "allocations and priorities." The principles of allocations and priorities particularly apply to the allocation of transportation resources.

The more efficient and responsive the transportation and movement control system the lower can be the levels of overseas supplies necessary to support combat operations.

Port and port clearance capacity are necessary factors in all overseas logistic planning.

All the foregoing matters are related to the question of combat force versus logistic force buildup, to the question of centralization versus decentralization in organization, to the development of strategical-tactical momentum, to flexibility, to the growth of the logistic snowball and to readiness for combat.

Finally, for "logistics to be responsive to the needs of combat," the interplay of all these factors must be understood by command at whatever level it is being exercised. However, it is fruitless to understand these matters and to plan correctly if the command is lacking in logistic discipline.

Chapter 12
Logistic Discipline

It appalls me to think how many failures occur in this very last link of the logistic chain. Equipment is manufactured at great expense. It is shipped 5000 miles by train, ship, and truck. It is issued to the troops and eventually, with great labor, carried to the top of a mountain in Korea. How many times, at that last point, has this whole enormous effort been thrown away, as carelessly as a burnt match, by the happy-go-lucky negligence of the very people whose lives depend on keeping the stuff in shape?[1]
—LIEUTENANT GENERAL W. B. PALMER

It is obvious that nothing is more important to combat effectiveness and efficiency than military discipline. However, the effects of inadequate discipline on logistic efficiency are not always fully appreciated. It is therefore appropriate to discuss these further effects under the term logistic discipline.

Logistic Discipline and Supply

The term logistic discipline has a broader meaning than the more commonly used term "supply discipline."[2] While it includes all that is implied in the latter term, it goes further and takes in the more indirect effects on the entire military establishment.

Logistic discipline is attained only through self-control on the part of command. It may be considered as the application of the principles of military discipline to the logistic aspects of war. It should not be considered as a thing apart, a matter of concern only to officers charged with logistic duties. It is a matter of concern to all those who are engaged in military work.

As discussed in chapter six all three Services are developing new supply concepts which attack the roots of the logistic snow-

---

[1] Lieutenant General W. B. Palmer, "Commanders Must Know Logistics," The Quartermaster Review, July-August 1953 (reprinted from the April 1953 issue of the Army Information Digest).

[2] An excellent terse discussion of supply discipline is contained in Vol. 3, No. 5 of "Officer's Call" published by the Department of the Army Troop and Education Division in 1951.

ball. The ultimate success of each of these is dependent on the development of logistic discipline.

Post war analyses of naval supply have indicated that a great majority of the requisitions originating in ships cover only a small percentage of the varieties of supplies in the stock catalog.

For example, one study showed that in general stores material with 75,000 items stocked, 12,000 items or 16% account for 96% dollar-wise of the issues. In ships' parts with nearly 276,000 items stocked, 14,000 items or 5.1% account for 90% of the issues dollar-wise and an estimated 17,000 or 6.1% account for 90% of the issues piece-wise.[3]

These studies indicate that by determining the location of stocks by their classification as "fast moving," "slow moving," and "insurance items," great economies can be achieved.

If forward area supply stocks are confined to fast moving military essentials, supplemented by a small supply of those slow moving items which are most critical in maintenance of combat readiness, *and if these stocks are backed up by a responsive, reliable, fast transportation system, efficient and effective support can be furnished at much less than the cost of attempting to provide all the items in the catalog.* This saving is measurable both in manpower and in the size of the supply facilities. The number of items in the forward supply system should be kept to the minimum, and the quantity of each item to be stocked must be determined by experience. Stripping the supply system to its essentials attacks the logistic snowball at its source and insures toughness and resiliency instead of fat and sluggishness in the logistic support operations.

While this concept may seem both obvious and simple, it is well to point out that it is directly related to discipline or self-control. The supply officers of any first class military service pride themselves on being "can do" men, men who think in terms of how the material needs of their unit can be met promptly and with the least discussion. It is sometimes difficult to reconcile the laudable "can do" spirit which has such a large influence on fitness reports, with the need for enforcing the supply disci-

---

[3] From "The Navy Conservationist" January 1954.

pline necessary for forward area efficiency. *The initiative and enthusiasm for such discipline must first come from command and it then will be loyally served by all others.*

The situation is analogous to sanitary discipline, which also has a profound effect upon efficiency. In this, while the medical officer is the technical advisor, the responsibility and initiative also comes from command.

In the matter of reducing the number of items in forward area stocks, the technical officers have an important reciprocal responsibility to insure that the method of supply demand control takes into account the difference between usage in peace and usage in war. A system based on only peacetime usage with no provision for quick wartime prediction, supplement, and adjustment will give a fictitious sense of economy.

Unnecessary Follow-Up

Studies of the requisition system in naval supply depots, for example, indicate that requisition follow-up letters and despatches may be self defeating and that the follow-up action may actually tend to impede the delivery of the material it supposedly expedites.[4] This comes about in a logical manner.

The modern large supply depot is designed to operate on a highly mechanized basis which is not unlike a mass production assembly line. The normal requisition is handled by means of a routine which is designed to produce the fastest delivery of the greatest number of items. This process normally may take from 5 to 20 days. If during the processing of a requisition through the "assembly line" a follow-up is received, it may be necessary to remove the requisition from the action system and to put it into another system in order to determine its status. If the follow-up action takes place in the earliest stage of the depot process it is possible that the item can be speeded up by changing its status from routine to exceptional. However, if the follow-up is received during the latter stages of the process it is likely that changing its status may even result in

---

[4] Oskar Morgenstern, *Note on the Role of Follow-ups in the Naval Supply System*, GWU-LRP, File PAM-43-1, December 1952.

additional delay for it may have been on the point of shipment when it was removed from the "assembly line."

Furthermore, if a large number of follow-up actions are required, personnel must be diverted from taking action to the duty of answering despatches about action. This diversion inevitably slows down the normal action time and causes more dissatisfaction and more follow-up despatches. It can indeed become a vicious cycle.

A principle now becomes apparent. In a well-organized, well-designed, and well-managed supply depot the efficiency of the depot is decreased by an increase in follow-up and expediting despatches and letters.

However, it accomplishes no good merely to deplore the use of a follow-up. As long as humans make mistakes follow-up will be necessary. It would be unthinkable not to expect follow-up on a needed item which in spite of being correctly requisitioned was still overdue. Obviously some judgment is necessary. Follow-up is not a substitute for timely and correct requisitioning. However, proper follow-up is an aid to a supply depot command in insuring that the depot is doing its job creditably. Nevertheless, two questions are posed: One, how to insure that our supply depots are well-organized, well designed and well-managed? While this topic is beyond the scope of this book it is well to note that the whole subject of supply depot efficiency is under constant scrutiny by able and devoted officers and as a result we are learning and instituting many improvements. The other is, how to reduce the number of follow-up actions? Consideration of this problem again shows the interdependence of logistic matters. A follow-up may be caused by lack of foresight lack of discipline, lack of confidence, or by an unforeseeable change of conditions.

If the initial requisition has been delayed in submission or if an unrealistic delivery date has been specified, it may be impossible to obtain quick delivery except by a change in priority or by specifying a higher priority than would have been justified had prompt initial action been taken by the originator. We have previously seen how inflated priorities quickly become self-defeating.

A lack of discipline may be evidenced when a guilty conscience attempts to compensate for lack of foresight by means of specifying an unwarranted priority, an unrealistic delivery date, or by sending an urgent follow-up despatch. In some such instances the specified delivery date may have passed even before the requisition reaches the issuing depot.

Lack of confidence sometimes causes commanding officers to take follow-up action on the theory that "the squeaky wheel gets the most grease." In other cases, they may feel that the supply system is so sluggish that a follow-up is necessary to obtain prompt action on routine matters. The general attitude of the operators of any supply system to a large extent governs the customer's confidence. Confidence is an intangible quality in human relations that does not respond to directives. *Confidence is always a mutual feeling.*

Of course when unforeseeable circumstances arise, a follow-up may be necessary. In this circumstance previous restraint and discipline in the use of the follow-up pays off in big rewards. If previous attitudes have been disciplined, if mutual confidence has been established, the legitimate follow-ups will receive prompt and effective action. But, if the customers have frequently cried "Wolf!" in the past, their frantic pleas in time of real need may be ineffective.

How Poor Discipline Snowballs

No one has any idea how much of the material shipped overseas in World War II was lost by theft or pilferage. It has been estimated that the losses in some Army areas ran as high as 15% of all material stored or shipped overland. The Arabs of North Africa were notoriously skillful thieves. In many instances the gasoline pipelines in France were hacked open by black marketeers. The losses to the Navy by theft in the Olongapo area of the Philippines in 1945 and 1946 were enormous. Even service men were known to sell military material in black markets all over the world.

In the shipment of naval material to advanced bases in 1942 to 1943, the extreme amount of theft created a dilemma as to how boxes of valuable technical materials should be marked. If the boxes were marked in plain English they were quite frequently pilfered; if marked in code they were hard to identify and in many instances were lost. Possibly the most exasperating instances were those in which a box would be pilfered and bricks or old newspapers substituted for the original contents, the box closed up and then shipped to its destination thousands of miles away.

In this situation we again can see the snowball effect. The direct cost of expensive material (about $1,000 per measurement ton purchase price) was only the first loss. Added to this was the shipping space; the loading, unloading, and manifesting costs; the storage costs before and sometimes after pilferage; and the paper work. Furthermore, there was the loss in working time of equipment made inoperative for lack of spare parts. Probably the most important costs were those deriving from the reduction in work output and efficiency of the unit for whom the material was intended and the consequent upsetting of schedules and plans.

It would be naive to expect to eliminate theft in overseas shipments in merchant ships or to prevent theft by impoverished and starving citizens of war-devastated countries. However, it is not unreasonable to expect our military discipline to be adequate to safeguard valuable material while it is in military hands in military areas. Time after time, pilferage was sharply reduced when commanding officers of naval and Army units recognized its menace and took drastic preventive and disciplinary action. The control of pilferage can be a significant contribution to future logistic efficiency.

But, not all the losses of material and efficiency were due to theft and pilferage. There was frequent unauthorized diversion or the official commandeering of material by responsible commanding officers. And this too reduced logistic efficiency. In 1942 and 1943 it was extremely difficult to guarantee the delivery of advanced base materials or even units to the naval bases in the combat zones of the South Pacific because of the frequency with which they were removed from ships or otherwise commandeered by the commanding officers of the bases in the rear areas of the South Pacific. Forward area operations were hampered by such rear area irresponsibility and lack of logistic discipline. Rear areas were built up to too high a level and great time and effort wasted before the forward bases were completed. In other words, a sense of logistic discipline was lacking.

This, in turn, set in motion the under-planning over-planning aspect of the snowball. For, thereafter, many base commanders tended to make overly generous estimates of their future needs and tended to build up excessive reserves.

In September 1944, transportation of supplies from the Normandy bases to the combat front in eastern France was severely handicapped by the forcible commandeering of the trucks and truck companies by combat commanders. The Army historian in discussing the shortage of gasoline during the pursuit in late August says:

> The Third Army even resorted to commandeering the extra gasoline which the Red Ball trucks carried for their return trips to the base areas. As a result of this short-sighted practice some convoys were stranded and available transportation facilities were consequently reduced. It is hardly surprising that the Communications Zone which was already losing entire truck companies through diversions became wary of sending its truck units into the Army area.
> . . . and at least one division, the 5th Armored, admitted resorting to hijacking gasoline, a practice of which other units were also guilty.[5]

This situation poses a serious problem. In the discussion of strategical and tactical momentum it was pointed out that the vigorous exploitation of a tactical success is of the greatest importance. Nothing should be done to hamper the intelligent initiative of an aggressive combat commander. However, an in-

[5] R. G. Ruppenthal, *Logistical Support of the Armies,* Office of the Chief of Military History, Department of the Army, Government Printing Office, Washington, D. C., pp. 505-506.

herent requirement in the use of initiative, particularly when it involves the commandeering of scarce transport units in a grand pursuit, is to be able to judge the ultimate effect of the action as well as the immediate benefit. It is difficult to draw up rules; it is vital to understand cause and effect relations.

Historical Illustrations

In the planning for the Marshall Islands operations in early 1944 there had not been adequate recognition of the need for boats for the service of the fleet in the captured atolls after the withdrawal of the amphibious forces. While the high-level plans called for certain ships of the amphibious forces to be designated to transfer boats to the naval base forces, this provision was not fully appreciated or emphasized in the development of the low-level detailed plans.

The subsequent breakdown in discipline was serious and expensive. Not all the designated transports received adequate warning that they were to leave boats behind on departure. Few of these transports made any effort to select boats in good condition for this duty. Few made any provision for leaving good crews or for equipping the crews with adequate clothing or with tools or spare parts. In some instances, boats that were broken down or in an advanced state of deterioration were left. In other instances, incorrigible enlisted men were left to man the boats. In certain instances the crews reported to the naval base for permanent duty clad only in shorts or trunks with no other clothes or personal equipment.

Cause and effect operated inexorably. Although the base commanders made heroic efforts to correct the situation, boat service to the fleet was bad. The boats and crews that could operate were overworked to the extent that in some instances boat coxswains deliberately ran their boats on the coral heads so that they would be laid up for repairs and the crews could get some sleep. The base boat repair facilities were overloaded before they could be set up for efficient operation. The combat forces of the fleet were deprived of recreation and logistic services because there were not enough boats.

Some of the transport commanding officers who had left poor boats and poor crews probably considered it surprising that anyone should expect them to leave behind their good boats and good crews. In other words, they did not fully understand the meaning and implications of the terms cooperation and loyalty.

This same basic lack of understanding of the far-reaching effects of poor discipline was also illustrated in our European operations.

The Army Transportation School in its analysis of the transportation aspects of the Normandy invasion came to the conclusion that a series of failures in the marshaling and movement of the American forces through the British ports threatened the collapse of the operation. In summarizing the lessons learned by this analysis their 1955 monograph says:

> The third problem was the almost universal lack of logistical discipline on the part of the units to be moved. There was, and continues to be today, a marked tendency for commanders at all levels to *disregard competent logistical orders*. In many cases these units failed to comply with published POM directives and brought excesses in both personnel and equipment into the marshaling areas in direct violation of the published instructions. The resultant congestion within these areas created a bottleneck that was a major factor in the threatened collapse of the operation.[6]

Confidence and the Limitations of Resources

"The quality and state of orderliness gained through self-control" is how the dictionary speaks of discipline. It is a responsibility of command to look to the ultimate effects as well as to the immediate effects of all actions. When we review these illustrations of the meaning of logistic discipline we can see again how interdependent are all areas of military action. Confidence and good faith tend to inspire confidence and good faith. Suspicion and selfishness always breed similar reactions in our associates. But the valuable intangibles which we seek need the fertile ground of competence and good fundamental thinking and planning if they are to grow.

---

[6] *Operation Overlord,* an historical analysis by the United States Army Transportation School, Monograph No. 3, p. 2.

Our fundamental thinking must start with the basic premise that *logistic resources are always limited.*

The apparently obvious plenty with which the United States fought World War II and the vitality of our economic system may lead some persons to challenge such a premise. While there are many tricky variables in the equations of war potential, it is clear that logistic resources consist primarily of trained man power, raw materials, facilities, and transportation. Regardless of what kind of a war situation we face, the basic problem is to achieve the maximum over-all combat effectiveness within the limitations imposed by resources and by the vital factor of TIME. This requires a searching analysis of the conflicting or related requirements of civilian support, basic industry, logistic forces, and combat forces. While we cannot expect to attain a precise optimum balance among these claimants for resources, nevertheless we should realize that an excess in one area means that over-all combat effectiveness has been reduced. Unthinking logistic waste is an avoidable waste of combat effectiveness.

If one command or one area has an excess of any resource, this has been attained in several possible ways. It may have been attained either by depriving another area or command of its required share of that resource, or else it has been attained by a faulty program that has not been balanced as between combat forces and logistic forces and resources. Or else the commander himself has not utilized his combat forces to the full extent of their capabilities. Any one or combination of these causes of excess is evidence that the full combat potential has not been attained or else has not been utilized.

A further factor related to logistic discipline is the principle that *unneeded material or resources clog the distribution of needed resources.* That is to say, if a forward area supply system delivers unneeded material to a forward area activity it has done so by the expenditure of material, or transportation, or effort, that should have been expended for the provision of needed material.

Since in war signal communications are always limited, unneeded dispatches block the flow of needed dispatches. And since administration personnel is always limited, unnecessary follow-up blocks the action on needed follow-up. In the light of the requirement to be prepared to fight either a group of brush fires or a major global conflict in which our base of production could be seriously damaged, the foregoing points are particularly important.

Finally, consideration of the factors involved in logistic discipline emphasizes the importance of good planning factors based on an up-to-date analysis and evaluation of usage data.

Summary

The previous discussions of priorities and allocations, on momentum, and on flexibility all point out the importance of well planned and located logistic reserves. Good planning factors utilized with judgment provide an estimate of what constitutes an adequate reserve in any particular situation. *Just as logistic discipline is essential in the planning and the proper employment of these reserves, so the knowledge that the planning is sound and that adequate reserves are available when needed is essential to the development of the confidence on which true discipline is based.*

Part III

ORGANIZATION AND READINESS

Chapter 13

Organization Problems and Issues

The work of organization is never done, and the structure has to be continually adapted to new and anticipated conditions."[1]
—RALPH J. CORDINER

In the last ten years the organization of the Department of Defense and of the Armed Forces has been the subject of much public discussion, executive action, and legislation.

Complexity and Its Causes

The causes of this turmoil are complex. Part of it is due to the natural play of the power factors which are inherent in our American system of government and part of it is due to different basic concepts of strategy. Another major cause of the controversies is found in the ultimate effects of the industrial revolution, particularly as they involve the economic and logistic aspects of national defense.

The interplay of natural power factors and strategic concepts has been very well brought out in a recent book by Samuel Huntington, *The Soldier and the State.* In it he points out that the nature of our government, particularly our concept of civilian control, the separation of powers and the ensuing differences between the Congress and the Executive, prevent "reliance on a single strategic concept, weapons system or single military service as the means of achieving military security."[2]

---

[1] Ralph J. Cordiner, *New Frontiers for Professional Managers,* McGraw-Hill Book Company, New York, 1956, p. 54.

[2] Samuel P. Huntington, *The Soldier and the State,* The Belknap Press of Harvard University Press, Cambridge, Mass., 1957. *The Separation of Powers versus Strategic Monism,* p. 418. Presents a thorough discussion of this aspect of our government.

196

These opposing forces tend to create organizational complexity rather than organizational simplicity. This same general idea is also expressed by Timothy Stanley in his book, *American Defense and National Security,* which describes the intricate organizational relationships necessary to deal with modern war.[3]

Both authors show that industrialization of warfare has necessitated the integration of a vastly complex war machine with the national economy and with national policy and objectives. This applies particularly to Presidential decisions concerning foreign affairs and national security. It has created major problems of executive control, executive decision making, departmental administration, and operational command of the Armed Forces.

The National Security Acts of 1947 and 1949, the Department of Defense Organization Act of 1958, the various reports of the Hoover Commission on the organization of the Executive Branch of the Government, and many executive orders, such as Reorganization Plan #6 of 1953, form part of various official acts and studies dealing with these and related problems.

By reason of the industrial revolution, military economics or "logistics" has been an all pervading factor in the arguments on organization and administration. In those discussions, however, the term "logistics" has seldom been used and when used has frequently been carelessly applied. Instead, a great variety of terms such as "management," "economics," "administration," and "comptrollership" have been used without specific reference to the recognized terminology and fundamental relationships of war and strategy.

Thus, there has been a tendency to subordinate the basic principles of the military arts to the terminology and practice of a business world in which the basic criteria are quite different from the criteria of military excellence, or even of success in combat operations.

---

[3] Timothy W. Stanley, *American Defense and National Security,* Public Affairs Press, Washington, D. C., 1956. This book should be read by all students of national defense. Particularly pertinent to our discussion is the material found on pages 6, 7, 9, 16, 18, 23, 38, 45-58, 93, 107, 108, 111-121, 124, 127-130.

Over the years there has been a tendency to judge organizational questions primarily on the basis of how they will influence the peacetime budget.

Of course, there are very real connections between the most effective defense and the greatest economy. However, these connections must be looked at from the military point of view as well as from the business point of view. It is well, therefore, to review a few of the fundamentals of the military situation and of the art of war.

In the first place there is no such thing as absolute security. We live in a world of uncertainty and risk in which new situations and conflicts will continue to threaten our security and challenge our character. The determination of the kind of combat forces needed for the protection of our position and policies in the world depends on the nature of the conflict which we face.

Our economic position both in peace and in war limits the size of the forces we can create. Further, logistic considerations inevitably will limit the size of the forces which can be employed.

The greater the economy achieved in logistics, the greater will be the effectiveness which the combat forces can develop within these basic limitations.

However, the only way we can determine what is a true economy and what is a false economy is to evaluate the influence of any proposed step on combat effectiveness. For example, if a decision in the field of transportation lessens the cost or increases the efficiency of the transportation service, combat effectiveness presumably is benefited. However, if this transportation efficiency is attained at the eventual expense of stimulating the growth of the logistic snowball, then combat effectiveness is damaged.

Even if we had precise scientific knowledge we could not establish ideal organizations because too many factors influence them. Organizations must always yield to the modifications forced by personalities, by human aspiration and faults, and by the political realities in government.

Even when the appearance of agreement is achieved and

perhaps supposedly illustrated by clean lines on a chart, the fundamental conflict may persist beneath the surface. The agreement may be found to contain compromises and ambiguities which when tested will bring the conflict out into the open again.

The ensuing discussion is designed to present some of the more important military considerations which enter into this complex adjustment.

The most important fundamental is that the industrialization of war has made the organization for national defense so large that its sheer size creates special problems. The conduct and support of war now includes almost every activity and organization in a nation. Advanced technology demands more and more logistic support and greater logistic lead time while at the same time creating the possibility of stockpiling obsolescence. Increased technological development creates further problems not the least of which is the need for rapid large scale industrial and training operations ordered up on short notice. Thus we are faced with the real dilemma of creating a huge organization which is both flexible and highly responsive to sudden enemy action.[4]

Differing Philosophies

There is a basic conflict between the broad philosophies of centralization of command and of decentralization of command. However, the proponents of neither side believe in complete centralization or in complete decentralization. Therefore, in some instances, the difference is merely as to where in the chain of command should decentralization begin and how complete it should be at various levels.

Within this broad conflict between the advocates of more centralization and the advocates of less centralization, two further specific differences are found. One of these is between

---

[4] The full implications of this industrialization and growing technology have not yet been fully studied. The preliminary study of Dr. Herbert Rosinski, "The Evolution of the Conduct of War and Strategic Thinking," contains an excellent terse discussion of the relation of industrialization to strategy. Naval War College, 1955.

those who believe in a single completely integrated national armed service with a single dominant commander (or chief of staff) and those who believe in three independently operated armed services each with its own chief; but with all three working under the unified direction of a single Secretary of Defense and a Joint Chiefs of Staff group.

Another aspect of this same basic conflict is found in the disagreement between those who believe in a fourth (logistic) Service and those who believe in each Service having its own logistic organization responsive both to its own command and to the broad coordinating policies of the Secretary of Defense.

The contrast in points of view is well expressed by the two recent examples: One, an amendment to the 1958 appropriations act proposed by Senator O'Mahoney; the other, an address by Secretary of Defense Wilson to the National War College on 11 June 1957.[5] The Senator proposed the establishment of a civilian-managed agency charged with procurement and distribution of common supply items for all services. The Secretary warned against major changes in defense organization, particularly against those changes which would bring greater centralization.

This question of a fourth Service dealing with logistics leads into the analysis of the meanings of the terms "command control of logistics" and "logistic coordination." Both of these are directly related to another controversial aspect of defense organization, that is, the question of what is the proper relation between civilian and military in the direction and management of our national defense and our armed services.

The Analogy of Business

In reviewing the discussions of the last decade a startling paradox is found in the fact that the slogan of "business efficiency" (to be applied to the armed services) is sometimes invoked by persons advocating administrative practices which

(to page 202)

---
[5] *Congressional Record,* 1st Session 85th Congress, Vol. 103, Part 8, Senate, July 1, 1957, p. 10672.
  "Intended to be proposed by Mr. O'Mahoney to the bill (H. R. 7665) making appropriations for the Department of Defense for

the fiscal year ending June 30, 1958, and for other purposes, viz:
At the proper place in the bill insert the following new section:

Sec. .. For the purpose of achieving an efficient, economical,
and practical integrated supply system designed to meet the needs
of the military departments without duplications or overlapping
of either operations or functions, the President, within 180 days
after the date of enactment of this Act, shall submit to the Congress his recommendations for a civilian-managed agency, to be
under the supervision and direction of the Secretary of Defense,
which shall be responsible for the procurement, production, ware-
housing, distribution of supplies or equipment, standardization of
inventory control, and other supply management functions for
common supply items other than combat equipment, material, and
directly related combat items.

At the proper place in the bill insert the following new section:

Sec. .. Section 638 of the Department of Defense Appropriation
Act, 1955, is amended to read as follows:

'Sec. 638. (a) Notwithstanding any other provision of law, the
Secretary of Defense shall take such actions as are necessary to
achieve economy, efficiency, and effectiveness in noncombatant
services, activities, and operations through the elimination of
overlapping, duplication, and waste within and among the agencies
of the Department of Defense . . .' "

Secretary of Defense Wilson, in the graduation address at the National War
College on June 11, 1957, said:

"We are associates in the largest organization in the free world—
there are over four million of us, military and civilian. Our assigned
mission—the security of the United States—gives us many common
interests, an important one being the best type of organization
of the Department of Defense.

". . . Quite a few people with or without experience underestimate
the basic requirements of an effective organization. It is really a
problem which defies simple solutions. It is importantly influenced
by our type of government.

"Bigness in industry as well as in government requires decentralization—the delegation of duties, authority, and responsibility . . .

"The current organization of the Department of Defense has been
established not only to promulgate unified policies but also to facilitate this type of administration. I believe that it represents the most
effective and most effcient way to run a large organization in a
free country . . .

"A large and improving organization is necessarily a compromise
between an assumed theoretically perfect one, the traditions and
experiences of the past, and the capabilities of the men who will
fill the important assignments in it. Each of these factors is important and must be fully appraised and taken into account.

"I would like to clearly go on record with all of you that I
believe the present organization of the Department of Defense is
sound, incorporating at is does the separate Military Services and
Military Departments in an organization which is responsive to the
President, the Congress, and the American people. I would caution
those who recommend radical changes to advocate them only after
the most careful thought and when experience has proved that they
are necessary."

are contrary to the trend in our major businesses. At a time when some authorities are emphasizing the evils of overcentralization in government in general, and when other informed persons consider that many of our military deficiencies stem from overcentralization, there arises a demand for still greater centralization. All the while large companies are tending toward decentralization in their management. For example, General Motors operates its various automobile companies as autonomous units, each buying and selling its materials and products by means of independent supply and sales organizations.

The size of any enterprise can be roughly measured by the number of its employees and its sales or gross income. In 1951 General Motors, General Electric, American Telephone and Telegraph, and U.S. Steel together employed a total of about 1,630,000 persons. Their combined net sales or gross income was about $16,935,000,000.

In fiscal year 1951 the U.S. Armed Forces were composed of a total of about 4,500,000 persons both military and civilian, and had an appropriation of about $48,200,000,000. These figures come to about three times that of the four industrial giants combined. In fact the Navy alone, with its 1,400,000 personnel and $13,900,000,000 budget, was almost as large as this hypothetical industrial combination.

Now granted that statistics can be very misleading, nevertheless these figures do give us, in terms of well-known industrial concerns, the general magnitude of the problem of military management.

If we attempted a corporate consolidation of General Motors, General Electric, American Telephone and Telegraph, and U.S. Steel, and then insisted that the budget for 1960 be submitted by each division of the combined company before its budget for 1959 had been established by a five-hundred man board of directors of such a consolidation, there might be some areas of imperfection and the stockholders might become impatient. Some might even say that under those conditions such a corporation would be unmanageable in a democracy.

One of the basic reasons why complete centralization of a

huge enterprise is not an efficient method of management lies in the problem of information.[6] The sheer mass of data which must be collected, processed, and evaluated becomes so great that management action in response to changing technical and production developments and market situations becomes sluggish. The operating unit which is smaller, more flexible, and responsive has been found to be more efficient. The contribution of the larger parent company lies in its great assets of broad policy direction and coordination, financing, and economic and technological research.

The Contending Opinions

The basic plea for more centralization rests on a group of assumptions which at times take the form of specific allegations. Some of these are:

(1) That there is a great duplication of effort in the logistical organizations of the three Services;

(2) That there is great waste and inefficiency in the operation of these Services; and

(3) That these faults are due primarily to lack of centralized control of logistical operations in these Services.

Within the group who call for more centralization, the advocates tend to split, one school believing in more civilian control, the other in less.

The former school (i.e., those advocating more civilian control) is represented in many of the reports of the Hoover Commission, the latter by the extremists who advocate a single military service or a single chief of staff.

While admitting that there may have been *some* waste, duplication, and overlapping of functions in the armed forces in the last ten years, the opponents of more centralization generally contend that—

(1) Not as much waste exists as is charged; and

---

[6] President Cordiner of General Electric Company makes frequent reference to this problem of information in his book, *New Frontiers for Professional Managers,* particularly on pages 82, 83, 89 and 102. Published by McGraw-Hill Book Company, Inc., New York, 1956.

what sometimes appears to be waste is frequently merely the procedure or the reserve that is made necessary by the preparation for a sudden, large-scale war.

(2) Great efficiency is being gradually attained within the present system.[7]

(3) It is not true that faulty organization is the major cause of the greatest waste nor is it true that greater centralization of authority will necessarily decrease waste.[8] On the contrary, in many instances it may increase the waste, or in other instances it may create a greater waste in another area. For example, some of the Department of Defense instructions issued by various Assistant Secretaries not only have dealt with trivial operating details but also have required conformity solely for conformity's sake and have vastly increased the load of paper work without accomplishing any significant purpose.[9]

(4) It is not true that all duplication is harmful. Limited discriminating duplication may be very beneficial.[10, 11]

(5) It is not true that all overlapping is harmful. Intentional overlap of many functions is necessary to flexibility, to mobility, and to the efficient use of limited resources. This overlap is required both in combat functions and in logistic functions.

The resolution of these sharp differences is made difficult by the absence of any mutually acceptable criteria for judgment between the protagonists of the conflicting opinions.

Obviously the criteria by which we judge military organiza-

(to page 207)

---

[7] An example of the increasing awareness of the efficiency which is attained is found in *Forbes,* November 15, 1958 on page 10 where the Editor, Malcolm S. Forbes, says:

In short, the popular stereotype of the limited obtuse "military mind" is as much an anachronism as the cartoonist's version of a cigar-smoking, pot-bellied robber baron, or the bomb-throwing, unshaven union leader. The executives in the Navy, junior and senior, by and large have a better, broader perspective, more experience and capacity for management than their counterparts in most corporations.

⁸ An interesting example of the influence ascribed to decentralization in business was reported in the April 13, 1957 issue of the magazine *Business Week* on pages 63 to 74. It describes how the Safeway Company helped to increase its profits by decentralizing buying authority. Previously there had been central buying. However, it was found that decentralization not only reduced the purchase price but also greatly reduced expensive paper work. The over-all results were startling. In 1955 profits were $1.10 a share, in 1956 $1.61 a share. The first 12 weeks of 1957 showed a sales of $1.9 billion—a gain of 4% and a profit of 25 million, a gain of 87%. While not all of this improvement is ascribed to decentralization, it nevertheless appears to be a significant factor.

⁹ Specific illustrations are the following DOD directives, among others:

Number	Date	Title	Signed by
4140.8	November 2, 1955	"Procurement, Replacement and Utilization of Filing Cabinets"	T. P. PIKE Ass't Sec. of Defense
4150.8	October 20, 1955	"Refuse Collection and Disposal"	F. G. FLOETE Ass't Sec. of Defense
4165.19	August 1, 1955	"Use of Treated Wood in Buildings and Structures Maintenance"	F. G. FLOETE
4270.13	June 30, 1955	"Standards and Criteria for Construction — Requirements Criteria, Design Criteria, and Space Allowances for Parking for Nonorganizational Vehicles"	F. G. FLOETE
4500.16	September 1, 1955	"Loading Rules, Test Loadings and Test Shipments Governing Rail Shipments"	R. C. LANPHIER, JR. Deputy Ass't Sec. of Defense
6230.2	August 30, 1956	"Adjustment of Fluoride Content of Communal Water Supplies at Military Installations"	FRANK B. BERRY Ass't Sec. of Defense
6230.1	August 18, 1955	"Standards for Drinking Water"	C. E. WILSON Sec. of Defense

¹⁰ The current policies of the General Electric Company offer important information as to these questions. In *New Frontiers for Professional Managers,* McGraw-Hill Book Company, Inc., New York, 1956, pp. 44-46, 59, the President of the Company, Ralph Cordiner has said:

Up until 1939, the Company was able to operate efficiently under a highly centralized form of management. During World War II, however, General Electric began a period of almost explosive growth which caused its managers to question whether it might not be necessary to evolve new techniques of organizing and managing the Company.

From the beginning of the study, it was apparent that the Company was going to require increasingly better planning, greater flexibility, and faster, more informed decisions than was possible under the highly centralized organization structure, which was suited for earlier and different conditions. Unless we could put the responsibility and authority for decision making closer in each case to the scene of the problem, where complete understanding and prompt action are possible, the Company would not be able to compete with the hundreds of nimble competitors who were, as they say, able to turn on a dime.

To demonstrate that the responsibility, authority, and accountability of these Operating Departments are real, not window dressing, consider their pricing authority. The price of a product can be raised or lowered by the managers of the Department producing it, with only voluntary responsibility on their part to give sensible consideration to the impact of such price changes on other Company products. In one area of General Electric products, the major appliances such as refrigerators, ranges, and home laundry equipment, there are two Divisions competing directly with each other. The Hotpoint Division in Chicago and the Major Appliance and Television Receiver Division in Louisville have different facilities, different product designs, different distribution, and different prices. They compete at the market place very aggressively, and incidentally, very profitably. Other Departments compete with each other by presenting different types of products that perform essentially the same function. For example, there is the competition between electronic tubes and transistors, or between room air conditioners and central air conditioning.

[11] Much of the criticism of alleged duplication and overlapping of functions comes from members of the Congress. One of the ironies of this situation is that in Congress, itself, there is a great deal of duplication and overlapping of functions. Samuel P. Huntington in *The Soldier and the State,* The Belknap Press of Harvard University Press, Cambridge, Mass.: 1957, Chapter 15, "The Separation of Powers and Cold War Defense" pages 402-403, says:

Under the separation of powers, Congress and the President must both administer and legislate, That is the iron law of institutional survival. The power to govern cannot be restricted or divided. If each branch is to share in it, each branch must exercise it at every opportunity. The separation of powers thus leads inevitably to the duplication of functions.

The collapse of the separation of functions before the separation of powers is normally lamented by reactionaries who attack the President for usurping the policy-making functions of Congress and by academics who criticize Congress for busying itself with administrative detail. In reality, however, the widespread distribution of power rather than the efficient allocation of function is the central value of the American constitutional pantheon. Divided power results in continuous overlapping and conflicting jurisdictions between the national government and the states, among the three branches of the national government, among executive bureaus and agencies, and between rival congressional committees. Many people do the work of others, and the legal profession and the courts acquire exceptional importance because of the constant need to adjudicate rival powers and claims. Other results of the dispersion of power, however, are the need to secure the agreement of virtually all interested parties (Calhoun's concurrent majority) before taking action, the democratic multiplication of the avenues of access to government, and the mutual restraint which all groups and governmental bodies exercise on each other and which prevents the arbitrary and dictatorial use of power. In moving in on each other's functional preserves, Congress and the President exemplify the basic genius of American government.

tions must include considerations both of economy and of combat effectiveness. However, we still have a very imperfect knowledge of how organizational matters influence these factors. Since there has been little scientific testing, most of the views expressed are merely opinions. Depending on the experience, insights, and motivations of individuals, these opinions are good or bad. Nevertheless, in the absence of the willingness to spend the necessary time and effort on large-scale, war-game simulation of the influence of various logistical organizational schemes on combat effectiveness, these opinions and personal persuasiveness must be our chief guides.

Another important argument in these conflicts between centralization versus decentralization and between civilian control and military control is about as follows: Authorities at the seat of government do not believe that a theater or area commander has enough knowledge of national economics and enough of a national viewpoint in his military decisions to be trusted with full authority for his logistics.

On the other hand, the theater, area, army, and fleet commanders do not believe that the national authorities have enough knowledge of combat situations and combat requirements to be competent to control theater, area, army, and fleet logistics.

In this area of mutual distrust one group feels that the other lacks the "national perspective" while the other feels that the first one lacks the "combat perspective." Perhaps if both had a better understanding of the command perspective of logistics and a better understanding of the logistic process in the sense that it is the linkage between the national economy and the combat itself, this distrust might be reduced.

A striking illustration of philosophic difference lies in the differing concepts as to the position of the U.S. Joint Chiefs of Staff. Some persons contend that the Joint Chiefs of Staff should be a separate body devoted entirely to planning duties with its members having no authority for execution or for the supervision of the planned action.

Others contend that the very fact that the individual Joint

Chiefs must themselves supervise the execution of the plans is the best possible guarantee for their soundness.

This is an area where national policy, national strategy, and national economic and military capabilities all have to be evaluated and translated into national military preparations (logistics) and into strategic dispositions and ultimately into campaign plans.

The Implications of Command Control of Logistics

At the area, army, and fleet level we find that the understanding of the statement, "The commander must control his own logistics," is a matter of critical importance.

In considering the question of what command control of logistics means, it is helpful if we go back to the basic elements of logistics, i.e., requirements, procurement, and distribution. We must realize that these elements blend and overlap in a way that varies in each situation.

The commander has the task of fighting. He, therefore, has the right to say what logistic resources he needs to fight—requirements—and how he will allocate and distribute to his subordinates the resources his superiors give him to fight—distribution. By his control of distribution he exercises his responsibility to see that these resources are actually delivered at the right time and place to the subordinates who will use them in the accomplishment of the tasks he has assigned.

Part of this function of distribution is "allocations." Part of the element of requirements is "priorities."

Submission of requirements goes from the subordinate to the superior. Determination of allocations goes from the superior to the subordinate. When the subordinate states his priorities he is making a statement of the order of precedence of the various elements which in total make up his allocated resources or which comprise his total requirements to accomplish an assigned task. When the superior makes a statement of priorities he is in effect establishing an order of precedence of the tasks which he has assigned to his subordinates. Thus, command control is exercised in a variety of ways in accordance with the level of command of which one is speaking, for every commander is both a superior and a subordinate.

The third basic element of logistics lies in procurement which includes, among other things, the matter of "production." This is where the civilian properly has a dominant role.

Requirements and procurement both involve *specifications* or "quality control," and *amounts* or "quantity control"—both being related to time. Command states requirements and controls distribution in terms of quantity, quality, time, and (frequently) place.

Superior command either decides in terms of allocations, which settles the issue, or by a statement of "capabilities" or "availabilities" which gives the subordinate the option of modifying his requirements and his plans to meet the realities of the procurement and distribution situations. Since the commander's strategic and tactical plans depend on his logistic capabilities, all three must be modified in accordance with a single integrated intellectual process—the mind of command. Thus, it is obvious that this formulation of specific strategic plans is an area where the military has the dominant role.

The Interplay of Civilian and Military

Quality, quantity, and time cannot all three be optimized simultaneously. Nor does it seem likely that the effect upon combat effectiveness of changes in their relationships can be reduced to a formula. Many of these effects are quite obvious to any experienced man, be he civilian or military. Many other effects, however, are recognized only by a man who is both experienced and highly skilled in a technical specialty, a "materiel" specialty, a production specialty, or a combat specialty. *Thus, the interplay of civilian and military in control of logistics will always involve overlapping areas of a variable nature in which men must meet, work together, and share responsibilities in a spirit of mutual understanding and cooperation.* These areas are not definable by law. If the law attempts such definition it will either be ignored, or be circumvented, by those whose judgment and patriotic devotion will bring them together informally in spite of arbitrary and restricting legislative or executive dicta.

The authority to exercise command control of logistics carries with it the equally important reciprocal obligation to exercise competence, sound judgment, and restraint in the exercise of that control.

One of the chief weapons in the hands of those who advocate the increase of centralization and of civilian control of logistics has been the charge that military commanders are not competent to control their own logistics.

In addition to allegations of avoidable waste supposedly due to poor supervision, it is a common opinion that military commanders invariably overstate their logistic requirements. Whether this is done through deliberate intent or through incompetence is not important; the harmful effect is the same.

The pressure for the establishment of a "fourth Service of Logistics" is a continuing threat to the exercise of command control of logistics in the theater of war. Any indifference to logistic organization or planning or any incompetence in the planning and supervision of logistical activities on the part of the senior line officers of our three Services is an open invitation to the further erosion, or perhaps even the destruction, of their command authority.[12]

This reciprocal obligation of competence in the exercise of control of logistics applies regardless of level of centralization or the civilian or military composition of the controlling

---

[12] In 1956, a general officer (name withheld) who carried major logistic responsibility stated to the author that high civilian authorities were largely justified in their dissatisfaction with overseas logistic coordination; that the chief cause for poor logistic coordination was that, in general, senior commanders took their logistics for granted. He further believed that the military should form a fourth service of logistics under military control because if the military did not form such a service the Congress would order such a service established and would insist that it be civilian controlled and operated. In his opinion such a civilian logistic service would be a disastrous blow to combat effectiveness whereas a military fourth service would only be a severe handicap. He stated that the faults in our present system could be corrected and the necessity for a fourth service obviated if *senior line officers* in the armed forces would study logistics and take their logistic responsibilities seriously. However, he had come to the conclusion that line officers would never do this in peacetime and therefore it was a hopeless situation.

authority. Therefore, civilians occupying positions of power have further moral obligations. They should remain in office long enough to apply the experience which it is so costly for them to acquire. They should study the art of war in order to learn the relationships and purposes of the various elements of war. For if they do not understand the nature of human conflict and the nature and principles of combat effectiveness, the exercise of power by such civilians may well bring national disaster —just as much so as might inaptitude on the part of military commanders.

The determination of national policy and the major strategic decisions are, of course, made at the highest national-political level. The division of resources between the military and the civilian economy is a question so vital to the welfare of the entire nation that it also must be made at the highest political level. This decision in its broadest terms is made in the form of allocations *after* the military forces have submitted their requirements to support the national policy.

These major decisions which are the foundation of military affairs are made by civilians. In them they are advised by the military. Thus at the highest levels, the civilian exercises command; the military act as staff advisors.

But after leaving the seat of national government and finally reaching the area of combat operations, we find that the military exercises command and to some degree civilians act as staff advisors.

Cognizance and command are clear at two levels—the highest national level and the military combat operational level. In between, in the Department of Defense and in the top management and basic home establishments of each Service, there will always be areas of dispute and adjustment. To shed light on these it is desirable to examine other implications of "civilian control."

In the post-war period there has been increasing demand for and development of civilian control of the armed services.

Practically no one disagrees with the wisdom of this from the point of view of broad policy, or at the higher levels at the seat of government. However, the manner in which it is carried out has created some doubt as to the judgment that has been used in applying the policy.

The term civilian control is subject to wide differences in interpretation. At one extreme there are those who hold that with a civilian President as Commander in Chief, with civilians as Secretaries of Defense and of the military Services, and with a civilian Congress responsible for budget, for authorizations, and for legislation, the basic requirements for civilian control are fully met.

The other extreme has never been clearly defined nor does it seem possible to place a limit on the degree to which some persons would extend the direct authority of civilians. However, in recent years the number of civilian secretaries, undersecretaries, assistant secretaries, and special assistants to the secretaries in the armed forces has grown to an extraordinary degree.[13]

One obvious and legitimate cause for the increase in the civilian staffs of the Department of Defense and the Services has been the industrialization of military weapons and supplies. As previously stated, the civilian economy is the direct foundation of our armed forces and their activities and demands are a

---

[13] Timothy W. Stanley, *American Defense and National Security,* Public Affairs Press, Washington, D.C., 1956. Page 111.

The most significant yardstick against which to measure the progress of unification and evolution of the defense structure is the Office of the Secretary of Defense. That office has grown from a small personal staff under Secretary Forrestal to an organization employing over 1500 civilians and nearly 700 military personnel. Compare, for example, Admiral Nimitz' 1947 views on the size of the Office of the Secretary of Defense with the present situation. The Chairman of the Senate Armed Services Committee had confused the staff of the Secretary of Defense with the Joint Staff and had mentioned the figure of 100 during the hearings. Admiral Nimitz replied: "That is for the Joint Staff, the staff to the Joint Chiefs. As for the Secretary of Defense, I do not visualize him having a staff that large." From three special assistants in 1949, the office has developed a structure which includes ten officials with the rank of Assistant Secretary of Defense (ASD). Within the Department as a whole, some thirty individuals rate the designation 'Mr. Secretary.' (The *number* of civilians in the Office of the Secretary of Defense has not increased since 1949 as much as these statements might imply. On December 31, 1949 the figure was 1616, and on January 2, 1953 it was 2082. But by December 31, 1955, the number had been reduced to 1760.)"

significant part of the national economy. *Thus increased civilian participation in military producer logistics is warranted.*

Two other reasons may also be cited for increased civilian control—

First, civilian control is deemed necessary in order to prevent any possibility of the rise of a military dictatorship in this country; and

Second, civilian control is deemed desirable *in all management areas* because it is considered that civilians experienced in the business world or other civilian pursuits can and will do a better and more efficient job than will professional military men.

The first point is really not debatable because its validity as a basic philosophy of our government is accepted almost without question. Perhaps this is because so far there seems to have been no tendency among American military leaders or in our military philosophy to desire such control.

The second point involves many serious questions. For instance, there is a grave concern that if military budgets are drawn up by military men only, there will be a disregard of the over-all economic and social welfare of the nation as a whole. It is felt that these budgets are so complex and huge that unless the civilian influence is very strong before these budgets reach the late, intermediate, and final stages of preparation the moderating civilian influence will be overcome by the sheer mass of the items and figures presented.[14]

---

[14] Malcolm S. Forbes in the November 15, 1958 issue of *Forbes* magazine, page 9, commented:

This issue looks into the ten billion dollars a year that Americans invest in their Navy. It presents a closeup of its management—who runs it and how well—and a birdseye view of what, operations-wise, we have "in being," along with where it is and what it's doing; and, particularly, the impact of this vast expenditure on the economy in general and investor-held corporations in particular.

From personal study in many places, on many ships at sea as well as installations ashore, I have arrived at several conclusions:

First: The management of this immense, unique outfit is outstanding, far better than would seem possible in the conditions and circumstances under which it must operate.

Second: The billions annually invested are spent with a caution that, if anything, is perhaps overdone in view of the missions assigned. . .

The point of most concern lies in the area of the supervision of the actual day-to-day logistical operations of the Services. the "logistical process" is the physical link between the nation's economy and its combat operations. In studying this area, because the exercise of command must include supervision of the planned action, it is extremely difficult to draw the line between "policy" and "operations."

Few individuals are content to control policy only; it is only human nature to demand the personal satisfaction that comes through executive action. This feel of power which is such a dominant psychological force in man provides the satisfaction which makes a job worthwhile.

If one is advocating the extension of civilian control he should be prepared to accept *all* the practical effects of such policy, not merely the effects he desires to achieve. It is not enough to have a worthy motive—it is important to avoid self-deception.

It seems obvious that control of any administrative activity is achieved by determining what is the position in the chain of authority at which centralization takes place, and then by seizing or occupying that position.

In many instances, the authority to control an activity has been assumed before the amount of information necessary to the exercise of that control has been fully appreciated.

Reorganizations which may have been widely advertised as "streamlined," etc., and as saving personnel, have ended by requiring more rather than less people to operate than the group superseded simply because the staff, the clerical, and the space requirements to handle the information have been ignored or initially underestimated. Thus, by reason of this need to handle more information, increase in centralization always increases the size of the top management staff. This is turn increases the effect of "bureaucracy" and creates sluggishness.

Experience in the Department of Defense has shown that when an Assistant Secretary has increased the scope of his authority, he not only increases his own staff but this staff makes increasing demands for information on the lower staff echelons who formerly handled these matters on a decentralized basis. Thus overcentralization frequently increases not only the higher staff work but also the lower staff work. For the highest staff by itself can never accomplish the necessary work. In the end it must always pass it to a lower echelon for final execution.

Furthermore, since *civilian control is attained only by raising the level at which authority is centralized,* military command control of logistics is decreased. When this is done civilian command authority extends in fact, if not in theory, toward the assumption of command authority in combat operations in the combat zone by reason of the transfer of authority to a higher level.

Each layer of detailed administrative authority superimposed on an executive tends to decrease his breadth of concept and command initiative. He then tends to become more and more immersed in details and less and less a broad executive.

Functional versus Area Concepts

In addition to these philosophic differences we find that opinions may vary in accordance with the "area point of view," and the "functional point of view." Since there is a valid area point of view and a valid functional point of view, it is not easy to devise a command structure which will meet both requirements satisfactorily.

This is a very live issue as was brought out previously in the quotation from Ruppenthal:

> The problem of reconciling functional control with re-gional or territorial control was as old as administration itself and was to plague the ETO thruout its history."[15]

The organizational requirements for the exercise of tactical command differ considerably from those for logistical and ad-ministrative command. This fact is closely related, particularly at the highest level, to the difficulty of distinguishing between the function of command and the function of staff advice. Here again the very size of our organizations make it difficult to

---

[15] R. G. Ruppenthal, *Logistical Support of the Armies,* Volume I, Office of the Chief of Military History, Department of the Army, Washington, D.C., 1953, p. 87.

draw the line precisely and to avoid harmful encroachment. At this point it is desirable merely to call attention to these differences of point of view. Later chapters will discuss more of their influence.

The Natural Forces

We have seen how the factors of great size, technological advance, need for rapid action, philosophic differences, and variety of point of view, influence our organizations. In addition, certain natural forces work inexorably to complicate the problem. These are inherent in any attempt to define precisely the relationships and authority among human beings in matters dealing with national and personal interest. Some may seem so obvious as to appear trite, some may seem obscure.

The chief forces which affect all types of organization are themselves so interlocked that they seldom appear as single clear causes of organizational variation. Instead, *the magnetic effect of power, the force of individual personality, the desire for personal, Service, or national prestige and the need for satisfying political demands all have a marked influence on our organizations.*

When we look at our major administrative and logistical organizations—particularly on the departmental and area level and army and fleet levels—we find in varying degrees, complexity, overlap, duplication, and sometimes considerable confusion. Therefore, we find that in these levels of command there is a continued spirit of change and reorganization. Each of these changes illustrates the previously mentioned lack of unanimity of informed and responsible opinion.

While we all can see the advantages of stability of organization, we should not expect ever to achieve it in organizations as large, complex, and vigorous as our armed forces. Nor would it be wholly desirable should it be attained. The major point is that *organization defines the relationship between individual people; individuals change and individuals differ.*

In all national capitals and departments there is a continued struggle for power. This is so natural that sometimes it seems to be almost inadvertent rather than conscious. In thinking of this it is well to consider the *principle of the magnetic effect of power*. Power attracts power. Every day we see examples of how a man of great ability and leadership welcomes additional responsibility and frequently by picking up a free ball that someone else has fumbled or ignored, runs to a touchdown.

Rear Admiral Samuel McGowan, Supply Corps, USN, in World War I; and Admiral Ben Moreell, Civil Engineer Corps, USN, and General Brehon Somervell, USA, in World War II are three examples of men who unhesitatingly accepted new and unusual responsibilities. Their wartime accomplishments were outstanding. Unique, however, is Major General F. C. Ainsworth, USA, who after the Spanish American War rose from Major in the Medical Corps in the Pension Bureau to become Adjutant General of the Army. In that position he exercised almost dominant power until his clash with his intimate friend, another former doctor, the Chief of Staff of the Army, General Leonard Wood, resulted in Ainsworth's removal by Secretary of War, Henry Stimson, in 1912.[16] In recent years, Mr. Wilfred McNeil, the Comptroller of the Department of Defense and a man of great ability, has exerted an extraordinary influence on the situation.[17]

In the last few years we have seen a tendency toward greater

---

[16] An account of this prolonged controversy is in *National Security and the General Staff*, by Major General Otto Nelson, pp 112-166, Infantry Journal Press, Washington, D.C., May 1946.

[17] Samuel P. Huntington, *The Soldier and the State*, The Belknap Press of Harvard University Press, Cambridge, Mass., 1957, page 439.
A final factor enhancing the power of the Comptroller was the continuity in office of Wilfred J. McNeil. McNeil had been the Fiscal Director of the Navy under Forrestal. In 1947 he became the budgetary and fiscal assistant to Forrestal as Secretary of Defense. In 1949 he became Comptroller, a position he still held in 1955. He was unique among the higher leaders of the Defense Department in that he performed the same job for all of the first five Secretaries of Defense. It is not surprising that he was labeled the "virtually indispensable man" of the Pentagon. The Comptroller's office possessed knowledge and experience in a way which even the military could not rival and which was quite beyond the grasp of transient political appointees. Thus, McNeil was able to maintain his position as the principal balance to the JCS, despite occasional challenges from other civilian units, such as the general counsel's office, the Joint Secretaries, and General McNarney's Defense Management Committee.

concentration of power in Washington. As more power is given to the high echelons there is a great expansion in their personnel needs with no reduction in subordinate personnel. The great expansion of the Office of Secretary of Defense illustrates this.

Closely allied to the principle of power are two other very human and understandable tendencies, *the influence of personality and the desire for prestige.*

We spend many years developing the spirit of decision and leadership in the officers of the armed forces. If our senior officers are not strong-minded and ambitious, they will not be good leaders. We, therefore, can expect that our senior officers and leaders will think for themselves and will have differences of opinion. Anything else would be fatal to our national survival.

This element of personal determination is most important. If a man has power, a clear idea of what he wants, and a high spirit of determination, he may easily force his solution to a problem upon his associates regardless of its effect on the theoretical efficiency of the over-all organization.

A good illustration of this is the manner in which Sir Winston Churchill forced the acceptance of Lord Mountbatten in the NATO Mediterranean Command in 1952. This organizational setup was quite contrary to the realities of military forces available and to fundamental theories of command organization.

One aspect of this element of personality and national prestige is the reluctance of people who have major jobs to do to accept subordinate positions. Another aspect is the desire of special interests for prestige and rank commensurate with those interests.

The Necessity for Compromises

In summing up the general question of military organization, it seems evident that we can never expect either perfect or permanent specific solutions to the problems. Our present organizations are the result of many compromises and contain many ambiguities. The basic differences and conflicts which made these compromises and ambiguities necessary still exist in the minds of able, strong men and the effects of these inner convictions will emerge again and again.

In spite of these admitted uncertainties and difficulties we must always remember that not all organizational decisions which bring economy in peace will bring effectiveness in war. When war comes it may be too late to alter our organizations or to find men and procedures readily available to take the load of decision and administration.

While theory can be helpful in the study and analysis of organizations, the force and conflicts of strong personalities will always be vital factors. In the face of our incomplete knowledge of all the factors which apply, theory may be more useful in showing why things went wrong rather than showing precisely how they may be set right. Even so it is well to remember the principle of the objective and insist that the chief criteria by which we judge our logistic organizations should be: "Are these so constituted that they contribute most to the development of sustained combat effectiveness in war?"

A major military organization sometimes can be analyzed by placing one's self in the position of the subordinates and looking at the problems of coordination with one's equal echelon associates, one's own subordinates, and one's seniors in specific hypothetical cases. If there then can be confusion as to authority and responsibility, the organization is probably faulty.

Business has a rapid and ruthless manner of evaluating the efficiency of organization and people. The test is a simple one —is there a satisfactory profit?

Business has much more decentralization and much more freedom of action in the hiring and firing of management.

In the military, it is much more difficult to evaluate the efficiency of any organization for we do not have such simple criteria, nor such freedom of action. Furthermore, the evaluation is made even more difficult by the vast difference between peacetime and wartime activity.

Certain forces and pressures will operate regardless of the organization or of rules, directives, and definitions from higher authority. These forces spring from the nature of war, the nature of man and his aspirations, from the complexity of war, from the inexorable demand for economy, and from the imperfections of our means of exchanging ideas.

These forces cannot be prevented from acting. However, if well understood they can be directed toward useful ends or at least their harmful effects reduced or alleviated. This only occurs when the existence and nature of these forces is recognized in advance.

In translating these general ideas into specific application by command, we should remember that in any given force or command with any given objectives and situations, the tasks that must be performed will be essentially the same regardless of the manner in which they may be divided between and within the organizational structure. If one level of command does not do them, another level of command must do them. Regardless of organization, the basic cause and effect relationships of war will operate inexorably.

The responsibility for organization rests directly upon the commander. If he does not provide in peacetime an organization which will work in war, he will be burdened with urgent reorganization problems at a time he should be free to solve military problems, or else his combat efficiency will be reduced by reason of his poor organization. Furthermore, under these circumstances hasty organization changes will be made under pressure. In the past this has almost always meant great expansion both in staff personnel and in administrative commands and activities. It has built up the logistic snowball and it has meant the *expansion of paper work*. Thus at the very time when we most need simplicity we have introduced unnecessary complication.

In many instances, particularly where complex, joint, or allied commands are involved, the organization of the commands and the staffs may be decided before the nature of the tasks of the commanders has been clearly developed. No one pretends that this is the best way to do business; it just happens to be the way that the pressures of time and personnel limitations and considerations of national and service prestige force this sort of business to be done.

When missions and tasks make it appropriate, conformity to set standards of command and staff organization is desirable insofar as it facilitates the conduct of work and administration. *However, conformity should not be sought for its own sake alone. It has no inherent virtue.*

Summary

In the light of this brief discussion of an extremely complex question we perhaps should limit ourselves to the rather obvious conclusion that the successful management of our military affairs will come only when the extremes are avoided and a reasonable and flexible means based upon an understanding of the factors, problems, and principles involved is established.

In the ensuing chapters on the theater or area organization, logistic coordination, logistic staffs and the logistic systems and command relations, various instances of these basic differences in concepts of command will be brought out and viewed from various aspects.

Chapter 14

The Logistic System and Command Relations

In war the chief alone understands the importance of certain things; and he alone by his will and superior knowledge can conquer and overcome all difficulties.[1]
—NAPOLEON

In the previous chapters the general structure, attributes, and principles of logistics have been described and certain broad statements made as to organization. It is now appropriate to discuss the characteristics, the command, and the employment of combat forces as related to and as affected by their logistic support.

The Need for Harmony

Since it is the bridge between the national economic system and the combat elements of the armed forces, the logistic system obviously must partake of the characteristics of both. It must be in harmony with two quite different activities of man and with two different types of organization.

We have seen that logistic organization starts out with its roots chiefly in the economic system and in that area is primarily a civilian type of organization and activity with certain modifications of a military nature.[2] As we progress toward the combat forces we find that the nature of the process changes and its organization shifts as the military influence increases and as civilian influence diminishes. At the end of the

---

[1] Napoleon, *Napoleon and Modern War: His Military Maxims,* Col. C. H. Lanza, Military Service Publishing Co., Harrisburg, 1943, p. 89.

[2] *The Soldier and the State,* The Belknap Press of Harvard University Press, Cambridge, Mass., 1957, p. 326.
Samuel Huntington points out that in World War II this civilian area was not without its combat aspects in saying:
> The record of strategic policy making, enlivened only by inter-allied differences, was bland and dull in comparison with the opposite extreme which prevailed on the economic mobilization front with its constant organizational shifts, fiery personality clashes, dramatic resignations and firings.

line of logistics we find actual combat a purely military function.

In between the purely civilian management of a free economy operating under government controls and the purely military management of actual combat there is the complex system of power in our national capital. Here the concepts of command control of logistics and of civilian control of the military tend to conflict and produce organizational uncertainties that cannot be solved purely by conventional organizational theory and methods.[3; 4] The system can be made to work successfully only by the development of common objectives, the appointment of good men, the fast free exchange of vital information, and the development of mutual confidence, *plus the establishment of a reasonably good, even though admittedly imperfect, organization.*

In the course of the industrial revolution there has been a series or group of actions and reactions between combat and economics whereby the changes in the economic system have brought changes in combat. A similar reaction has taken place whereby the requirements of combat have brought changes in the economic system. The logistic process has been the vehicle by which these interacting changes have taken place.

A few simple examples illustrate the reactions between combat and economics.

In World War II our enormous military engineering effort

---

[3] *Ibid*, p. 437.
Huntington also comments on one aspect:
> The principal antagonist of the Joint Chiefs within the central defense organization was the Comptroller. Like the JCS, however, his office afforded an excellent illustration of the deceptive quality of formal legal structure. On the organization charts the Comptroller was lost among the crowd of nine assistant secretaries of defense. In the actual operation of the Department, however, he was a political force rivaled only by the military leaders themselves. He became the preeminent representative of the civilian demands for economy and efficiency in the military establishment. Just as the power of the Joint Chiefs extended beyond the purely military, the power of the Comptroller extended beyond the bounds of strictly administrative and fiscal matters. His influence rested on four pillars: theoretical, legal, functional and personal.

[4] The importance of the Comptroller is also emphasized by Timothy W. Stanley in *American Defense and National Security*, Public Affairs Press, Washington, D.C., 1956, pp. 93, 112-114, 118-120.

was made possible only by the vigorous heavy construction industry in the United States. Thus industry supplied equipment, the management know-how, and skilled personnel to the Navy "Sea Bees" and to the Army Engineers for the greatest construction tasks in history. The Pacific airfield construction program was a major contribution to the strategic-tactical momentum which defeated Japan. In like manner military railroads, petroleum distribution, and cargo handling benefited directly from civilian experience and techniques.

The reverse action is illustrated by the history of the development of our new Navy in the 1880's where the insistence of the Navy Department on higher quality of steel for new construction stimulated the industry to great technological advances.

In the 1930's the railroad diesel engine received a great stimulus from the competitive contracts for new type of submarine engines. Of course, the tremendous applied research and engineering development efforts of World War II, particularly in electronics and nucleonics, have had a remarkable effect on U.S. industry.

These instances are sufficient to suggest several points.

A logistic system should be in harmony with its supporting economic system. Among other things this implies that for the greatest effectiveness and efficiency the military should make the maximum practicable use of civilian equipment and techniques.

The use of commercially available equipment greatly simplifies the procurement of military equipment. However, this does not mean that all commercial equipment is suitable for military use. Quite the contrary—much of it is unsuitable for the specialized demands that overseas and combat operations make. For example, commercial light bulbs will not stand up under the shock of gunfire on board ship. Therefore, discrimination and good judgment must be used in the adoption of commercial specifications.

One of the most significant and oft-repeated lessons of World War II was that the combat commander must have control of his logistic support in order that his logistics might always be responsive to his combat needs. Corollary to this is the postulate that: *The logistic support system must be in harmony with the structure and employment of the combat forces it supports.*

This has the important implication that *since our combat forces are designed to accomplish different but complementary tasks, our logistic system must be designed for different but complementary tasks.* Furthermore, each segment of our combat forces makes *specialized and differing* demands upon the logistic system.

The Ideal Structure

From the above it is obvious that the structure, characteristics, and the nature of employment of military forces are major factors in developing the design of the most effective logistic system.

For instance, the broad characteristics of an ideal naval logistic system are clearly indicated. At one end we should have a system analogous to and growing out of our national economic system; at the other end we have this same system transformed to one with the same relation to a sea-going combat system. In between we have a changing logistic process which accomplishes this transformation.

Similarly, starting from the same economic base the Army and the Air Force each develop logistic systems responsive to their unique combat needs.

Broad Command Responsibilities

The logistic process itself is largely, the sum of many technical functions which are used in a great variety of combinations toward the support of specific forces working for specific purposes. The perfection of each technical function is the task of the specialist. The control, that is the employment of various combinations of these technical functions, is the task of command; for if the technical functions are divorced from a common purpose they are of no significance. However, the attempt to exercise control without a knowledge of the characteristics of the logistic functions to be performed and of the working of the forces which influence their behavior will result in frustration and waste.

Throughout this book there has been great emphasis on the subject of command and its point of view. However, the vastness of the problem and the inherent complication of the shift from civilian to military control should not obscure the fundamental principle involved. *Command transforms war potential into combat power by its control and use of the logistic process.*

As stated earlier, the conflict between the principle of civilian control of the military and the principle of command control

	TO CREATE	TO SUPPORT	TO EMPLOY
OP NAV	DIRECT & SUPERVISE	DIRECT & SUPERVISE	DIRECT & SUPERVISE
BUREAUS	BASIC ACTION	BASIC ACTION	————
SEA FRONTIER	PARTIAL SUPERVISION	MAJOR SUPERVISION	LOCAL FORCES
AREA & FLEET	ASSEMBLE & TRAIN	MAJOR DIRECTION & SUPERVISION	MAJOR DIRECTION & SUPERVISION
TYPE	ASSEMBLE & TRAIN	MAJOR ACTION	————
TASK FORCE & GROUP	————	MAJOR ACTION	MAJOR ACTION
UNIT	————	FINAL ACTION	FINAL ACTION

Figure 19. Command Responsibilities for Naval Forces

Note:
   While the Reorganization Act of 1958 substitutes the JCS for OpNav in direction of Unified Commands, it does not otherwise change these general responsibilities shown in the first item of the last column above. (See SECNAV INSTRUCTION 5430.45 of 23 Dec. 1958.)

of logistics can be resolved only by a flexible, broad approach. The fact that on the national level this situation does not conform to any ideal solution does not prevent us from seeking clarity on the operational level.

If we consider the command organization in terms of the responsibility for the creation of the logistic support of, and the employment of combat forces, the problems of "separation of powers" can be illustrated by reference to the chart of naval command responsibilities (fig. 19), and by referring again to figs. 9, 10, 11, "Logistics the Bridge" which present this same idea in a somewhat different manner. While these ideas are somewhat oversimplified, they help to show the relationship among these responsibilities. Figure 19 gives another illustration of the flow of emphasis from "administrative" to "tactical" cognizance.

Characteristics of Naval Forces

The logistic aspect of the employment of naval forces is clarified if we consider those forces in the three broad categories of "heavy striking forces," "sea frontier forces," and "logistic forces." While there is considerable overlap and interchangeability between striking and sea frontier forces, there are also important distinctions.

In general, the heavy striking forces are characterized by heavy power, long cruising radius and deep draft. The attack carrier striking force, the major amphibious forces, and the hunter killer forces are in this group. A nuclear-powered, guided-missile submarine also would be in this category. These forces are essentially offensive in nature and should be so employed.

The sea frontier forces, on the other hand, are predominantly of shallow draft, and small cruising radius. They are considerably smaller and more diversified than the striking forces, and their objectives are primarily defensive in nature.

Destroyers, destroyer escorts, and mine craft may well operate with both striking and frontier forces. While conventionally armed submarines may operate with either force, they more usually act as an independent, offensive striking force. The smaller varieties such as fast gun boats, patrol, and associated craft usually belong in the frontier force.

The heavy striking forces require large building yards and great expense and time to build. The United States and Great Britain are the only nations with both wartime operational experience and immediate construction capabilities for these heavy striking forces. On the other hand, almost all maritime powers have had operational experience with frontier forces and have excellent capabilities for their construction.

The striking forces are under constant demand both by nations and by area commanders who do not necessarily have a full appreciation of their proper use. Both striking forces and frontier forces are capable of lending direct combat support to ground forces.

The protection of oceanic shipping requires a judicious combination of striking and frontier forces.

Carrier based air is always in the striking force category. Long-range, shore-based naval air in many instances should be so considered because of its importance to the operation of a striking force which must have the control of its own vital reconnaissance.

The logistic characteristics of naval forces have an important bearing on their employment and on the planning in all areas. A naval force of any major importance always has a large inherent logistic endurance when it puts to sea after replenishment from a base. The large ships themselves carry food for from 60 to 90 days, enough fuel to cruise at moderate speeds for 5,000 to 15,000 miles, and enough ammunition to handle certain types of combat operations for a considerable period. Thus, naval forces usually have enough built in logistic support to cruise at length and to fight at a moderate rate without any specially planned accompanying logistic support other than oilers.

The naval logistic forces, in general, come under the categories of underway replenishment group, mobile support group, and advanced bases. Again as with the combat forces there is considerable interchangeability. However, while the replenishment forces are generally limited in type to oilers, stores ships, ammunition ships, carriers, sea-going tugs, and salvage vessels, the mobile support group has a bewildering assortment of tenders, repair ships, slow oilers, dry docks, tugs, barges, and boats of all varieties.[5, 6] Neither the striking forces nor the frontier forces can develop more than a small fraction of their combat power without well-designed and specifically allocated logistic forces backed up by a complex of advanced bases and continental bases. With the development of advanced concepts of logistic support as discussed in chapter 7 an air transportation system responsive to the need of the naval tactical commander becomes an essential element of the naval logistic system.

It is well at this point to come back to the previously expressed thought that the logistic support system should be in harmony with the structure and employment of the combat force it supports. For it is only when this harmony exists that combat effectiveness reaches its peak and fully develops the war potential of the supporting basic economy.

When we review the general attributes of navies we find that the outstanding capabilities are mobility, flexibility, and sustained striking power. We find that these are merely potential capabilities which become combat realities only when there is a further vital combination of correct concept of strategic employment coupled with command relationships which are designed to exploit rather than to restrict the capabilities of the forces.

These in turn must be supplemented by the correct logistic concept, command relations and facilities, forces, and planning in the logistic support of these forces. An essential part of this planning is to ensure the effective—but minimum—build-up of base facilities and supply levels in the advanced bases to support planned replenishments; to ensure the presence and adequacy of a mobile support system; and to ensure adequate and responsive transportation. This way lies harmony.

Hypothetical Illustration

A simple hypothetical situation will serve to illustrate a practical application of this discussion.

(to page 231)

_____

[6] While a future war may have many novel aspects it will not greatly reduce the demand for logistic support of naval forces deployed overseas. Few persons realize the variety of duties performed by the mobile support group Service Squadron Ten in World War II nor the similar function of

Service Squadron Three in the Far East in 1953-1956. Carter, in *Beans, Bullets and Black Oil* says on page 303:

Service Squadron Ten had grown up! By the middle of February 1945, its floating facilities, classified by functions, totaled 280 units: 26 repair ships, other repair facilities and tenders; 34 floating ammunition supply facilities; 48 floating supply and fleet freight units; 100 floating fuel and water supply storage vessels; 24 seagoing and salvage tugs; 42 fleet-service small craft and harbor tugs; 6 barracks ships and hotel barges.

This was quite a growth from the 50-odd units with which the squadron had started a year before. It was a growth beyond the 80-odd units the squadron commander had estimated to be needed at the time of organization—to be told he was dreaming or had his head in the clouds, and scoffed at about the big outfit he was trying to wangle. It is not becoming to say "I told you so!" because he was so far wrong himself that the difference between his underestimate and all the others did not alter the fact that no one in those earlier days was sufficiently posted on fleet logistics to make very good estimates of what the future would require. New calculations had to be made as the war went on, and some of these reestimated on sudden notice before having been fully met.

⁶ Captain Randolph Meade, Jr., USN. Lecture 20 November 1956 at Naval War College entitled *The Service Squadron* in which he said:

The responsibilities of the Service Squadron Commander in the forward area are almost limitless. The Service Squadron Commander is "Mr. It." He supplies and does everything. Admiral Biggs used to say that his title more appropriately would be "Vice President in Charge of Things and Stuff!" There is no job too small or too large for him to do or to be called upon to do. He is the Operational Commander of a number of types of ships as well as their Type Commander in the forward area. Along with his responsibility for repairs, and for supplying all common and technical stores from his stores ships and tenders, he is responsible for the coordination of *all* repair and maintenance services in the area, for towing services, and for all salvage. His hospital ship was the source of medical aid for the Marines in Korea and in the case of the Indo-China evacuation provided much needed medical assistance and for the evacuation of wounded at the objective area. In addition, the Service Squadron is called upon to provide a certain amount of administrative assistance, particularly in legal and personnel work. The Service Squadron is frequently a floating receiving station, and during extended fleet operations the handling of transient personnel becomes a major task, and, unfortunately, one for which the Service Squadron is least well fitted. The Service Squadron operates the fleet mobile post offices as well as a mobile movie exchange, and for a long time in Okinawa operated a fleet recreation facility at White Beach. The fleet beach in Indo-China represented almost the only recreational outlet for a large groups of ships for a considerable length of time and provided a most valuable boost to morale. A similar facility was operated in Subic Bay with the assistance of the Base Commander. The net tenders were his, as was a deperming vessel, a mobile boat pool, a mobile warehouse group of barges, along with two service units; the mobile electronics technical unit, and the mobile ordnance service units. Two detachments of the Cargo Handling Battalion on Guam were assigned to the Service Squadron at Sasebo and Subic, and they provided valuable stevedore training and supervision and some relief when crews were shorthanded for fleet replenishments.

Let us suppose that an oceanic area naval commander has divided his command into three sub-areas, each with a moderate land area with locations suitable for naval bases. Each sub-area commander would have local defense and patrol forces, and each would have naval bases or stations.

Under these conditions the oceanic fleet commander would assign his heavy striking forces to task force or task fleet commanders and under the broad direction of his service force commander and other type commanders he would assign service force squadrons or detachments to the task force commander to care for underway replenishment. In accordance with the needs of the situation the fleet commander can order mobile logistic forces into any area to supplement as necessary the logistic support capabilities of the naval and naval air bases in the sub-area.

Under these conditions and provided there has been time allowed for the movement of the mobile logistic forces, the entire oceanic fleet can move into any sub-area and find adequate logistic support. The mobility and flexibility of the naval forces and their floating support provide this freedom of action.

The command arrangements are similarly flexible. The task fleet commander together with the commanders of the mobile logistic forces can all report to the sub-area commander for operational control during the period of the special operations in that sub-area. Or else the sub-area commander can report to the task fleet commander for operational control for this period.

In each case the officer responsible for combat command will have logistic authority. In each case the question of who will have over-all responsibility for the conduct of the operation will have been decided in accordance with the necessities of the situation and the experience of the various commanders in the employment of the forces assigned.

In each case it will be necessary to take into account the relationship of the sub-area commander and the task fleet commander with the commanders of the forces of the other services in the same operation and in the area.

In each case the responsibility for coordinating logistic support for the period of the operation must be spelled out and *in each of these cases the ability of the staff of the coordinating commander to handle the information required to make the logistic decisions will be a major factor.*

In each case the command of the combat units will be unchanged and will remain in the hands of their normal commanders.

A temporary shift of staff officers from one command to another for the duration of the operation would greatly facilitate the establishment of a good command structure and would reduce the size of staffs required.

These same concepts can be applied to the movement of striking power between oceanic areas as well as within such areas. It is not necessary to build up the sub-area support facilities ashore to an undue extent. It is not necessary to tie down mobile forces to any particular area or sub-area. Combat power and logistic support can be concentrated where needed and quickly moved when and where another need becomes greater.

Logistics and the Functions of Command in an Area

Analysis of the specific command functions to be performed is the first step in organizing an area.

The general missions of a command do not in general vary from area to area. These missions are: control, defense, offense, and support. The area must be controlled, that is the forces must have freedom to establish lines of communication and bases within it. They must have freedom to move. The area, the bases, and the fixed lines of communication must be defended in order that they may be effectively operated. The area forces within their capability must be able to undertake offensive operations against the enemy. The area must be prepared to support other areas and to support logistically forces from other areas.

In order to accomplish these major missions many functions and tasks must be performed. The area must be organized and the forces disposed. The forces must be logistically supported.

The forces must be maintained in a state of combat readiness. The activities of the command must be coordinated with the national governments and with those civil authorities who exercise authority in the area. In order to perform these functions of command there must be effective area intelligence and area signal communications systems.

In making this estimate of the command problem it is important to ask—

(1) Which of these functions and tasks should be considered on a day to day continuing basis and which will be intermittent?

(2) Which functions and tasks are predictable and which will be subject to wide fluctuations?

(3) Which should be handled on a geographic basis and which on a functional basis?

The proper evaluation of these questions is the critical point of area organization and this evaluation requires a detailed written analysis.

A sound logistic organization and plan will be the foundation for the whole structure. On this will rest the day-to-day operations of control and defense as well as the fluctuating logistics of offensive operations. Naturally, this logistic plan stems from an integrated strategic-logistic concept in which it is not profitable to try to distinguish between the hen and the egg. The logistic scheme can and should be designed 'to support both "area" forces and "functional" forces. Such a basic logistic foundation will support a number of strategic concepts and a very great variety of tactical plans.

In every area there is a need for two types of transportation. First, the point-to-point, major inter-area systems such as those operated by the Military Air Transport Service and the Military Sea Transportation Service, over which the area commander has only limited control; and, second, the more flexible intra-area systems which are more directly responsible to the area commander.

The greater the development of mobility and flexibility of our combat forces, the greater will be the need for providing for their freedom of employment on a functional basis. The greater this development the greater will be the responsibility of task force commanders and the greater will be the tendency for component commanders to become primarily logistical and administrative commanders with little direct combat activity. The great speed of modern operations and the mobility and flexibility of enemy forces make it important that one's own chain of combat command be as simple as possible and that there be the maximum practicable degree of decentralization. This is particularly true in land areas of western Europe where sabotage, atomic weapons, and airborne operations pose a major threat to command, communications, and transportation centers.

Practical Problems in Command

Certain very real attitudes and considerations will affect the organization of an area.

In the past the Army has been inclined toward the assignment of command on a geographic basis and in general has advocated the centralized concept of unified command.

The Air Force has stressed the strategic freedom of the Strategic Air Command and properly insists that it be treated on a functional basis. The position of air defense is not so clear. It seems to be an area matter if the area is big enough; but it has strong functional claims, particularly as speeds and ranges increase. The Air Materiel Command is not a very mobile command. It thus fits into the area concept except for the paradoxical requirement that it be a highly-centralized, world-wide organization and yet be responsive to local and to tactical air demands.

As various types of guided missiles come into operation this situation can be expected to present many problems.

The continental U.S. organization of the Navy is a part of an area concept by reason of its well-established system of Sea Frontiers. However, the flexible mobile striking power of the carrier forces and the amphibious forces are not subject to exploitation under an area concept. Nor can this striking power be fully exploited unless these forces have their attached mobile logistic support. The smaller ships of the Navy such as mine sweepers, harbor defense craft, and certain types of ASW craft which have herein been classed as "Sea Frontier Forces" may well be assigned on an area basis.

The attack carrier forces, the major amphibious forces, and the submarine forces, all with their mobile logistic forces, previously classed as "Heavy Striking Forces" should not be *tied down* to any one area.

The priceless capability of the Navy is that major sustained striking power can be quickly formed and quickly moved to areas where needed, provided that mobile logistic support is furnished and provided that the command relations are designed to exploit rather than to restrict the capability of flexibility.

The standard Army organization with its combat zone and communications zone conforms to the concept of the area type organization. In large land areas this poses no particular conflict with Navy or Air Force concepts. However, in areas like the Mediterranean it is not so simple. In a stable situation it may not be too difficult to work out an accommodation where certain portions of the base section are assigned for naval use.

In time of war it may be quite different.

The hypothetical geographic picture shown in figure 20 is useful to illustrate this problem.

In this situation there may be a combat zone, a communications zone, a base section, and air material depot, a naval base, and mobile logistic forces. How best should the command relations among them be spelled out?

The three services will be competing for real estate, unloading priority, and construction facilities. If the base section of the communication zone is under attack, the problems of defense and quick rehabilitation require the same type of unity of command that is needed in the combat zone.

However, in our European and Mediterranean Unified and Allied commands, this desired unity is not always found. There are many objections to it and, therefore, this important aspect

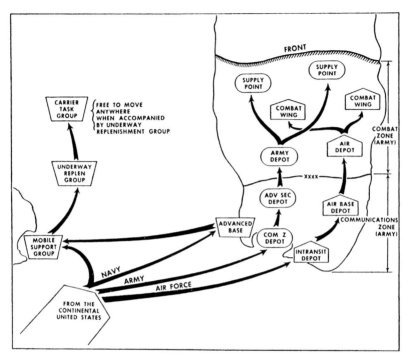

Figure 20. The Three Logistic Support Systems in an Area of Operation

of organization is frequently discussed in only the most general terms. In an Allied command structure this is further complicated by the need for spelling out the relations between the allied commanders and the national authorities both in war and in peace. These command relations include such problems as control of railroads, highways, labor, port facilities, local defense and security, and the control of coastal areas. The great problem of developing specific plans to cover these matters lies in the basic fact that the presence of an allied command on the soil of any nation constitutes a sacrifice of the sovereignty of that nation.

Personal Problem of a Commander

The *personal* problem of the commander of an area is very great. This is particularly true in a combined area where he, personally, is continually involved with "VIP's" and with conferences. Figure 21, showing the interlocking NATO and U.S. command relations in Europe as they were developed in 1952 and 1953, illustrates the responsibilities which General Ridgway and his successors have borne. This complexity, of course, is a further reason why great care must be taken to have a sound command organization and a sound and adequate staff organization. His personal problem is further complicated if he also commands one of the component forces, as has been the case when a naval officer has commanded an area.

Combat command is only one of the major problems of the area commander. True, he bears the responsibility for the proper exercise of command in combat. On the other hand, in most instances his work is primarily concerned with the over-all planning, the logistic, and the administrative aspects of command; actual tactical command of combat operations is usually delegated to task force commanders. While, in theory, the area commander assigns broad responsibilities and tasks, he must also be sure that his subordinate commanders organize in such a way that they fit together harmoniously.

This means that in some cases he may have to go into considerable detail in his directives and orders. In any event, major changes in subordinate command organizations frequently must be approved by higher authority because of their political and strategic implications.

Summary

In summary certain points should be emphasized.

The first and most important factor in the organization of an area is the determination of the decisive strategic areas and of the vital lines of communication.

The understanding and proper utilization of the attributes of geographical command and functional command are essential.

As the nature of an alliance changes, the nature of the organization must change to conform to reality.

Without a unified command, combat forces and logistic resources may be frittered away on unimportant tasks.

The command organization, the staff organization, and the

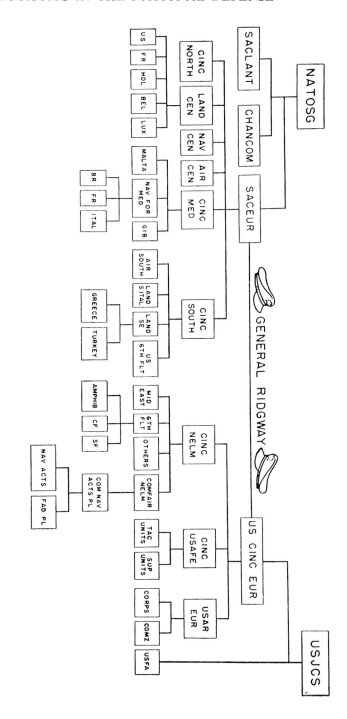

Figure 21. National-International Command Relationships (1952)

This oversimplified command chart shows a two hat national and international command. It need not be up to date nor do the subordinate units need to be spelled out to show the complexity of the command and staff problems which must be solved.

basic policy directives are all related and, in a well administered area, they form a harmonious whole. A failure in any one of these will disrupt the command of the area.

The larger the number of nations involved in an area command, the more complex becomes the task of organization; the greater the personal problem of the commander himself, and the greater the need for adherence to sound principles of command.

As danger grows or becomes imminent, the cohesive forces tend to increase. As the sense of danger diminishes, the disruptive forces tend to increase.

Compromise is inevitable, change is inevitable. It is only when the commander understands the principles involved that he can compromise and change wisely.

The application of the basic principles of unified command is essential to the good organization of an area.

An area organization and its plans must be examined from within and in the lower echelons in order to be evaluated. It is not enough simply to know that its upper echelon command relations conform to good principles.

The effectiveness of an area organization depends both on sound command relations in all echelons and on equipping each command with an adequate, trained staff which in itself is organized to do the tasks assigned.

Finally, effective area command can be exercised only after vast amounts of information are accumulated, screened, digested and evaluated. This requires staff working facilities and equipment, and communications. The absence or failure of any one can mean the breakdown of command, regardless of the perfection of the paper organizations and of the excellence of individuals.

As was indicated earlier, the question of control of logistics is of vital importance in any study of area command. This, naturally, leads to the next topic—the meaning and implications of the term "logistic coordination." The review of a major campaign in which such coordination was not practiced is therefore appropriate.

Chapter 15

Logistic Coordination

"Which are more important—facts or ideas?" White-
head reflected a while, then said, "Ideas about facts."[1]
—ALFRED NORTH WHITEHEAD

German-Italian Mediterranean Campaign

A classic example of how logistic considerations influenced
the outcome of a major campaign is found in the German-
Italian Mediterranean-North African operations in 1942.

Here several fundamental factors, primarily in the strategic-
logistic area, acted in combination to bring disaster in spite of
the brilliant strategic concepts and superb tactical leadership of
a field commander. Since many factors are involved in this situation it is necessary to go into some detail before drawing conclusions as to the logistic aspects.

The situation in June 1942 was as follows. There was no clear,
loyally-supported, Axis strategy. The Italian people were politi-
cally divided and had little enthusiasm for the war. Italian war
potential was low. The Army was ill prepared and its high command generally incompetent and hampered by jealousy. The
Italian Navy, which had never contemplated a war against the
British, was given only a secondary defensive role. The ships
had low fuel endurance, low oil reserves, and were without
radar[2] or effective air reconnaissance.[3]

Nevertheless, in spite of these handicaps, by June 1942 the
German-Italian Coalition had forced the British in the Mediter-
ranean into a desperate position. Malta was staggering, the
British Navy had suffered very heavy losses, and the badly de-

---

[1] *Dialogs of Alfred North Whitehead*, as recorded by Lucien Price, Little,
Brown and Co., Boston, 1954, p. 337.
[2] Admiral Franco Maugeri, *From the Ashes of Disgrace*, Reynal & Hitchcock, New York, 1948, pp. 8 and 9.
[3] Commander (R) Marc' Antonio Bragadin, *The Italian Navy in World
War II*, United States Naval Institute, Annapolis, Maryland, 1957, pp. 7, 21,
22, 43, 44, 123, 150.

feated Eighth Army was in retreat. When Marshal Rommel captured Tobruk on 21 June it was believed that Suez would soon fall to him.

The British had just made a great effort to replenish Malta in two convoy operations: "Harpoon" sailing from Gibraltar, and "Vigorous" sailing from Alexandria. The British historian has summed up the situation:

HARPOON

Two out of six merchant ships had arrived; but we had lost two destroyers, while a cruiser, three more destroyers, and a minesweeper had been seriously damaged.

VIGOROUS

Apart from the failure to revictual Malta we had lost a cruiser, three destroyers, and two merchant ships. The Italians lost the *Trento* and had the *Littorio* damaged. The enemy's success was undeniable, and no further attempt was made to run a convoy to Malta from Egypt until the Army had driven the Axis forces out of Libya.

As this was the last attempt made during the present phase to revictual Malta on a large scale, it will be a convenient moment to summarize the results achieved and the losses suffered. Compared with the three convoys run from the west in 1941, the degree of success achieved in the first half of the following year was very meagre. In 1941 thirty-one supply ships sailed for Malta from Alexandria or Gibraltar, and all but one arrived safely. In the first seven months of 1942 twenty-one ships sailed in major convoy operations and another nine took part in the smaller attempts from the east made in January and February. Of these thirty ships ten were sunk at sea (seven of them in the major convoys), ten turned back because of damage, or for other reasons such as inability to keep up with their convoys; and of the ten which reached Malta three were sunk after arrival. Thus only seven of the original thirty survived intact with the whole of their cargoes. Moreover, in this period the naval losses had been heavy. Quite apart from the large number of ships damaged we lost a cruiser, eight destroyers and a submarine.

The seriousness of these losses can best be realized by mentioning that the whole evacuation of the B.E.F. from

Dunkirk in 1941 cost the Royal Navy two less destroyers than were lost in these Malta convoy operations.

. . . By the 21st the enemy was in full possession of the base (Tobruk) which had been so stubbornly held throughout the long siege of 1940-41. For ,the Mediterranean Fleet the implications were most serious. The Naval Staff warned the First Sea Lord that "in view of the news that Tobruk had fallen we must prepare for the worst"—namely the loss of Alexandria. Preparations were put in hand to move some of the fleet to Haifa and others south of the Suez Canal. After the passage of the latter the Canal was to be blocked. Once before, in April 1941, we had prepared to face these dire consequences of defeat on land, but this time the threat was far more serious.[4]

The British picture was undeniably bad. It was clear that the whole of the British effort was endangered—first by the parlous condition of the essential base (Malta) and second by the military reverses and immediate threat to Egypt brought about by the length of the line of supply.

On the other hand, possibly unknown to them, the forces under Rommel were suffering even more acutely from logistic deficiencies.

Rommel reached El Alamein on 30 June and on 3 July, in his own words:

After three days vainly assaulting the Alamein line, I decided that I would call the offensive off for the moment after the next day's attack. Reasons for my decision were the steadily mounting strength of the enemy and the low fighting strength of my own divisions, which amounted by that time to no more than 1,200 to 1,500 men, and above all the terribly strained supply situation.[5]

The logistic struggle between the Axis and the Allies which had dominated the Mediterranean war since its start in June 1940 entered its climactic phase as Rommel and the new com-

---

[4] Captain S. W. Roskill, D.S.C., R.N., *The War at Sea*, Volume II, "The Period of Balance," Her Majesty's Stationery Office, London, 1956, pp. 67, 71, 72, 73.

[5] B. H. Liddell Hart, *The Rommel Papers*, Harcourt, Brace and Company, New York, 1953, pp. 248-249.

mander of the British Eighth Army, Lieutenant General Montgomery, raced desperately to build up their forces.

Realizing that time was working for the British, Rommel attacked at Alam Halfa on 31 August and was finally repulsed on 3 September.

He had come to the end of his resources. He had lost the initiative and when Montgomery attacked at El Alamein on 23 October, two weeks before the Allied landings in Western North Africa, Rommel's brilliant campaign was finally lost.

Two of the men involved, Field Marshals Kesselring and Rommel, write their personal analyses.[6; 7] In some important respects they differ sharply; in others they agree.

The chief differences are three. (1) Kesselring was in agreement with the Italian Navy which had held that the capture of Malta was essential to the conduct of a war against Great Britain;[8] Rommel emphasized the maintenance of his own momentum. (2) Kesselring, while admitting many deficiencies in Rome and in the Italian organization, felt that Marshal Ugo Cavallero, the Italian Chief of Staff, was competent, loyal, and reliable. Rommel thought Cavallero to be incompetent, unreliable, and without any strategical grasp or administrative energy. (3) Kesselring, while admitting Rommel's great leadership and tactical brilliance, thought him reckless and over ambitious.

Both agree that the German high command failed to grasp the strategic importance of the Mediterranean. They agree that the German and Italian high commands failed to grasp the life or death nature and the critical periods of decision of the desert war. They agree that the campaign was primarily a "logistic battle." They agree that the margin of victory was very small and that it was essentially a matter of striking before the British

---

[6] Albert Kesselring, GeneralFeldMarschall, A.D. *Kesselring A Soldier's Record,* William Morros & Company, New York, 1954, particularly pages 116, 119, 121-122, 124, 126, 129-131, 133-135, 137-138, 140-143, 147-149, 151-154.

[7] B. H. Liddell Hart, *The Rommel Papers,* Harcourt, Brace and Company, New York, 1953, pp. 233, 235, 241, 243-245, 250, 261.

[8] Bragadin, *The Italian Navy in World War II,* U.S. Naval Institute, Annapolis, Maryland, 1957, pp. 19, 20.

had time to build up their logistic support at the critical area. Thus, in effect they agree that logistic effectiveness was the decisive factor. They agree that at the critical time in early and mid 1942 when opportunity for decisive victory was present, the Mediterranean sea transport was badly planned and badly organized, and that *there were no clear channels of logistic coordination.*

Rommel's comments on the confusion in command authority and the lateness of the high command recognition of the nature and importance of the logistic problem are borne out by the analysis of Captain R. E. Krause, U.S. Navy.[9]

---

[9] Captain R. E. Krause, U.S.N., *The German Navy Under Joint Command in World War II,* U.S. Naval Institute Proceedings, Vol. 73, No. 9, September, 1947.

Until 1943, the supply of the German and Italian armies in North Africa was the major problem in the Mediterranean. It was primarily a naval task to get these supplies across, and the German Navy, in liaison with the Italians, had set up an organization to cope with this problem. The German air force was also called in to help with this supply problem, but it was primarily a naval task. As the Fuehrer aptly pointed out in a conference on March 14, 1943. "It is impossible to supply armies by air. A single 9,000 ton steamer, for example, can carry as much on one voyage as a whole air fleet can carry over a longer period of time. Protection of convoys by the Air Force *alone* is not possible; ships continue to be required. The Straits of Sicily must teem with patrol and escort vessels. Good organization is essential. Only the German Navy can organize this on the basis of its experience and success in this field."

As Deputy for the Four Year Plan, Hermann Goering took a hand in the transportation problem. He had appointed the Nazi party leader, Gauleiter Kaufmann, as Reich Commissioner for Merchant Shipping, usually referred to as "RKS." Early in December, 1942, Goering and Kaufmann made an inspection trip to Italy. There Goering signed an order drafted by Kaufmann, establishing under the jurisdiction of "RKS" a new office, the Deputy for Transportation in the Mediterranean, abbreviated "BVM."

These administrative actions became of most immediate concern to the German Naval Command, Italy when on December 24, 1942 Goering issued a directive by which:

(a) BVM was to function under the authority of the Commander in Chief, South;

(b) BVM was authorized to give direct orders to all naval commands, offices, and technical personnel with regard to shipping.

Commanding German Admiral, Italy, immediately informed Naval Staff that "this move restricts the authority and responsibility of the German Naval Command, Italy, and will, in the long run, eliminate its function completely since the chain of command now runs from Commander in Chief, South, via 'BVM,' directly to Naval Transport Offices, Harbor Captains, and so on. I cannot

Another writer throws additional light on this campaign. In his history of the Italian Navy,[10] Commander Bragadin emphasizes time and again the failure of the Italo-German high command to appreciate the strategic importance and characteristics of the Mediterranean Sea. This strategic blindness was aggravated by four other major factors:

(1) Consideration of political prestige and jealousy among allies;

(2) The lack of naval air arm responsive to the needs of naval operations;

(3) Gross underestimates of the logistic requirements of the war, particularly for land operations in Libya; and

---

accept responsibility for the deterioration of the over-all war situation which will result from this order."

Consequences of the Goering directive were not limited to this urgent protest by German Naval Command, Italy. This command now received orders directly from the Commander in Chief, Navy, and the Commander in Chief, South. This situation resulted in the clash recorded by Naval Staff on December 25, 1942:

"Telephone call from General Deichmann, Chief of Staff to Commander in Chief, South.

'General Deichmann declared that the Grand Admiral (Raeder) has issued orders to the German naval offices in Italy which cannot be carried out. The Commander in Chief, South has ordered that his own directives are to be carried out without paying attention to the orders of the Grand Admiral, if this is required for the conduct of the war in the Mediterranean. The Commander in Chief, South, will arrest any admiral who does not obey this order.' "

Under date of December 28, 1942, the War Diary of the Naval Staff records: "The Commander in Chief, Navy, reported personally to the Fuehrer by phone on 25 December that he was rescinding his order, after the Armed Forces High Command had sanctioned the orders of the Reichsmarschall (Goering) which are now being carried out."

On December 28 the matter was discussed during the daily staff conference of the Commander in Chief, Navy. The Chief of the Navy's Quartermaster Office pointed out "the impossible attitude which the Commander in Chief, South, or his staff, has adopted vis-a-vis the Commander in Chief, Navy." In answer to this statement, the record says that "Commander in Chief Navy, is disregarding such all-too-human failings for the sake of the cause."

[10] Commander (R) Marc' Antonio Bragadin, *The Italian Navy in World War II*, United States Naval Institute, Annapolis, 1957, pp. 5, 7, 9, 10, 12, 13, 19, 35, 41, 81.

(4) Lack of integrated strategic-logistic planing in a high command dominated by a single service.

While it may be difficult to unravel all the threads of this campaign, certain very significant facts should be borne in mind.

Comments on the Campaign

The 7th and the 12th Panzer Divisions destined for Rommel in the summer of 1942 were diverted to Russia. These would have doubled his German armored force and could easily have tipped the balance.

German industry was not fully mobilized until 1943-44. Up to that time it had been largely on a one shift basis.[11]

There was a lack of unity of logistic effort in the German-Italian Headquarters in Rome.

Rommel requested 60,000 tons of supply for June of 1942. He actualy was able to obtain only 3,000 tons that month.

Rommel was unable to get these supplies delivered at points advantageously related to his tactical operations.

The operations of the Italian Navy and thus the effectiveness of North African supply convoys were always limited by fuel shortages.

In March-June 1943 it was found possible to deliver 195,171 tons of fuel to the Italian Navy, a great increase over past performance. If this same effort had been made by the Italo-German high command a year earlier the Libyan supply flow could have been greatly increased.[12]

Finally, in mid-November 1942, only after the African Campaign had been lost and when the Western Allies had a much greater preponderance of naval and air power in the Mediterranean than they had in June and July, the Italian-German high command was willing to make the degree of military effort necessary to accomplish the delivery of large quantities of supplies to Tunisia.

Thus, it is clearly evident that Rommel's defeat was not due to any basic inability of the Germans and Italians to furnish

---

[11] The U.S. Strategic Bombing Survey—Over-all Report (European War) September 30, 1945, "The German War Economy," pp. 31 and 34.
[12] Commander (R) Marc' Antonio Bragadin, *The Italian Navy in World War II*, United States Naval Institute, Annapolis, 1957, p. 194.

him with troops and logistic support. *His defeat in this campaign was due to the faulty strategic concepts of the Axis high command, to faulty logistic concepts, and to faulty command organization of logistics.*

In this one campaign we have illustrations of the strategic-logistic relationship and the tactical-logistic relationship as discussed in chapter 2.

We have an example of the vital importance of correct strategic concepts and strategic objectives. In particular, we have an example of the nature of the problems of attaining unity of effort in a military alliance.

We have an illustration of the inability to convert a tactical success into a major strategic success because of a failure of logistic support.

We have an illustration of the importance of priorities and allocations and of proper command control in this field.

We have an illustration of the relation of transportation to over-all logistic efficiency and to the attainment of sustained combat effectiveness, and an example of the importance of command control of intra-theater transportation.

And, finally, we have an illustration of the problems of logistic coordination in an allied theater of war.

The fundamental requirements for logistic coordination in his particular situation are very well stated by Rommel in his discussion of the North African situation in the summer of 1942.

> Nevertheless, the worst difficulties were with bulk supply. Here there existed serious weaknesses of organization which worked heavily against us. Control of shipping across the Mediterranean lay in the hands of the Commando Supremo. The only German office which could exercise an influence on supply matters was under the charge of General von Rintelen, who had been German Military Attache in Rome for years. Field Marshal Kesselring and Admiral Weichold were only called in on questions con-

cerned with the air and sea protection of convoys and ports.

The only influence which the Panzer Army Command could exercise on the supply question was the production of a "priority list"—that is to say a list showing the order in which the material stored in Italy should be brought to Africa—if at all.

We had no influence whatever over the shipping lists, the ports of arrival or—most important—the proportion of German to Italian cargoes. In theory this was supposed to be a ratio of 1:1; in fact, it moved steadily to the German disadvantage. A good example was the case of the Pistoia Division. This division, which was scheduled to arrive in mid-September and was intended for use in Libya instead of at the front, was shipped across with two-thirds of its men and between three and four hundred of its vehicles at the beginning of August, although only 60 vehicles had then arrived for 164th Division, which already had units in the line. Then again, while many of the Italian units in the Alamein line were being refitted at an astonishing speed and were exchanging their vehicles one after the other for new ones from Italy, not one German replacement vehicle left Italy for the Panzer Army up to the beginning of August.

Cavallero, who from time to time visited the front, often promised to have all manner of things put right. But it just as frequently happened that on his next visit he would say with a laugh that he had made many a promise in his time and not all of them could be kept.

The unloading of shipping in Africa was also a terribly leisurely affair. It was only too often a triumph of antiquated ideas, lack of initiative and a total absence of any sort of technical ingenuity. Thus we found it completely impossible to get the port capacity of Tobruk increased—600 tons a day was all it could handle, with the result that ships were kept far too long in the harbour exposed to the danger of destruction by British bombers. We made repeated demands for increased port construction, the building of unloading facilities in neighbouring inlets by Italian labour, the provision of larger quantities of Italian dock equipment and stronger air defences for Tobruk—all, of course, with little success.[18]

---

[18] B. H. Liddell Hart, *The Rommel Papers,* Harcourt, Brace and Company, New York, 1953, pp. 266-268.

In his final remarks on the disaster which finally overwhelmed him at El Alamein, he said:

> No one can say that we had not given warning, months before the British offensive, that the army would be unable to fight a successful defence, unless a minimum specific build-up was created in Africa and unless certain specific quantities of reinforcements and replacement material reached African soil. That this was not done, was very well known to the people who later flung the most mud. To quote only one example—instead of the thirty issues of petrol I had demanded, we had had three. The figure I had given for our material requirements had been based on the anticipated increase in British strength. I could not of course have foreseen just how great the strength of the British was actually to be.[14]
>
> We had still received no strategic decision from the supreme German and Italian authorities on the future of the African theatre of war. They did not look at things realistically—indeed, they refused to do so. What we found really astonishing was to see the amount of material that they were suddenly able to ship to Tunisia, quantities out of all proportion to anything we had received in the past. The urgency of the danger had at last percolated through to Rome. But the British and Americans had meanwhile multiplied their supply shipments many times over and were steadily increasing their strategic command over sea and air. One Axis ship after the other was going down beneath the waters of the Mediterranean and it was becoming obvious that even the greatest effort could no longer hope to effect any decisive improvement in the supply situation; we were up to our necks in the mud and no longer had the strength to pull ourselves out.
>
> The mismanagement, the operational blunders, the prejudices, the everlasting search for scapegoats, these were now to reach the acute stage. And the man who paid the price was the ordinary German and Italian soldier.[15]

Summary

When we realize how close was the balance of victory and defeat in this campaign and when we weigh the advantages

---

[14] Liddell Hart, *op cit*, p. 333.
[15] *Ibid*, p. 358.

which the Axis powers would have gained, the importance of efficient logistic coordination becomes obvious. We can apply this lesson to our times and to the future only by first making a general analysis.

Chapter 16

Logistic Coordination Analyzed

The search for and establishment of leading principles—always few—around which consideration of detail group themselves, will tend to reduce confusion of impression to simplicity and directness of thought, with consequent facility of comprehension.[1]
—ADMIRAL ALFRED T. MAHAN

In the last ten years, with the development of unified area commands, both with purely U.S. forces and with allied forces, the term "logistic coordination" has come into frequent use.

Need for Coordination

However, there has been little common understanding as to how this term should be interpreted. Therefore, in each case where it is used, the responsibilities and authority implied must be spelled out in detail or else the various elements of the commands whose logistic activities are to be "coordinated" may be working at cross purposes.

All commanders, be they unilateral, joint, or allied, have certain combat forces, logistic forces, and logistic resources allotted to them by higher authority. Each commander has the duty to make the most effective use of these allotted resources.

Since it is not reasonable to expect a commander to plan or to execute a scheme of war without understanding and controlling the means for its accomplishment, it naturally follows both that: (1) Logistics is a responsibility of command; and (2) a commander must have control over his logistic operations comparable to that which he exercises over his tactical operations.

If these principles are neglected, one of two results is likely: Either military disaster will ensue, or else victory will be at-

---

[1] Admiral Alfred T. Mahan, *Naval Strategy*, Little, Brown and Co., Boston, 1911, p. 118.

tained only after an unnecessary delay and with unnecessary waste of life and material resources.

No element of command is more important than loyalty, yet loyalty cannot be fully effective unless it is based on a common understanding of purposes and objectives and a common concept of how they should be attained. This is the reason why all analyses of military thought place so much emphasis on the OBJECTIVE.

The purpose of all logistic effort is the creation and continued support of combat forces which may effectively carry out our national strategy. The nature of modern war is such that its effective conduct requires economy in the provision and support of these combat forces.

Economy of force in any one operation results in the ability to increase the scope and tempo of other operations and thus to increase the over-all pressure that is exerted upon enemy forces.

The Nature of Logistic Coordination

Webster defines the word *coordinate* thus: "To regulate or combine in harmonious action."

The purpose of unity of command is to obtain unity of effort. *Unity of command by itself has no virtue. It is valuable only as it contributes to unity of effort in the accomplishment of the war objectives.* Similarly, logistic coordination is useful only as it contributes to harmony, to unity of effort, and to economy of forces and resources in the accomplishment of these war objectives.

Responsibility for coordination must include *authority to make decisions.* Because of the limited authority granted to certain commands in peacetime it is desirable to discuss this statement at some length.

First, it is important to realize that the official rules and regulations which in peacetime govern our military affairs sometimes represent compromises in conflicting philosophies of command. These official rules do not themselves represent fundamental principles or cause-and-effect relationships, nor do they necessarily represent the rules which will govern the wartime conduct of our armed forces. Instead they represent merely the best compromise, as of the moment, that it has been possible to achieve among a variety of differing opinions. These rules can, and will, be changed any time the authority which promulgated them decides to do so. They are not immutable.

Therefore, a distinction should be made between a discussion of the actual directives which are currently effective, and a discussion of the basic forces and principles which apply in war. In war the broad problems are: (1) to create and to give continued support to effective combat forces, and (2) to attain unity of effort and economy of forces and resources in the accomplishment of war objectives.

For various reasons, combat commanders are naturally reluctant to depend in any way on another nation or service for their own support or to surrender any measure of control of their own resources. This reluctance is responsible for a considerable difference of opinion as to what the term "logistic coordination" means. One narrow interpretation is contained in two terms "coordinating authority" and "coordination with."

To act as a "coordinating authority" is to perform a specifically defined and very strictly limited function which under our present official limitations includes power to require consultation between the parties involved, but provides no authority to compel agreement. In case agreement cannot be attained by discussion the only recourse is to refer the matter to higher authority.

Similarly, the term "coordination with" is interpreted to mean, "in consultation with." There is mutual active participation between all the parties who act in "coordination with" and while concurrence is sought, if this fails, the next higher common authority makes the decision.

While these two terms may be adequate and appropriate for certain special situations, they in no way express the meaning or requirements of "logistic coordination," if the term is to describe the authority which "command" requires over its logistic operations in war. As previously stated, the needs for economy of resources and for unity of effort have developed a broader interpretation.

It is probably impracticable to lay down specific rules for logistic coordination which will apply equally to all joint or combined commands. Therefore, the directives which govern all such commands are expressed in general terms which are specifically interpreted in each area depending upon the circumstances, the situation, and the personalities concerned. There is a hazard that some individuals, having seen how a weak compromise solution worked well in a particular area, may assume that similar solutions will work equally well in all areas and circumstances.

In all cases, however, the basic governing philosophy is that there should be centralized control, centralized planning, common doctrine, and decentralized execution. The question is: How do we actually apply this doctrine in the area of war? In other words, where is logistic coordination needed and what are the organizational and intellectual bases for its exercise?

Where Coordination is Needed

In the case of a unilateral commander the question of the authority to exercise logistic coordination does not arise, for in the United States services, both the combat force commanders and the logistic force commanders report to a natural, common superior.[2] He exercises unquestioned and direct command over both the forces and their allocated resources. However, when we consider joint or combined commands, various complicating factors must be recognized. In all commands certain human forces come into play to a greater or lesser degree depending on the circumstances. For instance—

---

[2] The fact that a commander-in-chief of a unilateral force has authority to prescribe the channels of logistic coordination does not mean that controversies are eliminated. On the contrary some naval officers firmly oppose the suggestion that a fleet commander should delegate the tasks of forward area logistic coordination to any single subordinate commander. This is the result of the contention for position among the type commanders. Each type commander strives to maintain his own administrative authority regardless of where his forces operate. The question is particularly acute in regard to operation of aircraft, destroyer, and submarine tenders.

(1) There is always the natural desire on the part of each man and leader in combat to have an ample factor of safety in his resources;

(2) Service pride and national pride are qualities which we work hard to cultivate, yet they frequently produce jealousy and suspicion;

(3) Differences in background and in training develop different concepts as to tactics and organization and prejudices as to the superiority of the methods to which one is accustomed;

(4) The nation with the greatest resources feels that its resources may be unduly exploited by its allies if it does not retain a very close control over the resources it supplies to the common effort. Furthermore, frequently there is the feeling that the over-all commander will tend to favor his own national or service interests; and

(5) Finally, the differing nature of naval, land, and air forces require that many parts of their logistic support conform to the special characteristics of the element in which they operate; and that they be tailored to fit the special vehicles, planes, ships, and weapons used.

All of the above factors combine to make combat commanders reluctant to depend on another nation or service for their logistic support. The larger the forces involved in a joint or combined operation the more difficult it is to overcome these handicaps and to achieve effective logistic coordination. Joint and combined education and training and standardization of methods and materials can do much to reduce or to moderate these factors but can never completely eliminate them, for they stem from the very pride and eagerness for competition which we work so hard to cultivate in our fighting units.

These same factors also apply to the problem of command or control of tactical forces. The age-old reluctance of services and nations to submit to a single unified command of combat forces was epitomized in the Dardanelles operations in World War I; it was only overcome, in that war, by the final reluctant acceptance in 1917 of General Foch as an over-all Allied commander in France. In World War II, after the American entrance, the principles of unified area command became established and were successfully practiced. In spite of these successes and the long history of previous command squabbles, a highly respected writer, Captain John Cresswell, Royal Navy (Retired), in his book *Generals and Admirals,* published in 1952, makes a last ditch defense of the traditional British preference for command through cooperation. The most prevalent American view is that the unified command concept is the result of the inexorable logic of war experience and that it is here to stay. This feeling is particularly strong as it applies both to over-all strategic direction and as to tactical command in the combat zone.

In the application of this concept special provision is made for the formation and command of joint forces. This provision is based on the concept that unified command is best carried out by means of centralized over-all control, the establishment of common doctrine and centralized planning, but with decentralized execution. This concept naturally leads to the further provisions that the actual tactical command of combat units of any service be exercised by an officer of that same service and that the logistic support of any unit be the responsibility of the parent service.

However, the demands of economy both from the standpoint of the national budget and from the military principle of economy of force dictate that logistic support be furnished with the least possible waste and in such a way as to develop the maximum fighting power of the combat units. Therefore, in general, the U. S. unified commanders have been given the responsibility to "coordinate" the logistics of the component forces of the command.

The foundation for logistic coordination on any level must always be the basic agreements which have been made between services and between nations. The details of these agreements will specify the limits and areas of the logistic control authorized. In general, however, the responsibility for logistic coordination normally includes responsibility for establishment of the general organization of the command, preparation of general logistic plans, review of requirements, and establishment of general logistic policies and procedures.

The *general logistic policies and procedures* include such matters as: construction policy and standards, standards of living, housing, feeding, and recreation facilities, supply levels, cross supply, cross servicing, medical and evacuation policy, maintenance and repair, control, pay and allocation of local labor, and local purchasing.

The power of *review* covers the requirements as submitted by subordinate commanders, particularly as to combat forces, supporting service forces, and certain critical or common use items such as petroleum products, ammunition and certain types of technical spare parts. This broad power of review also includes the review of servicing and transportation requirements, recommendations as to priorities and allocations, and, within limits assigned by higher authority, the administration of priorities and allocations. In addition, it is necessary for the commander to have authority to delegate, and authority to establish subordinate joint and combined commands and staff agencies to handle special problems.

One of the most important tasks of coordination is to maintain appropriate balance among the various programs, logistical and otherwise, which combine to make the forces of any command ready for combat. An example of this may be found in the problem of creating a new armored division in an allied army which is receiving U. S. military aid. Here, recruitment, basic training, housing, preparation of training areas, supply, weapons and heavy equipment, communication equipment, instructors and material for advanced training, all must be phased so that men and equipment are ready for employment at the right time. Few things are so wasteful and so disruptive to morale as men who are in enforced idleness in time of emergency.

If large combined or joint operations are contemplated, the various national and service programs that create, make ready, and replenish the combat forces must also be coordinated and brought into harmony.

This whole process depends upon an appreciation of logistic lead time, and upon a flow of information to a central supervising agency. The control and harmonization of the programs requires a continuing process of alternate speed up and slow down. While perfect timing and accord are impossible, the difference in combat readiness and combat efficiency between a haphazard program and a coordinated program can indeed be tremendous.

A very important part of logistical coordination must take place in those coastal areas and major ports where land, sea, and air forces of various nations will be demanding real estate, ship berthing and unloading facilities, transportation, labor, and construction materials.

If these areas are subject to enemy attack, (and most of them will be), it is essential to provide for the local adjudication of the conflicts that will inevitably result. The problems become too urgent to be passed to a higher common authority several hundred miles away.

The Basis and Elements of Coordination

The *intangible* bases of coordination of logistics lie in the same fundamentals which form the basis for any other exercise of command. This is stressed because some people seem to think that "miracle men" and "perfect organizations" can exercise effective authority without these fundamentals. No attempt is made to arrange them in any order of priority.

Professional *knowledge* is essential. The person charged with assisting the commander in the exercise of logistic coordination must have a knowledge of war as a whole. He must have a good knowledge of strategy, a thorough knowledge of logistics, and enough knowledge of tactics to recognize the logistical implications of tactical events and developments.

Regardless of the competence of any man, he is helpless if

he does not have access to *information*. This information is in two broad categories. The first of these is information concerning the logistical situation, logistical resources, and dispositions. But, equally important is that he have full information as to strategical and tactical plans. He cannot operate in a vacuum with someone else deciding how much he needs to know. In any major command, the accumulation, processing, and evaluation of logistical information requires time, space, equipment, and personnel plus the authority to determine what information is needed.

Under the best of circumstances it takes at least six months for a new organization to begin to exercise effective logistic coordination. This fact alone should give pause to those persons who think that you can set up one system for peace and then shift to another system in war without first establishing duplicate staffs and duplicate files.

Coupled with knowledge as part of the over-all quality of competence, comes that great intangible—*professional judgment*. This, of all characteristics, is of the utmost importance in logistic coordination. It involves wisdom in when to act and when not to act; when to control and when to delegate. In this respect it is almost impossible to overvalue the importance of exercising wise restraint in the use of power. *The fact that members of one service are sometimes reluctant to trust the professional judgment and restraint of officers of another service is the one greatest obstacle in the process of reaching agreement as to the manner in which logistic coordination is to be exercised.*

Finally, *cooperation*. This simple term includes both loyalty and good faith; it stems from character and from common understanding of common objectives. It is stimulated by the use of good judgment and restraint on the part of others and it is an indispensable element in any successful process of military command. It is only when mutual understanding, mutual confidence, and mutual respect are established that full cooperation can be achieved. The human relations problem is always present and always important.

For all of the above elements to be effective there must be adequate channels of *communication* provided for a coordinating authority. Major logistic coordination requires an enormous amount of correspondence and dispatches. If this is not recognized well in advance the whole system can bog down in war. Peacetime correspondence and radio traffic give little clue to the demands of war. The communication load can be reduced only if the coordinator delegates to the maximum degree, if he establishes clear coordinating policies and systems of cross-supply and cross-servicing, and if the commands involved have faith in the efficiency of the system under which they are operating.

An important factor in the exercise of combined and joint command is the political situation in the national capitals. This is strikingly illustrated by the Mediterranean Campaign of 1940-43 where the political antagonism and jealousy of Mussolini and Hitler had a disastrous influence on the conduct of the campaign. In our own country the psychological climate of the national capital in peace is quite different from what it is in wartime. In peace there is a continuous public struggle for power among the political parties and among politicians. Top administrative officials, all theories to the contrary notwithstanding, must keep a close eye on the political fortunes of their elected or appointed superiors. Members of the legislature are eager to uncover real or alleged wrongdoing or waste, and a free press and radio and television are avid in pursuit of both malefactors and headlines. Furthermore, an atmosphere of personal and inter-party contention and of personal aggrandizement is not conducive to developing the sense of dedicated selflessness that we might wish to see among the working level executives of government. Very great attention is paid to immediate cash economy, and the benefits of long-range military planning may not be fully appreciated.

Under these conditions, while lip service may be given to the doctrines of centralized control and decentralized execution, practically all the changes made by legislative or executive order actually result in greater centralization of authority. That is to say, more and more decisions affecting military preparations and operations are actually made in the national capital.

In war in a healthy nation these conditions change. The actions and danger of a common enemy over-shadow and tend to reduce the more selfish attributes and quarrels of men. The need for secrecy restricts the flow of information to the public and censorship reduces criticism. In most men, patriotic instincts are strengthened and unselfish dedication to the nation becomes the expected norm. The rapid development of the most effective fighting power of our combat forces rather than the effect on the budget, becomes the most important criterion by which to judge logistic effort and organization. Eventually, the impossibility of running everything from the capital becomes obvious, and a proper amount of real power is delegated to area, army, and fleet commanders.

In considering these conditions it is well to bear in mind two further important factors which affect unilateral, joint, and combined operations. First, modern war can be so devastating and can come so swiftly that we must plan on little or no warning period in which to shift from peace organization to war organization. This makes it mandatory that our lines of authority and planning organizations in peace be such that they can shift to war conditions in a matter of a few days. Second, modern logistics is so complex and its elements are so interrelated that no single officer, regardless of his energy and genius, can ever hope to exercise control until after he has been equipped with a trained staff, a vast amount of evaluated information, and an extensive communication system.

Lastly, it must be reemphasized that the objective of all logistic effort is the creation and continued effective support of the combat forces; while economy is essential to the attainment of that objective, economy, in itself, is not the objective. If the wartime effectiveness of our combat forces is jeopardized by false economy, disaster may ensue. *Therefore, all measures affecting the control and coordination of logistics must be judged by their effect on sustained combat effectiveness under war conditions rather than by the sole criterion of peacetime economy.* An economy of a million dollars a year may be swept away in the first hour of a war and may cost a billion dollars in the first year of the war, not to mention its possible disastrous effects on the ultimate outcome of the war.

The evaluation of logistic effectiveness is one that requires the finest kind of mature and fully informed professional judgment. It is not an area where amateurs and the use of superficial statistics can contribute to our national security. This careful evaluation is particularly important in connection with those organizations and procedures which were established in response to the clear lessons of previous war experience.

Exercise of Command Control

Certain other important factors will enter the picture. In military affairs the factors of personality must always be taken into account. No amount of theorizing and no legal directives will ever alter this requirement. All great military leaders must of necessity be of strong character and must have confidence in their own ability and judgment. This fact, coupled with the basic principle that commanders must have freedom of action to use their own initiative, particularly in face of the enemy, makes it impossible to lay down rigid lines over which a commander may not step. The manner in which General MacArthur stretched his authority in World War II is one illustration of this. The disaster which overcame the German armies in Russia when Hitler interfered in the tactical decisions of his field commanders is an example of the harm which may come from refusing to grant freedom to field commanders. So also, in the area of logistics we can expect wide variation in the interpretation of directives by reason of the differing personalities of commanders.

With the great emphasis on electronics, guided missiles, airplane speed and lift capabilities, and atomic energy, certain requirements for success in future wars are obvious. The combat forces themselves must be flexible, and they must be mobile. If they are to retain their firepower, flexibility, and mobility in the face of modern attack, their logistic support itself must be flexible and mobile. These qualities must come not only from an improved system of supply and transportation, but also from cutting the logistic requirements of the combat forces to the essential bone and muscle.

Tactical flexibility is dependent almost wholly on the flexibility of the logistic support system. With the increased use of joint task forces and the greater need for cooperation and mutual support among unilateral task forces, there is a greater need than ever before for flexibility in tactical plans. *This means that the basic design and the control of the area logistic system must be in the hands of the commander who will design, shift, and control the task forces in accordance with the strategic and tactical needs of the situation.* Thus the element of control and coordination of logistic effort becomes a vital factor in the attainment of combat effectiveness.

All military students are familiar with the manner in which a tactical commander may divide his forces, assigning certain forces to his subordinate commanders for their complete disposition, but retaining other forces under his own command or control as tactical or strategical reserves. In this, the wise commander varies the nature and proportions of his disposition in accordance with his capabilities and the situation he faces rather than by arbitrary rule.[3]

In logistical matters the same general principles apply. However, because the lessons of our logistic experience have not been fully appreciated, there has been a tendency to swing toward the extremes of either overcentralization or complete decentralization. This point was well illustrated in the Pacific in World War II, where in the initial stages of advanced base development there was almost a complete decentralization of construction effort. When the inefficiency of this was exposed, the policy in the Central Pacific swung to such complete centralization of construction command that other wasteful evils were caused. Actually, the most efficient operations were those in

---

[3] This is an extension of the principles of priorities and allocations discussed in chapter 10.

which there was a combination of a major centralized force, with certain small decentralized construction forces operating under other commands. Similarly, the wise commander will allocate his logistic resources in accordance with his capabilities and his combat situation. Here, again, arbitrary preconceived decisions may be fatally defective or may result in gross waste.

In considering how logistical reserves can best be established and managed, it is well to note that in many instances all that is necessary is to grant allocating authority and movement control to the coordinating authority. It is not always necessary for that authority to take actual physical possession. The fear that actual physical possession may be insisted on, and that the original owner or provider of the resources may be deprived of them at the time of his greatest need, is an important factor in the reluctance to yield any real authority.

This dilemma emphasizes the fact that good faith and mutual confidence in the professional competence and professional judgment of associated commanders are vital, indispensable factors in joint or combined commands.

The Special Problems of Combined Command

Combined command includes all the problems of joint command and in addition the special problems that are involved in an alliance. These are so great that some officers feel that an alliance of more than two nations is impossible of effective effort under one military command.

While the exercise of combined command requires certain compromises of strict military logic in the strategic and tactical field, most of the headaches stem from logistical causes. If there is ever to be an effective military alliance of a multi-national nature, these logistical problems must be recognized and brought out into the open where patient good-will can be brought to bear upon them.

International logistic coordination must always involve some invasion of the economic rights, independence, and sovereignty of each nation in the alliance. No amount of semantic acrobatics can change this basic fact of modern war. It is sheer delusion to think that an effective alliance can be built on any basis other than that of mutual accommodation, mutual sacrifice, and mutual confidence. The only real question to be posed can be stated simply: "Is the enemy threat to one's economic, military, and political position sufficient to justify the sacrifices which a true alliance demands?" If the answer is "yes," then these compromises of complete sovereignty should be made with a full knowledge of their nature, their magnitude, and their effect on the capacity of the alliance to fight.

The first element which enters into this calculation is to determine the proportion of a nation's economic resources which can be devoted to the raising and maintaining of combat and service forces. Next, the proportion in which this effort should be divided between combat and service forces and the requirements for facilities and installations to support these forces should be determined. Then it is necessary to determine the facilities and installations necessary to support the allied forces which may be brought into that country in peace or in war.

These all boil down to what is now known as the "force commitments" and the "infra-structure programs." These commitments and programs are so large that they have an important effect on the economy and internal political situation of each country involved and, therefore, they must be decided at the highest political level. However, these same programs are the basis of the allied commander's ability to fight; and they constitute the foundation of all his strategic and tactical plans. If the allied commander is to plan and command effectively, he must have a major voice in the development and supervision of these logistical programs in time of peace. Furthermore, in time of war his authority should be greatly extended.

It is in the nature and degree of this wartime power that we find the major differences of current opinion. Even if nations agree readily to the required political and economic concessions demanded by military logic, there still remains the problem of spelling out the relations which should be established between the allied military and the national civilian authorities. In this area there are certain command and tactical problems to be solved such as the coordination of local defense, the control of subversion and sabotage, and the coordination of land, sea, and air command relations in matters concerning communication zones, base areas, and sea and coastal areas. In addition there are the previously mentioned problems of control of railroads, airlines, highways, and the operation of coastal shipping. There are also the problems of civil defense and the control, care, and evacuation of refugees. The enemy capabilities for airborne operations and for using atomic and guided weapons vastly increase the difficulty and importance of these logistical problems.

These problems all require coordination and in each case there must be a blend of civil and military authority. In each case the international military authority has a decided interest. All these problems involve the economy and sovereignty of the country concerned. In all cases special organizations must be formed to determine policy and to lay down the local ground rules for their management in war.

This all sums up to "international logistic coordination," a process in which the allied area commanders and their staffs must play a vital role.

Summary of Problem of Coordination

What are these tasks which together comprise the whole of logistic coordination? They were mentioned earlier but are here recapitulated to aid in further appraisal of the problem—

(1) To establish the general organization;

(2) To prepare general plans in the twin fields of logistics and strategy;

(3) To establish general logistic policies and procedures; including policies and procedures for cross-servicing and cross-supply;

(4) To review requirements for forces, both service and combat; for critical and special materials; and for stockpiling, for advanced bases, and for transportation—land, sea, and air;

(5) To make recommendations as to priorities and allocations in these same fields, and within limits assigned by higher authority, to administer priorities and allocations;

(6) To form subordinate commands to which the operation and administration of central control or co-ordinating functions may be delegated;

(7) To provide a centralized source of up-to-date logistic information and a staff adequate to evaluate and use this information; and

(8) To provide an informed staff which can represent the commander on the extensive inter-service and international military-civilian committees which are so important in a major war.

If we are to employ our combat forces most effectively, and if we are to make the best use of our invariably limited logistic resources, the commander who has over-all combat responsibility must have commensurate responsibility and authority for the performance of the foregoing essential logistic tasks. *He has the reciprocal responsibility to utilize this authority with good judgment and restraint.*

Each of these logistic tasks should be considered on its own merits and a series of questions asked about each one—

(1) Is the task pertinent to the problem at hand?

(2) Is the task vital, important, or merely desirable?

(3) Will the over-all logistic support of combat forces be made more effective if this task is done by central direction, or will it be done better by leaving it to individual component, or type, or task force commanders to handle for themselves?

(4) In each particular case do you wish to give power to act or merely grant power to recommend? (This can be a fine but important distinction in the international area.)

(5) Should the power to recommend or to act in any particular area be extended or restricted in the event of war? If so, how?

In all of the foregoing, certain basic considerations and factors need emphasis. For example, in peacetime the details of area logistic systems are controlled by the budget officers of the three Services in Washington who exercise a close, detailed supervision which is impracticable in war. Peacetime maneuvers don't really test logistic systems. War transforms this situation. Time, skilled manpower, and the availability of industrial facilities, raw materials, and transportation become the governing factors, with time being the most pressing. The fact that peacetime maneuvers have not really tested our logistic system becomes immediately apparent. The unpredictability of enemy action makes flexibility a paramount consideration.

The ability to improvise of course is a priceless requirement, but improvisation on a large scale is more indicative of poor planning and lack of forethought than it is of inventive genius. Large-scale improvisation is always very expensive.

And finally, it should be kept in mind that the development of an effective logistic system makes exceptional demands upon the staff of every major commander.

It is obvious that General Rommel as an active tactical commander could never have had the staff to perform all the functions listed as essential to proper logistic operations in a theater. It is equally obvious that neither General Kesselring nor the Italian Commando Supremo ever even understood the nature of the problems or the functions.

In this connection it is well to note that in the United States these problems were recognized only belatedly. For instance, it was not until 1943 and 1944 that the logistic division of the staff of Admiral Nimitz, Commander in Chief Pacific Ocean Areas, was developed. From this group a sound doctrine and excellent techniques of integrated planning grew. However, before such coordination was achieved many mistakes were made and strong differences had to be reconciled.

The Army historians commenting on the early days of the war said:

> The clarification of supply and administrative responsibilities within the Army's own organization was but one facet of the problem of logistical organizations in the Pacific. In this area of joint operations, supply of Army forces was intertwined with the supply of Navy forces. Both services had to recognize the necessity for some measure of logistical coordination.
>
> Progress toward a more integrated system of joint logistics was slow, halting, and the subject of acrimonious dispute between the two services.[4]

Clearly, unity of combat effort requires harmony and logistic coordination; and the latter rests upon the authority of the commander and its intelligent use.

---

[4] Richard M. Leighton and Robert W. Coakley, *Global Logistics and Strategy,* Office of the Chief of Military History, Department of the Army, Washington, D.C., 1955, pp. 187-188.

Chapter 17

Logistics and Staff Organization

*To a very significant degree the art of command con-
sists of the art of using people to the best of their
abilities and in the right field.*[1]
—ADMIRAL R. L. CONOLLY, USN, RET.

The organization of the staff of a commander who has
major logistical responsibilities presents problems that are far
beyond the scope of the usual discussions of staffs.

Anticipation of Problems

This is especially true in naval education and training where
most of the emphasis has been placed on the staff organization
of the sea-going tactical commands. The system whereby the
forces afloat are commanded by fleet, type, and task force
commanders is flexible and permits the combat task force
commanders to concentrate on the *tactical* aspects of their
duties with a minimum of preoccupation with matters of logistics and administration. Therefore, in peacetime the significance
of many elements of wartime logistics and administration are
not apparent; and consequently, officers can be lulled into a
false sense of security insofar as these matters are concerned.
In particular the question of the nature and amount of logistic
coordination required by war is seldom recognized either in
the Army, the Air Force, or the Navy.

As Ruppenthal says of the situation before the Normandy
Invasion:

> Fundamentally the issue thruout was clear: Who was
> to be responsible for the over-all coordination of logistic
> support both in planning and actual operations?[2]

If war comes unexpectedly the staff problem in all its aspects

---

[1] Admiral R. L. Conolly, USN, Retired, February 1951.
[2] Ruppenthal, R. G., *Logistical Support of the Armies,* European Theater
of Operations, Volume I, Office of the Chief of Military History, Department of the Army, p. 201.

blows up like a huge balloon. Tactical matters must receive immediate and competent staff consideration twenty-four hours a day, seven days a week. The communication channels become clogged and intelligence reports and the flow of general information, both logistical and administrative, increase twenty to one-hundred-fold in a matter of a few days. The assimilation, evaluation, and executive disposition of this mass of material is possible only in commands in which the staffs have been organized and manned on a basis of a realistic appraisal of the problem of major wartime command.

Experience has shown that in the case of a newly established commander of a major area it may take from six to eighteen months to assemble the staff, organize the information, and begin to exercise effective control of logistical matters. This presupposes no unusual delay in acquiring a suitable headquarters site and in obtaining the assignment of competent officers. If the problem has been carefully thought out in advance and if conditions are particularly favorable, this period may be shortened somewhat. Under unfavorable conditions it could even happen that a war can be lost before the major staffs can begin to function effectively. While no one can anticipate all the complications that may develop in future staffs, a discussion of some of the fundamentals of the logistic aspects of staff organization may aid in a more effective control in the future.

Growth and Conflict

One of the most striking illustrations of the logistic snowball is found in the expansion of the logistic staffs in wartime. This applies both to the logistic divisions of area and fleet commanders and to the staffs of logistical commanders. In many instances these staffs have become so large that they are difficult to manage. With great increase in size of staffs, paper work grows and slows down and signal communications become more and more overburdened.

The psychological factors are interesting. As the staffs grow, charges of "empire building" are bandied about with enthusiasm. There is no lack of energy in the senior staff officers of the American armed forces, and much of this energy sometimes seems to be expended in justifying the need for the further expansion of the authority and personnel of each staff division or section. (When the junior commanding officers of the tactical units meet for relaxation in a rear area this seems to be the burden of their recreational conversation. "The staffs are too big." "They all take in each other's washing!" "I never can possibly read all the papers the staffs send to me!") Complaints of this sort are common and in some instances are justified. In spite of these complaints most officers recognize the need for large staffs in wartime. However, they may not understand the reasons why the *over-expansion* takes place.

The entire history of the U.S. Army participation in World War II in Northern Europe was marked by the struggle between the Service of Supply (SOS) and other commands for control of logistical planning and operations. At various times the other participants were: European Theater of Operations U.S. Army (ETOUSA), Supreme Headquarters Allied Expeditionary Force (SHAEF), First U.S. Army (FUSA), and First U.S. Army Group (FUSAG). From time to time the U.S. Army Air Force was involved in the controversies. This struggle for power caused confusion and was accentuated by confusion. It involved both the commanders and their staffs.

Ruppenthal comments extensively on the situation, pointing out how controversies as to authority between staffs and command echelons were long-drawn-out and caused waste and confusion. He speaks of how ". . . the hodgepodge of effort and confusion continued . . . If this setup is difficult to understand . . . it was not always completely understood by the people involved in it. . . ."[3]

---

[3] Ruppenthal, *op cit*, pp. 159, 168, 191, 192, 193, 209.

The problem of developing an efficient logistical organization with workable delineation of authority between the various staffs and command echelons continued throughout 1943. The initial attempt by the SOS to take over theaterwide supply and administrative functions had resulted in an unsatisfactory compromise with ETOUSA, providing for a division of responsibilities between the two headquarters, creating over-lapping agencies, and permitting

There were two fundamental causes for this confusion. In the first place, officers must have ambition and a desire for responsibility if they are to be effective in war. Therefore, struggles for military power are inevitable and should not be condemned per se. However, the struggles must be watched carefully by senior authorities in order that they not interfere with the conduct of war.

---

considerable wasted effort and confusion.

The crux of the problem from the start was the position of the special staff and the split of the services between London and Cheltenham. The first attempted clarification of the relationship of the two staffs, shortly after General Eisenhower's assumption of command, was admittedly a makeshift arrangement and not intended as permanent. It solved nothing in the fundamental conflict for the simple reason that it did not give the SOS control of all theater supply and administration. Partly because of this unsatisfactory definition of relationships and powers, and partly because the SOS was split between Cheltenham and London, the hodgepodge of agencies, duplication of effort, and confusion continued.

But while the need for reorganization was widely recognized, there was little agreement as to what the changes should be, probably because any fundamental alterations inevitably involved surrender of authority by one headquarters or another.

Colonel Landon asserted that it was necessary that the SOS continue to issue instructions in its own name to the entire theater if it was not to be reduced to the position of a minor staff section of a huge G4 office. He admitted the necessity of avoiding delicate matters which other commands might consider an infringement of their rights, but it would be intolerable to have the service chiefs, for example, in their theater capacity pass on recommendations from the office of their own superior, the Commanding General, SOS. Colonel Landon therefore recommended that the SOS continue to issue instructions within its province to the entire theater in the name of the Commanding General, SOS. This procedure was adopted, but it resulted only in an increase in the number of matters which had to be submitted to the theater staff for review, and therefore increased the duplication of effort in the two headquarters.

Relation of Army and Army Group (FUSA and FUSAG) vis-a-vis ETOUSA and SOS was to be a matter of considerable confusion and produced many conflicts over responsibility and authority in both planning and execution of the continental operation.

The struggle over control of supply and administration at theater level had been largely duplicated within the Air Forces . . . (1943).

As in the theater command, therefore, the desire to concentrate all administration and supply services in one command and the adaptation to continental operational conditions had an inevitable influence on the organization and control of the U.S. Air Forces.

If this setup is difficult to understand some consolation may perhaps be derived from the knowledge that it was not always completely understood by the people involved in it and that in practice it often became somewhat difficult to operate.

In the second place, the magnitude and nature of the logistical tasks were not fully appreciated by most of the senior planners who outlined the command organizations and who set up the staffs of the various commands. This is clearly indicated by the fact that in the early stages of planning the ratio of service troops to combat troops was absurdly low. The commander of the SOS, Lieutenant General J. C. H. Lee, on the other hand, did have an excellent grasp of the task confronting him and proceeded to organize in such a way as to make clear control possible.

By reason of these inadequate concepts the delineations of command and logistical responsibilities were foggy. As a result, when the realities of the tasks became known, all staffs tried to handle them by expansion and by seeking responsibility. Staffs themselves snowballed, confusion reduced the efficiency of planning, over-all logistic support snowballed, and combat effectiveness was reduced.

As an illustration of the size of staffs employed to handle logistics it is well to note that the logistic division of the general staff of the Supreme Commander, Allied Expeditionary Force on 12 July 1944 had an authorized strength of 178 officers and 261 enlisted men.[4] This did not include the special staff.

AUTHORIZED STRENGTH OF HEADQUARTERS SHAEF

DATES	TOTAL	TOTAL U.S.	TOTAL BRITISH	OFFICERS U.S.	OFFICERS BRITISH	WARRANT U.S.	WARRANT BRITISH	ENLISTED U.S.	ENLISTED BRITISH
July 1944:									
Total	4914	3476	1438	764	421	52	49	2660	968
G4*	439	266	173	97	64	7	10	162	99
H. Q. Command ..	1574	1574	....	114	....	8	....	1452	....
February 1945:									
Total	16312	9992	6320	1581	1229	67	88	8344	5003
G4*	500	297	203	106	76	9	12	182	115
H. Q. Command ..	4635	4635	....	215	....	8	....	4412	....

* G4 does not include Special Staff.
Since the numbers of many staff divisions are omitted on this abbreviated chart, the figures do not equal the totals shown.

Figure 22. Growth in Authorized Strength of a Headquarters

[4] Forrest C. Pogue, *The Supreme Command,* United States Army in World War II, the European Theater of Operations, Office of the Chief of Military

With the Navy in the Pacific, there is no question but what a better analysis of the staff problem would have resulted in greater effectiveness with reduced personnel.

Admiral Nimitz formed his joint staff on 6 September 1943, nearly two years after the outbreak of war and thirteen months after the invasion of Guadalcanal. Up to this time there was no section nor even an officer on his staff who was charged with supervision of the over-all logistical and supply situation.[5] By July 1945, however, the logistic division of CINCPOA's staff was composed of 145 officers of whom 9 were flag officers. At the same time the details of the area logistic planning and operations were handled by the staffs of the type commanders. Commander Service Force was the largest of these with a staff of about 1100 officers. Commander Service Squadron Ten had the largest staff afloat in the Pacific.[6]

The problem posed is not that of getting enough bodies to fill these billets, but of getting officers who can exercise both imagination and sound judgment in the planning and conduct of major operations. This is quite a problem. Men with these qualities are scarce and are urgently needed in the combat forces as well as in logistical staffs. Moreover, the snowball effect of mediocre logistic planning is very expensive to the combat forces' effectiveness.

The Design of Staff

An appraisal of the logistic aspects of any staff organization depends on an understanding both of the fundamental tasks of the command and of the basic factors in the design and organization of a staff.

In an area, a fleet, or an army, the assignment of tasks and

History, Department of the Army, Washington, D.C., 1954, Table 4—Authorized strength of Supreme Headquarters Allied Expeditionary Force, 12 July 1944, p. 533, 534.

[5] Charles H. Owens, Jr., *The Logistical Support of the Army in the Central Pacific: 1941-1944,* A dissertation submitted to the Faculty of the Graduate School of Georgetown University in partial fulfillment of the requirements for the degree of Doctor of Philosophy, Washington, D. C., June 1954, p. 114.

[6] RADM. Worrall Reed Carter, USN, Ret'd, *Beans, Bullets, and Black Oil,* Washington, D. C., 1953, p. 273.

the command relationships can be and frequently are changed quickly by a brief directive from proper authority. This is particularly true when using the task force system which seems to be the simplest and most flexible general system of command. When the individuals concerned are commanding similar types of tactical forces within a fleet or an area, these shifts of responsibility are relatively simple. All individuals probably are up to date on the background situation, the current intelligence and the basic operational directives and information.

However, when a major shift in logistical responsibility takes place, and particularly where a commander who has been primarily concerned with tactical matters is given logistical duties, the situation is quite different. As shown earlier, major logistical staff action is dependent upon the acquisition and evaluation of vast amounts of information. If logistical command responsibilities are to be shifted, this information must either be duplicated or shifted from one command to another. Either process is lengthy. Unless the cognizant personnel are transferred *with the information,* months of confusion and uncertainty will ensue. The information factor alone makes it important that the problem be very carefully analyzed prior to final decision as to the assignment of command responsibilities and the organization of the associated staffs.

As was previously stated, the performance of basic tasks will require certain plans, certain information, and certain facilities regardless of the organizational structure. If one branch or level of command does not carry out these tasks, another branch or level of command must. The point is that while a commander can delegate he cannot divest himself of his responsibility.

It is neither wise nor profitable to attempt to establish a command and staff organization without providing for some overlap of functions and responsibilities. Inadvertent duplication is harmful but intentional overlap is essential, for organization is like a brick wall—the overlap of the bricks lends strength. But like the brick wall, the overlap should be part of the design. The only way to distinguish between good overlap and wasteful duplication is to analyze the general responsibilities, the specific tasks, and the information situation of each command.

Because of the pressure of officer personnel ceilings and a fear of "empire building," staff billet structure is usually strictly controlled by each military service. This tends to make it difficult to make major changes in the structure of a staff once it is established; and this control increases the tendency on the part of various commands to "play it safe" and to ask for the maximum number of officers which can be obtained.

The tendency in favor of too-large staffs again emphasizes the importance of analysis on the basis of wartime responsibilities and tasks throughout each command. The development of the necessary intuitive understanding between the commander and his staff becomes more difficult as staffs expand. As staffs grow, informal contacts become difficult. A natural tendency toward mediocrity in the quality of work sets in.

In the past it has been customary to establish the staff of a new command on a conventional basis and then to expand the staff as the demands of the situation develop. In peacetime many adjustments are possible to permit all of the tasks of the commander to be accomplished reasonably well without varying from established patterns in too drastic a manner. However, there is a tendency to forget that peacetime operations are not a test of the logistic situation nor of the adequacy of the logistic staffs. If in peacetime we are to develop staff structures adequate for war, it is necessary to take into account the basic principles which affect the design of staffs in general.[7]

The first of these principles is that staff organization is not a fixed and predetermined entity. Rather, the organization should be tailored; it should be derived from (and it depends upon) a group of factors: The tasks of the commander; the forces assigned and the manner in which they are organized; the command relations with superior and coordinate commands;

---

[7] One of the greatest problems to be overcome by the U.S. Naval Forces Far East on the outbreak of the Korean War was to provide adequate competent staffs to handle the explosion of tactical, logistical, and communication activity. No one can estimate what would have resulted had the enemy attacked our bases in Japan or our ships at sea.

and geographical and communication considerations, particularly in relation to the location of forces and headquarters and the ease and reliability of communications.

Derived From War Tasks

The second principle is that the staff should be basically designed for its war functions. In order for it to meet purely peacetime needs and limitations, it may be appropriately modified, but only within the framework and concept of its wartime operations. If the staff should have to be reorganized at the outbreak of war, the administrative effort of this reorganization would distract the commander, his chief of staff, and division chiefs from their primary tasks at the very time when concentration on the primary tasks is most important. This bad effect would, of course, be compounded by the very inadequacy which made redesign of the staff necessary.

It is an illusion that peacetime economy precludes designing the staff for war. Peacetime economy merely means that the staff cannot be kept fully manned for war. Furthermore, peacetime economy should mean a greater emphasis on the careful study of staff design rather than the casual acceptance of conventional procedures.

General Types of Staff Organization

Since no standard staff organizations are prescribed, there is a wide variation in the manner in which various commanders choose to organize their staffs. From the logistic point of view two general types of organization can be recognized.

The service force of a fleet is an illustration of the first type. Here the *principal function* of the commander is logistics. In his force the individual major functions such as fleet personnel, supply, maintenance and repair, medical, base development, plans, and operations are usually each established as a separate staff division. Fuel, electronics, and ammunition usually require special arrangements which vary according to circumstances. Since the whole task of the commander is a logistic task, the whole staff is a logistic staff. Therefore, the chief of staff has the fleet logistic situation as his major concern. He, assisted by the plans officer, coordinates the entire logistic task of the command. This coordination is based on the strategic and the broad logistic guidance provided by the fleet or area commander. Under these circumstances there may be no need for a separate logistic division on the service force staff.

A second type of organization is found in commands where logistics is only one of several major responsibilities of the commander. Area and fleet commands illustrate this type. In these it is important to group the major logistic functions under a single logistic officer who is the principal staff advisor to the commander in logistic matters. During World War II this was done with notable success by Admiral Nimitz as Commander-in-Chief, Pacific Ocean Area. However, this sound practice has not always been followed in our post-war organizations. Instead, in peacetime, there has been a tendency to diffuse the logistic function throughout the staff. In an area or fleet staff, the chief of staff has many urgent concerns other than logistics. Therefore, he cannot act as an effective logistic coordinator. If no single officer is given specific responsibility and authority for logistic planning and coordination within the staff, many loose ends or "holidays" develop. Under such conditions, it is probable that both the strategic-tactical and the logistic plans will be defective.

The need for centralizing logistic staff work in a single staff division does not imply that type and force commanders with major logistic responsibilities do not also act as advisors to the area or fleet commander. *There are two legitimate sources and channels of advice; one the commander's staff, the other the chain of command. Both are necessary.*

Logistic staff organization is complicated by the very human and understandable desire of each technical bureau to have its staff representative report directly to the commander, without dealing through a "logistic officer" or through the commander of a logistic force. This brings up the question as to the desirability of a staff officer wearing two hats. Two systems are in use, one where a staff officer has his primary duty in one staff division and a collateral duty in another staff division. This frequently results in the collateral duty being done in an unsatisfactory manner. If this method must be used, allowance or compensation for unsatisfactory performance of the job must be made.

The other method is one in which the commander of a subordinate unit acts as a principal staff officer on the staff of his own commander. The Army uses this system in some of its general staff and special staff organizations. It is sometimes used by the Navy where the commander of the service force acts as a principal logistic advisor to the commander of the whole fleet. A modification of this occurs when the supply officer, the medical officer and the ship maintenance officer of the service force act in a similar capacity on the staff of the fleet commander. While this system works reasonably well, it may develop personal friction and lost motion.

How War Expands Staff Work

Many of the above variations and deficiencies in staff organization spring from the laudable desire to operate with a minimum staff. Except for war planning, area and fleet staffs in peacetime have relatively little to do and what they do is diffused and scattered among several major staff divisions such as plans or operations or communications. These divisions can probably handle certain current logistic matters with no undue effort *and with no apparent harm*. However, war instantly transforms this situation. The above divisions become swamped with their own primary duties and have no time for anything else. In fact, they urgently require additional personnel to handle their extra load.

When war breaks out, fleet and area logistic problems literally explode to huge size and great urgency. However, if the logistic responsibility has been diffused rather than concentrated, the logistic division will not be prepared to handle the emergency. Therefore, confusion, serious trouble, and major waste ensue. These are the minimum results of the hasty improvisation which inevitably occurs. At the worst, a major military disaster can take place.

The mission of the commander and the type of operations which his command must be prepared to undertake provide a basis for the analysis of the staff problems and organizations within the command. In addition, the level and nature of the commands being studied, the nature of the command functions to be performed and the logistical category in which the command functions are to be performed are pertinent. When these factors have been related to the operational tasks and when it has been determined which command will perform what function in each category, the basis is laid for both the size and the organization of each logistical staff or staff section.

Inventory of Tasks

That this is not a simple process is indicated by the following inventory of command, functions, and categories which may be involved. This inventory should be expanded or contracted to the degree of detail necessary for the analysis of any particular command.

COMMAND ECHELONS (NAVY):
>   Commander in Chief of an Area.
>   Commander in Chief of a Fleet or other Component Commanders.
>   Commander of a Sea Frontier or Sub-Area.
>   Type Commanders.
>   Task Fleet Commanders.
>   Task Force Commanders.
>   Other Unit Commanders.
>   Note: Examples from corresponding Army and Air Force command echelons could be listed as appropriate.

THE COMMAND FUNCTIONS:
>   To organize:
>   Own commands and staffs.
>   Review subordinate commands and staffs.

>   To plan:
>   Prepare future plans.
>   Prepare current plans.
>   Coordinate plans of other commands.
>   Review plans.

To establish policy:
    General logistical policies.
    Cross-service and cross-supply policy.
    Levels of supply.
    Standards of living.

To execute plans:
    Initiate requirements.
    Consolidate requirements.
    Review and screen requirements.
    Local purchase and services contracts.
    Establish priorities and allocations.
    Administer priorities and allocations.
    Operate logistical services and establishments.

To supervise and to inspect:
    Collection, evaluation, and dissemination of information.
    Analysis of operations, equipments, and techniques.
    Conduct maneuvers and exercises, and develop training
        policy.
    Conduct necessary inspections.

To provide representation on:
    International committees and agencies.
    Interservice committees and agencies.
    Civilian controlled agencies.

THE LOGISTICAL CATEGORIES:

Supply:
    General
    Electronic
    Aviation
    Ship technical
    Ordnance
    Food
    Other special
    Messes, commissary, and exchange

Maintenance and repair:
    General
    Engineering
    Ordnance
    Electronic
    Ship repair by types
    Ship salvage
    Damage control
    Fire fighting and prevention

Transportation: (Including control, operation, and equipment):
    Land:
      Rail
      Highway
      Pipeline
    Sea:
      Intra-area and inter-area
    Air:
      Intra-area and inter-area

Port operation:
    Cargo facilities
    Stevedoring and lighterage
    Transit depots

Movement control:
    Personnel
    Cargo

Budget and fiscal

Petroleum:
    Storage and transportation by types

Medical:
    Hospitals
    Equipment
    Sanitation and preventive
    Epidemiological
    Nuclear, chemical, biological
    Evacuation

Ammunition:
    Aviation
    Land
    Naval
    Small arms
    Guided missiles
    A. S. W.
    Special weapons
    Depots

Construction: (Base development—infrastructure)
    Air fields
    Tank farms
    Pipelines
    Roads
    Utilities
      Water

    Power
    Telephone
  Depots
  Ports and harbors
  Shipyards and dry docks
  Communication facilities
  Construction equipment
  Nuclear, biological, chemical defense
  Acquisition of real estate
Personnel:
  Forecasts
  Housing
  Transportation

While the following functions are usually handled by the Administration division of the staff rather than by the logistic division, nevertheless, they all have a major effect upon logistic planning and all are wholly dependent on good logistic planning for efficient operation:

  Mail
  Legal matters
  Recreation and welfare
  Military government
  Refugees
  Prisoners of war.

In a somewhat similar manner both signal communications and intelligence make heavy logistical demands. Unless this is recognized and allowed for in the development of staff organization and instructions, it is quite likely that serious deficiencies will develop at critical times.

Problems of Headquarters

The question of the logistical support of a major headquarters presents some interesting problems of staff organization. The Army has had well-developed headquarters organizations for years. Until the later part of World War II the Navy had no regularly established shore headquarters organizations. Flagships had always been designed to handle sea-going commands and a small additional staff had been adequate to handle the situation afloat.

Naval logistic planning on major staffs has a tendency to

fall into a quiet routine in peacetime. Then problems of shore headquarters planning and operation may become the major task of the logistic division. In fact many naval officers on large staffs have taken this situation for granted.

Planning for a new major headquarters is a proper function of the logistic division of the staff just as is the planning for any other major logistic task. However, headquarters administration or operation is not a proper function for a logistic division, but properly is a function of a separate organization. The logistic division with specially qualified officers can properly act in a supervisory staff capacity. However, if the logistic division becomes engaged in the day-to-day operations of a major headquarters it will do so only at the expense of its major function.

Logistic Analysis

While the analysis of tactics and weapons is usually undertaken in an orderly manner by major commands and staffs, the importance of analysis and assessment of current logistical practice and equipments is not always fully recognized. The chapter on information and programming indicated one approach to the broad problem of information and showed its relation to readiness. How much logistical analysis should be done by a readiness division or a programming division and how much should be done by the logistical division is a matter for determination by the specific commander concerned. The point is that logistical analysis is an important staff function which requires specific and skilled treatment. Those charged with it should be prepared to travel extensively and to work with considerable informality in order to obtain a complete picture of the situation within the command. The performance of this function is essential if the technical bureaus and technical services are to be given adequate guidance as to the service needs and problems.

Inevitable Adjustments

This initial anaylsis of logistic staff organization on this basis gives only the first approximation. The next steps of compromise and refinement on the basis of sound professional judgment must follow.

Invariably many compromises will be required; inevitably it will be necessary to combine billets and functions in order to achieve economy and efficiency in the use of personnel and staff equipments and facilities. But, only when the war problem is analyzed and the peacetime staff established on the wartime structure, can economy be achieved without sacrificing combat effectiveness in war.

To some subordinate commands there will be delegated certain special logistic planning or the actual operation of specific functions. In such cases the staff of the subordinate command will be increased to the degree necessary to handle these functions and the staff of the delegating authority may then be appropriately decreased. However, since the delegating authority always retains responsibility and the power of review, enough staff in that particular category should be retained for supervisory purposes in any event. Just what will constitute "enough" depends on the category and the situation.

A final check of the staff organization and plans of a major commander is necessary to determine that each normal command or operational function for each logistical category is allocated to a specific command or commands for accomplishment. Within each command to which such function is allocated, there should be a specific staff section charged with its cognizance. Furthermore, it is regrettably necessary that there be a positive check to insure that the requisite staff action and planning is actually being accomplished.

Need for Analysis of Staff

The problem is big. It is important. To some it may seem bewilderingly complex. However, its apparent complexity is due to the nature of war and the nature of the problem of providing the tangible means for the creation and support of combat forces.

If such an apparently complex problem is approached in an orderly manner, it can be broken down into a large number of individual problems each of which is relatively simple when the advice of experienced specialists is sought. Yet, if the commander fails to recognize that all these problems are related and that their correlation is the special task of command, the technical specialist may exercise an unwarranted degree of control simply through the abdication of command. There are two major evils to avoid: one is to ignore the advice of the technical specialist, the other is to turn the whole problem over to the technical specialists.

The thorough analysis of the staff of a major commander must relate his staff to the manner in which he has retained and delegated logistical tasks and to the staffs of the commanders to whom he has delegated these tasks. The nature and flow time of the decisions and paperwork incident to these tasks must then be considered.

Such analysis of the logistical staff problem of a major command may require the concentrated attention of several experienced officers for some weeks, but once it is done it furnishes a permanent background for future adjustments. Furthermore, it brings the fundamentals of the command problem to light most effectively. Nothing wastes more time than the refusal to make a thorough analysis in the early stages of this type of command problem.

However, to be fully effective an analysis of this nature should extend throughout the whole command. As previously pointed out, "any military organization can be analyzed only by placing oneself in the position of the subordinates and by looking at the problems of coordination with one's equal echelon associates and one's seniors in specific hypothetical cases."

The analysis not only furnishes the basis for establishing staff billets but also it provides the essential outline of the staff instructions. Furthermore, it automatically develops many of the elements of the area basic logistical plan.

Many of the foregoing statements made as to relationships and principles may appear to some people to be so simple and obvious that they do not merit serious discussion. However, in the ten years following the end of World War II there were many costly examples of the disregard of these very simple matters. Also what may be obvious to an experienced staff officer may not so appear to the inexperienced one.

The will of command is determined by the interaction of the commander's concepts with the situation. The staff is the instrument for the detailed development of this interaction and the transmission of its results.

If staffs are merely modeled blindly on previous forms they will not become effective instruments of command in situations that are new. But if the missions and tasks of command are reviewed and modified to meet changing concepts and conditions of war, and if the organization of the staffs are based on an analysis of these tasks and missions, the spirit and effectiveness of the command and its staff are maintained regardless of changes that may take place in war. This does not necessarily imply constant change. It does demand constant scrutiny, frequent analysis, and the willingness to change when conditions warrant change.

The most important factor in logistic staff organization is the identification of the tasks of coordination and planning. These tasks stem from the commander's mission. They must be done if logistic support is to be efficient and fully effective. An understanding of the relationships of these logistic tasks to the strategic planning and tactical operation of the command is also necessary.

It is of secondary importance how these tasks are labeled and grouped and to whom they are assigned, provided that the officer to whom a logistic task is assigned understands logistics, and provided that somewhere on the staff there is an officer who, with the whole logistic picture clearly in his mind, acts as the primary staff logistic advisor to the commander.

Chapter 18

Logistic Readiness

What has never before been tried within the profession of arms invariably invites more opposition than support.[1]

—S. L. A. MARSHALL

In the last ten years the question of the readiness of our armed forces for immediate combat has been of increasing concern. Time and again we have been warned that war on a very large scale may be suddenly precipitated. As a result all Services have placed more emphasis on realistic combat training; and special organizations and staff sections have been set up to supervise the inspections and reports which deal with combat readiness.

In the Navy the *techniques* of replenishment at sea have been studied and improved by constant practice. In the Army the annual LOGEX (Logistical Exercise) maneuvers have been very valuable. In the Air Force air refueling *techniques* have been developed in an excellent manner. In all Services the *techniques* of peacetime supply have been thoroughly overhauled. In spite of these and other worthwhile developments, there are many additional areas of logistic planning and operations that are of great importance to the rapid development and maintenance of maximum combat effectiveness *which are not regularly examined* and tested. It is, therefore, appropriate to discuss the question of "logistic readiness" and to indicate a few of the major practical matters with which a commander should concern himself to assure that he is logistically ready for combat.

What It Is

First, what do we mean by the term? Logistic readiness might

---

[1] S. L. A. Marshall, *The Fatal Decisions*, William Sloane Associates, New York, 1956, p. viii.

well be called the logistic aspects of combat readiness. *It is the ability to undertake, to build up and thereafter to sustain, combat operations at the full combat potential of the forces which are assigned to the combat commanders in those areas that are vital to the security of the nation.*

The determination of the logistic aspects of readiness consists of obtaining the answers to a few very practical questions. If these questions can be answered affirmatively, the command or the service is logistically ready for combat. If the answers are negative or unknown to any degree, then to that same degree the command is not ready for combat. Perfect logistic readiness will never be attained but the difference between good and poor logistic readiness may well be the difference between success and disaster.

Factors in Attainment

There are six major factors in the development of logistic readiness; the mental attitude of command, the balance of logistic and combat forces, the logistic plans and policies, the logistic organization, the state of material readiness, and the program of training and exercises. Again, as in all other studies of war, we will find many areas of overlap. Furthermore, each command will find that it has its own areas of special emphasis.

Mental Attitude

The mental attitude of command is the first measure of logistic readiness. In this we are interested in both the combat commanders and the logistic commanders. We seek a state of mutual understanding which produces confidence. This state of mind recognizes the nature and magnitude of both the combat task and the logistic task, and their interdependence. It recognizes the effect of time and distance factors in the performance of these tasks. It recognizes the timeliness and nature of the critical information which must be exchanged between them. This favorable state of mind should extend from the commanders to their staffs and to their subordinate commanders in order that the necessary cooperation may be instinctive.

The Balance of Forces

No problem presents more difficulty than trying to determine in advance the most efficient balance of logistic resources and combat forces that will be needed for any campaign. In commenting on this aspect of Korean logistics the Army historian says:

> Perhaps the general problem from which it was most difficult to draw definite conclusions was the question of personnel to perform all the logistical functions needed. It has become common to make the ratio of combat troops to service troops the measure of efficiency in the Army. By itself this ratio may mean nothing. The important factor is the total amount of effective firepower which can be brought to bear against the enemy. If the greatest total of effective power can be delivered with one combat man for each service man, then this is the desirable ratio; but if 1,000 service troops for one combat man are needed to achieve that maximum, then that is the desirable ratio.

> The entire field of administration and logistics was one in which the Army had been forced to excel in modern warfare. In the mid-20th century fighting was becoming, for the Army, secondary to administration. Becoming noticeable in World War II, this trend received further acceleration in the Korean conflict.

> Much to their consternation, a great many old soldiers who longed for the smell of gunpowder and the chatter of machine guns faced the more likely prospect of having to settle for the smell of mimeograph ink and the chatter of typewriters. Officers and men who felt they were contributing nothing to a war effort if they were not on the firing line had to develop a broader view of the requirements of modern war.

> Most of the Army was not in the combat arms—the infantry, armor, and artillery; most of it was in the technical services—the engineers, quartermasters, medics, and chemical, signal, and transportation units, and in the administrative services and the headquarters which guided and supervised the tactical and service units from the combat zone to the Pentagon.[2]

---

[2] Dr. James A. Huston, "Korea and Logistics," *Military Review,* February 1957, Issue No. II. Taken from Dr. Huston's study on "Logistical Support for the Conflict in Korea."

Over the long range it may seem easier to build up logistic support forces than it is to build up combat forces because the training of personnel is sometimes not as difficult and the procurement of equipment is usually easier. The reason for this is that many logistic operations closely resemble industrial operations, and consequently the conversion in most cases is relatively simple. However, this apparent differential in ease of buildup should not blind us to the need for carefully planning conversion from peace to war and for allowing adequate lead time for its accomplishment. To take a buildup for granted is folly. Furthermore, the increasing automation of weapons makes the training of the supporting technicians a critical factor. However, the balance of logistic forces and combat forces at the beginning of war is another matter. In the initial stage of a sudden war the emergency conversions are of little help. At this time fully trained and equipped logistic forces must be available, properly disposed and in adequate number to render immediate sustained support to the combat forces in being. A combat force with no logistic support is ineffectual and represents a waste of effort.

In the mobilization of operating forces, it is essential that the logistic support forces be mobilized with the correct phasing relative to the combat forces they will support. *In many cases the logistic forces should be mobilized first.*

The critical questions to be asked are: Is the time phased buildup of logistic support adequate in quantity to support the buildup of combat forces? Are both of these in harmony with strategic deployment and tactical operations?

Logistic Plans

The next requirement to insure logistic readiness is to examine the plans. While the questions to be asked are simple and obvious, obtaining accurate answers entails rigorous and searching study.

We should ask—

(1) Are the logistical plans based upon, and do they support, the strategical and tactical concepts of

the combat plans and the most probable courses of action in time of war?

(2) Are they drawn so that the basic logistic framework will support alternate strategical and tactical plans?

(3) Are they within the capabilities of the forces assigned?

(4) Are they complete and harmonious from the most advanced command back through the armies, fleets, areas, and frontiers to the zone of the interior, (or shore establishment) which forms the ultimate source of logistic support?

(5) Do they assign specific responsibility for the performance of logistic tasks without placing conflicting responsibilities on any single command? If it is necessary to place conflicting responsibilities on any single commander he should be given separate staff and subordinate command to accomplish the tasks.

The preparation of logistic plans presents the serious hazard of the substitution of format and bulk for quality of content. Since logistics deals with many details, the plans must be bulky and both standard forms and check-off lists are frequently required. *These factors of standardization, check-off lists, and bulk make it only too easy for logistic planning in peacetime to become a routine task of a perfunctory nature. When this happens the commander may have the illusion of readiness without the substance.*

Logistic Organization

The next test of readiness comes with a study of the assignments of logistic responsibility and the organization of the logistical commands and staffs. Here we ask—

(1) Are these organizations structurally based on war requirements?

(2) Can they be expanded to wartime strength without a drastic revision of lines of authority and of the filing and information systems?

(3) Are they such that no commander in wartime must serve two masters?

(4) Are they such that no commander has two or more conflicting tasks without staffs and assigned forces to whom he can delegate the conflicting tasks and their immediate supervision?

(5) Are the logistic staffs adequate for the planning and supervision of the tasks assigned?

(6) Do combat command and logistic responsibility and authority go hand in hand throughout the chain of command?

(7) Is there clear and unequivocal responsibility for the allocation of materials and services in the area of war?

There is no area of military activity where so many departures from the theoretical ideal are required by circumstances as in organization. Yet the fact that compromises which produce defects are inevitable should not lead us to ignore them. Instead we have the task of recognition and compensation.

Experience has shown that where there is uncertainty as to authority or where there is unnecessary duplication, staffs tend to grow to such inordinate size that confusion and delay snowball. The logistical system becomes so sluggish that it no longer responds to the needs of combat even though its size is enormous, and its over-all resources more than adequate.

In other words, the command and staff relations and organization have a direct influence on logistical responsiveness which, in turn, is the foundation for tactical and strategic flexibility.

The Test of Logistic Organization

The question arises: How should we test various organizational proposals to determine which is the most effective and efficient?

With any given strategic situation and availability of logistic resources we can assume that the most desirable organization for logistics will be that which most completely fulfills the needs of the combat forces in the shortest time with the smallest number of personnel. The question of relative monetary cost normally is not so important because, other things being equal, the cheapest organization is that which provides the needed resources to the combat forces in the shortest time and in so doing uses the least personnel. The best understanding of the problem requires a general appraisal followed by a specific analysis.

The general questions most pertinent to the analysis of the administrative excellence of organization are—

(1) What decisions are to be made?

(2) What is the nature of the factors and considerations which enter into these decisions?

(3) What flow of information is necessary to provide the statement of these factors?

(4) What is the quality and number of staff personnel required to assist the commander in making these decisions?

(5) How long does it take to recognize the need, make the decisions, transmit the decisions, and carry them out?

(6) What are the needs for feed-back of information in order to provide supervision of action and to insure that decisions are based on current, rather than past situations?

In other words, if we are to understand the state of logistic readiness of any command we must be able to state and evaluate in terms of people and time, the decisions, the recommendations, and the action which the various commanders must assume by reason of the logistical responsibilities assigned.

The logistical effectiveness of any command will to a large degree depend upon the speed with which certain actions of a cyclic nature are taken under wartime conditions. What may be an acceptable peacetime logistical cycle of, say, 180 days for a particular action, may be intolerable in war.

Therefore, it is useful to construct flow charts of logistical decision and action throughout the various commands in the organization under study. From these flow charts estimates can be made as to the number of staff personnel and of the time required at each step of the over-all logistic process or cycle.

The various logistical and technical functions of supply, maintenance and repair, transportation, medical, engineering, etc., will each present different situations, personnel problems and time cycles.

In some command analyses it may be sufficient to test the personnel and time requirements by measuring the flow of action papers in a few representative items or classes. In other instances a more thorough breakdown should be made.

Cycle of Paper Work

In all technical functions, however, staff preparation and command decision involve the following broad actions:

> Prepare plans
> Approve plans
> Formulate policy
> Allocate resources
> Establish priorities
> Supervise execution of plans and policies.

In each of these a vast amount of logistical information is required and in each case the opinions and problems of the subordinates must be considered. This requires time, qualified staff personnel, staff files, and staff facilities. Command supervision of the ensuing action requires a continuous feedback of information to insure that command action is based on reality in a typically changing war situation. The logistic time cycle is the total time taken by these procedures, by the decisions, and by the transmission of information and decisions, plus the time taken by material procurement, handling, and transportation. Therefore, when logistic authority and responsibility have been assigned to any commander the question should be asked:

Does his staff normally have available the logistic, strategic, and tactical information necessary to make these logistic decisions or will the accumulation and processing of such information require augmentation of personnel, space, and equipment?

In most instances certain elements of the situation such as geography, basic strategy, and basic availabilities will remain the same regardless of the command structure. The variable elements, which can be reduced by good organization, will be the time it takes to prepare, to transmit, and to act on the staff paper work concerned. "Communication" by mail or by dispatch, including headquarters administrative routines such as clearances, registration, and coding, as well as basket-time waiting signature, must be taken into account and added to the time of actual transmission by mail or dispatch. *Thus, whenever a piece of paper must go to and through an unnecessary office, unnecessary time is added to the logistic action cycle.* In complex logistical organizations these administrative delays can snowball and become the most important element of the cycle.

The situation which existed in the War Department in 1942 illustrates the time consuming aspects of staff procedures.[3] In the operations division "Secret" action mail took nearly 26 hours to go from the receiving clerk to the action officer. There were about 100 detailed steps in this process. After reorganization and simplification there still remained 53 specific steps.

State of Material Readiness

One of the most important aspects of readiness is the insistence on maintenance of a high state of material readiness at all times. Insofar as the Navy is concerned, this has always included the insistence on the maximum degree of self-support in ship maintenance. This implies a knowledge of material maintenance and repair on the part of ships' officers and their retention of responsibility for supervision of repair during navy yard overhauls. This indoctrination in peacetime pays great dividends in war for it not only insures a high state of material

---

[3] Major General Otto L. Nelson, Jr., *National Security and the General Staff*, Infantry Journal Press, Washington, pp. 473-480.

readiness at the outbreak of war, but it also provides a backlog of experienced officers to handle the tremendous increase in mobile repair requirements that war brings.

The development and maintenance of the supply system is the backbone of material readiness. This includes not only the design of the system and its procedures but also requires the maintenance of overseas stock levels of adequate size and proper location. In the case of the Navy, these must be both ashore and afloat. The desirability of maintaining stocks in afloat storage for the Army and Air Force is one which under circumstances of geography, local destruction or contamination, or other special situations, may well be considered.

These problems should be solved on the basis of determining what level and distribution of stocks will best support the basic plans of the commander. In this regard it is well to remember that a good logistic plan will support several strategic plans and a great number of tactical plans. We therefore should not seek the perfect solution for one particular plan but rather we should seek a distribution that will provide the best foundation for flexibility.

In considering forward area stocks it is well to avoid placing major stocks in locations that are vulnerable to enemy attack. *An important part of logistic readiness is the ability to absorb the shock of an enemy attack and still support the combat forces.*

The questions to be asked relative to material readiness generally are as follows—

(1) Are the combat forces practicing the maximum practicable amount of self maintenance?

(2) Are the repair facilities located properly in relationship to areas of combat operation?

(3) Is the mobilization buildup of repair facilities, both fixed and mobile, properly phased in relation to buildup of combat forces?

(4) Are the stocks of supplies immediately available to the combat commanders adequate in quantity and variety to supply their critical needs until supply reinforcement can be accomplished?

(5) Are these forward area stocks protected by location, construction, and local security from excessive initial loss by capture, bombing, or sabotage?

(6) Are the back-up stocks which will furnish supply and reinforcement identified and are they available in adequate quantity and with adequate assigned transportation to insure no delay in initiating supply reinforcement?

(7) Are there adequate cross-supply and cross-servicing agreements in effect to insure that there will be no administrative delays in the necessary allocation and use of critical facilities and supplies?

(8) Is there an adequate system for the flow and evaluation of material information?

Training and Exercises

The programs of training and exercises form the final test of logistic readiness.

Since the majority of junior officers and enlisted men in the logistic services are specialized in a technical field, sound technical training is their fundamental preparation for war. In addition, however, specific attention should be paid to the development of fundamental discipline, leadership, and personal versatility which are so vital to efficient logistic service under wartime conditions. World War II showed that too many technical specialists were unable to care for themselves under adverse conditions and that too many were so narrowly trained that they were of little use under combat conditions. *The ability to adapt and to improvise are just as important to the logistic forces as to the combat forces; and it is just as important to maintain military discipline.*

Too often in the past, fleet and field maneuvers have been

based on the assumption of the ready availability of complete logistic support. Too seldom have the reports of these exercises included a realistic appraisal of the logistic problems and situations that would have been encountered under wartime conditions. Most peacetime exercises make little pretense of having realistic logistic aspects. The usual excuse is that to do so would detract from tactical training, or otherwise unduly complicate the maneuver. The deficiencies in logistical organization and planning which were disclosed in the early stages of the Korean War illustrate this and should serve as a warning to all commanders. To a large degree these deficiencies were similar to those which plagued us from 1942 to 1944. Many of these came about because senior officers had ignored the logistical analyses of World War II operations.[4]

One method of training for logistic readiness would involve the carrying out of exercises designed specifically around logistic problems and the functioning of logistic commands and staffs. As has been previously mentioned, the Army annually carries out such an exercise on the zone of interior level. This practice could well be extended in all the military services, and to a much lower level of command.

In any event, whenever we make an appraisal of training and exercises we should ask—

(1) Does the logistic personnel of the command get specific training under simulated wartime conditions?

(2) Are realistic logistic considerations fully incorporated in the tactical and strategical maneuvers of the combat forces?

(3) Are the tactical commanders required to keep

---

[4] For example, practically every logistic deficiency in staff organization, theater planning and coordination, port operations, and similar matters which occurred in the summer of 1950 had been anticipated and remedies described in the pamphlet, "Joint Overseas Operations" prepared by the Joint Board of Operational Review convened at the Army Navy Staff College in 1946. To attempt to place the blame for these deficiencies wholly on national policy and budget restrictions is an evasion of command responsibility.

their maneuvers within the limitations of their logistic capabilities?

(4) Are the bases which would be supporting actual operations tested as to planning, staff, communication, and material readiness by being brought into the maneuver fully and by conducting complete supporting exercises under simulated war conditions?

(5) Are the logistic aspects of the manuevers as fully analyzed in the reports and critiques as are the tactical aspects?

One effective way of improving the logistic adequacy of maneuvers and exercises is to require that at the conclusion of each phase of the maneuver each tactical commander be required to submit a dispatch report as to his current state of logistic readiness and as to his specific plans to restore it to the level necessary for continued combat. If this logistic report be extended to include several echelons of tactical *and logistic* commands, invaluable information as to true readiness for combat can be obtained.

General Factors

There is no way precisely to define or assign relative weights to any specific factors in logistic readiness. These will vary according to circumstances. However, there are certain elements that are of fundamental importance in any situation.

A good logistic plan based upon a careful estimate of the situation will support a great variety of tactical courses of action and a number of strategic courses.

The commander of any force—however small or however large—should have personal knowledge of those logistic deficiencies and situations which are critical in the consummation of his plans. He should assure himself that he has done all in his power to overcome them, that his superiors in the chain of command know what these major deficiencies and situations are, and what effect such deficiencies or situations may have on his actions.

Some of these matters may depend on factors such as appropriations or other things which are beyond the control of the commander. However, many more are within his control and involve not money and resources but merely the application of sound principles of command and planning.

General Trends

The study of the lessons of the past has value only as it provides guidance for the future. While no one can accurately predict what the future will bring, it is nevertheless important to note the general trends which are becoming apparent. These trends, growing out of fundamental human factors, combine to produce specific military results which themselves create puzzling and at times contradictory further effects.

THE FUNDAMENTAL, ECONOMIC-POLITICAL, HUMAN DEVELOPMENTS ARE—

(1) Continuation and acceleration of scientific research and technological development.

(2) Greatly increased world population.

(3) Continuation of economic-social-political turmoil as underdeveloped nations strive toward independence and industrialization.

(4) Increased spirit of nationalism occurring at the same time.

(5) An increased demand for centralization of authority as the "easiest way out."

(6) Continuation of pressure for monetary inflation.

(7) Increased speed of travel and communication.

THESE COMBINE TO PRODUCE CERTAIN SPECIFIC MILITARY RESULTS—

(1) Greater speed, greater range, and greater destructiveness of weapons.

(2) Increased mechanization and automation of weapons and military equipment.

(3) Increased complication of weapons and equipment.

(4) Need for greatly increased technical training of personnel.

(5) Increased use of weapons systems.

(6) Increased mechanical and electronic computation of logistic requirements.

(7) Increased centralization of authority in certain areas coupled with *increased need for decentralization*.

(8) Increased civilian control of military affairs at all levels.

(9) Increased availability of nuclear power in all fields.

(10) Extremely rapid obsolescence of military equipment.

(11) Mounting increase in military costs—for old as well as new equipment, and for personnel.

THESE IN TURN TEND TO CREATE THESE FURTHER EFFECTS, SOME BEING CONTRADICTORY—

(1) Increased need for dispersal of combat forces, of military installations, and of industrial installations.

(2) This need for dispersal and the possibility of electronic jamming and of the destruction of command facilities creates a need for decentralization of command authority.

(3) At the same time the speed and range of modern weapons create a need of centralization of certain types of command authority.

(4) Continued demand for greater centralization of administrative authority.

(5) Continued demand for greater civilian control of military affairs.

(6) Greater need for technically trained personnel at all levels both in armed forces and in industry with resulting competition for talent.

(7) Continued pressure for economy in military administration.

(8) Finally, the enormous danger to civilization and to the human race, inherent in thermonuclear warfare, has forced exploration of the concepts and practices of limited war.

A detailed examination of all the interactions of these forces and trends is not practicable. However, as the performance characteristics of weapons and equipment continue to advance, several specific results which are of great importance to the understanding of command and logistics become evident.

First, technological intricacy stimulates the formation of new weapons systems. At the same time, it greatly increases the cost of initial procurement and of upkeep.

As units and personnel become grouped in weapons systems each system tends to demand its own specialized tactical command and logistic support.

Along with this, while there is a *decrease of combat personnel* in contact with the enemy, there is also a great *increase in total personnel* required.

In other words, three vital changes are taking place: direct combat personnel is decreasing, logistic requirements are more complex, and logistic personnel is increasing. In terms of numbers of men, in fact, it is worthy of note that the center of gravity of military personnel is moving back from the enemy toward the logistic base.

A critical logistic paradox is found in the communication situation. On the one hand, our logistic systems are being modernized to take more advantage of electronic communications, while on the other hand the demands of tactical communications are cutting down the allocation of radio circuit time for logistic use.

A further effect of advanced technology is to reduce the capacity of combat forces for self-maintenance. A generation ago a good mechanic with a few tools could repair or build a needed spare part. Today most of such improvisations are impossible. Instead a new part or component must be installed. This increases the dependence of the combat force on the logistic organization.

While these changes create complex logistic problems, more subtle and less obvious psychological problems are also shaping up. Because more and more computers are being installed, and used to assist in making many tactical decisions as to course, speed, target selection, weapon selection, and firing data, commanders must devote more and more attention to the material readiness of complex command equipment.

At the same time, as the combat officer becomes more and more involved in the logistics and readiness of weapons systems, strategic decisions and major tactical decisions tend to be elevated in the chain of command in accordance with the trend toward greater centralization of authority throughout the military service.

However, modern weapons have created a need for both tactical and logistic dispersal. These in turn demand greater decentralization. In a case of such an obvious contradiction a wise blend of centralization and decentralization must be sought and this requires a knowledge of logistic cause and effect. Realistic war games provide, in peacetime, our best test in dilemmas such as these.

The development of nuclear power for military propulsion raises logistic questions of grave importance. While nuclear propulsion will change the limitations imposed on operations by fuel it by no means eliminates the problems of logistic support. It merely changes them, for when one logistic limit has been overcome another one takes charge.

The Army history of the Korean War points this up in the following terms:

> Almost never will all logistic requirements be satisfied in an exact balance, and as long as that is true, and as long as military operations are governed by the finite, some phase of logistics is bound to be a limiting factor.[5]

---

[5] Dr. James A. Huston, "Korea and Logistics," *Military Review,* February 1957. Issue No. II.

The greatest paradox and therefore the greatest danger, lies in the fact that we must be prepared to fight both an unlimited thermonuclear war and a variety of limited wars while at the same time we must maintain our position in the cold war. *We must deal with the entire spectrum of conflict. Those extremists who say that we can or should prepare for only one kind of conflict are courting disaster because they are implicitly rejecting the concepts of flexibility and change which are fundamental characteristics of humanity and nature.*

The contradictions between *preparation* for the thermonuclear and for limited conventional war are primarily in the logistic field. Therefore, it will be largely in the field of logistics that our *readiness* for future conflict will be determined.

This problem can be illustrated by the requirements for a war which it is hoped will be fought as a "limited war," but which is under the threat of enlargement to thermonuclear war. These will include—

(1) Limited objectives.

(2) The recognition that the exercise of strategy is the art of control.

(3) Careful restraint in the limits of destruction.

(4) The employment of such forces and tactics as can effectively control the actions of peoples *without widespread destruction.*

(5) The availability of, and the readiness to use, all types of weapons and forces.

(6) The need to be able to use *all the tools of power,* including non-military tools in the economic, political, and unconventional fields.

One basic ingredient of this kind of controlled power is *men* —highly trained, well equipped, able to move and to be reinforced more quickly than those of an enemy. The combat training and organization for thermonuclear war in many respects is quite different from the training and organization for conventional war. It also differs markedly from the preparation of forces for guerrilla war and other forms of covert action.

Furthermore, in thermonuclear war one great task—new to this nation—would be that of civil defense and rehabilitation. This is an enormous logistic task.

Transportation is another basic ingredient of the flexibility necessitated by dual preparation.[6,7,8,9] The inherent limitations of air transport make it mandatory that air, sea, and land transportation be wisely combined as appropriate to each operation.

Since we will continue to have global commitments, control of the sea will be essential to this transportation capability.

In spite of the incalculable logistic demands of atomic war and the increasing logistic support required for conventional war, we find a final paradox. We are cutting our conventional forces because it is alleged that modern atomic weapons require less combat personnel than do conventional weapons while at the same time some are saying that modern atomic war will inevitably lead to suicidal thermonuclear war.

In reporting this situation the *New York Times* said:

> For weeks the National Security Council has been debating policies that concern the ability of the United States to maintain both a conventional and nuclear arsenal. The decision to cut the armed forces by 100,000 has reinforced the view that the United States would not be equipped to fight any but a nuclear war because for reasons of economy, it had reduced the equipment and forces that could be used in so-called "brushfire wars."
>
> Army officials are known to be in the vanguard of the fight against the nuclear strategy. General Maxwell D. Taylor, Army Chief of Staff, has not spoken on this subject recently, but he has stressed in the past the importance of being prepared for so-called "little wars." This

---

[6] The most recent examples of the decisiveness of transportation in modern conflict is found in the British reports and comments on Suez in 1956. The Franco-British inability to act decisively in July when Nasser seized the Canal was almost wholly due to logistic deficiencies. Of these deficiencies, transportation was the most critical.

[7] "Operation Musketeer," *The Economist*, Nov. 24, 1956, pp. 668-669.

[8] Dispatch by General Sir Charles F. Keightley, GCB, GBE, DSO, Commander in Chief, Allied Forces, "Operations in Egypt—November to December 1956," Supplement to *The London Gazette*, 10 Sept. 1957.

[9] Paul Johnson, *The Suez War*, Greenberg, New York, 1957.

would indicate that he has been strongly opposed to the nuclear war concept.

On the other hand, the belief that another war inevitably would be a wide-scale nuclear war has been attributed to Admiral Arthur W. Radford, the outgoing Chairman of the Joint Chiefs of Staff, and Donald A. Quarles, Deputy Secretary of Defense.[10]

These trends are merely those which are most apparent. They interact with each other in very complex ways so as to defy sure prediction. In some instances several of the factors which underlie the dilemma of strategic and logistic courses of action dampen the effects. In other instances they may accentuate each other. *In all cases simple extrapolation of our present statistical data will produce misleading and perhaps dangerous results in planning.* Nevertheless, we should remain keenly aware of the nature and significance of those trends which we can recognize and we must adjust our thinking and planning to their development. We must retain mental flexibility and imagination.

A Summary of Paradoxes

Before concluding this discussion it is well to restate and summarize these paradoxes which make wise decisions so difficult.

The need for fast, efficient logistic support operations is growing, yet the threat of new weapons dictates a greater dispersal of logistic installations; and dispersal in turn reduces their efficiency.

The use of thermonuclear weapons may be detrimental to the attainment of our national objectives. On the other hand, *the need for being prepared to use them* grows with every shrinkage of our cold war defensive periphery and with every increase in enemy thermonuclear capability.

---

[10] Jack Raymond, "U.S. is Debating 2 Defense Issues," *The New York Times,* Monday, July 22, 1957.

While enemy capabilities greatly increase the hazard of concentrating our top command and administration in one location, the size and centralization of power in the Office of the Secretary of Defense tends to grow.

While there is a greater emphasis on the control of 'military authority by civilians, it is difficult to maintain continuity of high-grade civilians in positions of authority.

It has been repeatedly and conclusively proven that rapid fluctuations in the scale of our preparations for war produce great waste and yet our political system is such that these fluctuations are almost inevitable. It is particularly ironical that these fluctuations are so frequently alleged to be instigated by the need for economy.

While the free flow of scientific ideas and information is important to technological progress the need for security tends to restrict this flow.

At a time when there is the greatest need for imaginative creative thinking there is some confusion in the public mind as to the distinction between political, economic, and ideological unorthodoxy as opposed to subversion or sabotage.

There is a need for fighting a cold war in the economic, political, and psychological areas in which the nation must seek the understanding and cooperation of nations who have very different political, economic, and sociological ideas from those we hold.

There is the need for being prepared to fight both cold war guerrilla war and cold war "brush-fire" wars while at the same time remaining ready to fight large-scale wars either of limited weapons or of unlimited weapons.

The type of tactical unit suitable for one type of war may be quite unsuitable for the other type. This poses the question of how we can remain prepared without maintaining large-scale forces of both types with an excessively high cost for this apparent duplication.

While these and other factors indicate the need for flexibility in policy and in the organization and equipment of our armed forces, from some quarters there is a demand for an inflexible military policy which would assign an overriding priority to one fixed strategy and to one weapon.[11]

There are the demands for improved technology in weapons and at the same time demands for greater simplicity for the sake of economy. Yet history shows that the improved military technology leads to increased costs and personnel.

There is the demand for maintaining a state of readiness, for instantly undertaking large-scale warfare while at the same time technological advances are so rapid that any equipments that are produced in large quantity will soon be theoretically obsolete.

The fear of obsolescence restrains our effort at stockpiling of equipment, yet the threat of atomic attack on our industrial facilities makes it imperative that we maintain large dispersed stockpiles of finished equipment.

While a purely defensive strategy is foreign to our military philosophy and to the nature of our people, there is nevertheless a great need for the commitment of a large part of our resources solely for the defense of the North American continent.

Appreciation of Fundamental Principles

Underlying and causing the variables in today's situation are the intangible motivations and aspirations of men, their creative imaginations and their refusal to be bound by either man-made laws or statistical forecasts. Deep within all the paradoxes and contradictions in life today, which are obvious to one who studies human conflict, there are fundamental cause-and-effect relationships. Recognition of these by our future commanders and executives may well make the difference between haphazard improvisation and sure guidance.

No military commander or high civilian executive, operating in the fields of strategy or logistics, can hope to deal effectively with these contradictions unless he has acquired an intuitive appreciation of fundamental theory and principle. In recognition of this Sir Julian Corbett said:

---

[11] See Mr. Finletter's articles in the September and October 1954 *Atlantic Monthly.*

. . . it is of little use to approach naval strategy except through the theory of war. Without such theory we can never really understand its scope or meaning, nor can we hope to grasp the forces which most profoundly affect its conclusions.[12]

This appreciation cannot be acquired by hasty scanning of military literature. It comes only when one has thought deeply about these matters in the light of the evidence of history. But such appreciation of fundamental principles is of little real value unless the commander exercises critical supervision of those matters which in summation create readiness for combat.

[12] Julian S. Corbett, *Some Principles of Maritime Strategy,* Longmans, Green and Co., London, 1918, p. 9.

Chapter 19

Conclusions

The outcome of every war is not a question of power-
ful means, war material and war potential in them-
selves, but is dependent on the mental capacity of
the High Command.[1]
　　　　　　　—Vice Admiral Eberhard Weichold

The earlier chapters of this work have shown how modern conflict, strategy, logistics, tactics, command decision, and organization are related to each other.

The Need for and Nature of a Theory of War

Modern war is so complex that no one mind can master all the detail. Therefore a commander should rise above technical detail. Through development of the perspective of command, and the study of the theory of war, he should qualify himself to be able to control the essentials of war.

Before we can appreciate the full significance of logistics in this context we should briefly examine the situation at the highest levels of national decision.

In the early fall of 1957, *The Atlantic,* commenting on the induction of a new Secretary of Defense, said in part:

> The task facing McElroy is simply this: to devise a new military doctrine and to create the military forces necessary to carry it out in the light of the changed and changing nuclear facts of life and the nature of the Communist threat. . . .
>
> According to informed Administration officials, Eisenhower sought a new Defense Secretary who not only could handle procurement (hence he wanted another businessman) but who also could tackle the doctrinal problem. Departing Secretary Wilson, fortunately for McElroy, took care of the unpleasant chore of chopping down the existing military machine to fit the new budget levels set

---

[1] Vice Admiral Eberhard Weichold, Commander German Naval Forces Mediterranean 1941-43, *ONI Review,* September 1946, p. 47.

by Congress—cuts in manpower, moth-balling of naval vessels, stretch-outs in aircraft procurement, and so on. The deck thus is relatively clear for McElroy to tackle the main job.[2]

In contrast on November 15, 1957 the leading editorial of the *New York Times* said in part:

> President Eisenhower has now spelled out some of the iron imperatives of this great but troubled age. As he has pointed out, the Soviet challenge is symbolized not so much by the sputniks, important as these are, but rather by what lies behind them. And what lies behind them is the attempt of another dictatorship to conquer the world by the forced development and regimentation of the scientific and economic capacities of the nearly one billion people in the Communist bloc. . . .
>
> All this, Mr. Eisenhower made plain, calls for increased defense expenditures which may require increased taxes and the elimination of "entire categories" of other activities. A healthy American economy is, of course, the mainstay of free world defense, and that economy rests in the long run on a balanced budget and growing trade. But for the present it is to be "more guns and less butter," and the budgeteers will not be permitted to hamper our scientific progress. This will call for new sacrifices. But these sacrifices will have to be made lest we come to a pass where we have nothing left to sacrifice.[3]

Thus in the space of about two months the basic attitude toward national security seems to have been transformed, in fact almost reversed.

In this short period there had been no significant change in the tangible aspects of national security. There had, however, been an enormous change in the manner in which these tangible aspects were recognized and evaluated. In the early fall a large number of our citizens were complacent in their faith in a "weapon strategy" based on a supposed technological superiority. In the late fall many of these same persons were awed by

---

[2] The Atlantic Report on World Today, Washington. *The Atlantic,* October 1957.

[3] *The New York Times,* November 15, 1957, p. 26.

an enemy weapon capability. In their preoccupation with technology and its logistic concomitants they gave little thought to strategy. This swift change in attitudes poses a challenge to our basic concepts of national security.

Clausewitz pointed the way to clear thinking when he wrote:
. . . theory serves to pull up the weeds which error has sown everywhere . . .[4]

Obviously no theory or set of theories, however persuasive, can by itself obviate or reconcile differences of opinion. *However, the search for comprehensive theories is the best way of shedding light on these problems and of developing the understanding of principles and of cause and effect relations which may guide the responsible men who must choose among conflicting ideas.*

A comprehensive theory of war should include a description of—

(1) The nature and structure of modern conflict and of the elements which comprise it.

(2) The manner in which these elements are related to each other.

(3) The manner in which war is related to other parts and actions of human society.

(4) The nature of the various forces which act throughout the whole structure and the description of the way these forces act and interact.

In somewhat different but more specific terms this can be expressed as the following group of interrelated theories:

A general theory of modern conflict;

A theory of strategy;

A theory of logistics;

A theory of tactics;

A theory of command decision;

A theory of military organization.

---

[4] Karl Von Clausewitz, *On War,* Book VIII, Plan of War, Introduction, p. 568. Infantry Journal Press, Washington: 1950.

Logistics as Related to the Theory of War

The foundation for the exercise of modern high command responsibility lies in the appreciation of modern war as but one phase of the whole spectrum of an unceasing human conflict. If we are to survive as a free nation we must be prepared to use military force appropriately throughout this spectrum; and to use such military force in harmony with the other elements of power: the political, the economic, the psychological, and the ideological. These tools of conflict are interwoven and they should be used selectively and flexibly as appropriate to our political objectives and to our moral values. When, for one or another reason the use of one tool is limited, then the importance of the other tools is proportionately accentuated.

The military aspects of this conflict are strategy, logistics, tactics, communications, and intelligence. The decisions of command are governed by a blend of strategic, logistic, and tactical considerations. Intelligence sheds light on the situation and communications transmits both information and the will of command. At the highest level of command, strategy and logistics are so entwined that they seem to merge. *Thus command must see strategy in relation to logistics and must see logistics in relation to strategy.* These interrelations are well expressed in broad concepts such as—

(1) The exercise of strategy is the comprehensive direction of power and becomes a means of exercising control in the pursuit of objectives. Strategy determines objectives and the broad methods for their attainment.

(2) The exercise of tactics is the immediate direction of power. Tactics determines the specific employment of forces to attain the objectives of strategy.

(3) Logistics provides the means to create and to support combat forces. Logistics is the bridge between the national economy and the operation of combat forces. Thus, in its economic sense it limits the combat forces which can be created; and in its operational sense it limits the forces which can be employed.

Thus strategy and tactics are always limited and at times are determined by logistic factors. Obviously, therefore, in order to support the combat requirements of strategy and tactics the *objective of all logistic effort must be the attainment of sustained combat effectiveness in operating forces.*

The concept of the exercise of strategy as being the comprehensive direction of power toward the attainment of control establishes the primacy of *control* in the *conduct* of affairs, as opposed to a philosophy of destruction as the only tool of strategy. The analysis of the various aspects of control points up the need for flexibility and discrimination in the employment of forces and weapons. It rules out the fallacy of the "weapon strategy."

Strategic flexibility and mobility can only be based on a logistic foundation. Therefore, if a commander is to establish flexible concepts and exploit opportunities, he must have adequate control over his logistic support. The understanding of the nature and degree of logistic control which commanders at various levels should exercise over their logistic support is essential to the attainment of combat effectiveness in war.

It is self-evident that the practical application of a strategic concept requires very specific deployments and tactical operations. The study of ancient and modern wars and of current crises shows that these deployments and tactical operations must be *preceded* by specific logistic action. This consists first of an economic-logistic buildup to create the combat forces, and second the further very specific logistic deployment to support the tactical operations. This vital relationship requires that strategic, logistic, and tactical planning and control be completely integrated in the mind of command.

Regardless of the manner in which the authority of civilian and of military executives are blended, command is exercised through planning and by control and adjustment of the ensuing action.

In logistics, the commander is always seeking to coordinate a variety of technical functions toward the attainment of combat effectiveness. The technical specialist on the other hand is seeking to perfect the performance of his own specialty. This distinction is important for two reasons: First, command must sometimes sacrifice the efficiency of a particular function in order to increase the effectiveness of a combination of functions; and second, the objectives and concepts of command must be clearly understood by the technical subordinates in order that they may support them with both loyalty and ingenuity.

This means that the commander must understand the cause and effect relationships which exist in logistics in order that he may estimate how the gain or loss of efficiency in any particular technical function will influence the efficiency of the other functions which in combination determine his over-all combat effectiveness.

This study has emphasized that modern conflict requires many areas of overlap in the command and management of logistic forces and systems. This in turn requires that those exercising authority have common concepts of objectives and common criteria of judgment. Only then can there be harmony and flexible adjustment in the management of strategic, logistic, and tactical affairs.

In looking to the future we can expect a continuation of the present "cold war" conflict for an indefinite period of perhaps ten years, perhaps fifty or more years. No one is wise enough to know. All of the forces which influence the situation are variable and as they increase or decrease in intensity the situation will change. The accurate measurement of the situation and its precise evaluation are beyond the reach of any science.

Technical Superiority Not Decisive

However, an improved knowledge of the forces and of how they probably will work will assist us to effectively adapt our policies and methods to the changing situation. We can expect accelerated technological progress to continue in all parts of the world. While we will make every effort to protect the security of our own military technology, we cannot expect to be wholly successful in this nor can we expect to prevent our enemies from making at least equal progress. Furthermore, a technological superiority in itself cannot guarantee national security.

It can be a fatal error to depend wholly on a supposed technical superiority for the preservation of security and for the accomplishment of national objectives. It can be equally disastrous to feel helpless or defeated in a situation where one is technically inferior.

From the logistic point of view these basic principles have the corollary that for every logistic advantage which a technological advance may give to us, one can expect that a compensating logistic disadvantage will accrue to ourselves by reason of an improved enemy capability.

Warfare seems to be developing in two opposite directions simultaneously. With the development of electronic controls for guided missiles, nuclear weapons, and nuclear power, we seem to be approaching a push-button type of war. In this the major effort might go into preparation for a war in which the decision would rest on the relative ability to give and to absorb devastating blows in the first few hours of a war. In such a war the major logistical effort *after war broke out* might well be in the logistics of relief and rehabilitation of the homeland and its industry. This would entail an effort of the same type as the development of an advanced base on an area devastated by an amphibious assault.

At the other extreme there is the prospect of a continuance and intensification of a politico-economic-psychological cold war with overtones of guerrilla warfare, subversion, and sabotage. This would require the maintenance of large, modern, relatively conventional military forces on a ready basis. It might not ever require their large-scale active participation. In any event, the demands of the economic war would require logistic efficiency to support any guerrilla type of warfare, and to create and support the larger forces standing by.

Somewhere between these two extremes lies the possibility that we may fight a conventional war of considerable scope and of great technological complication, with limited weapons.

This again would demand logistic efficiency to improve the combat effectiveness of our engaged forces, to survive the simultaneous economic struggle, and at the same time to remain prepared for the explosion of an unlimited war.

Our national security will depend on our ability to act effectively in any continuation or extension of the conflict in which we are now engaged regardless of whether or not it be confined to the psychological-political-economic area, of whether it bring on a number of "brush fire" wars, or of whether it burst into a major but limited war or into an all out unlimited war.

Need for Study and Research

It is sometimes considered that the word "research" should be applied only to what is generally known as "pure research," i.e., the determination of new facts in the area of specific sciences such as mathematics, physics, etc. Because of their "practical" back ground, some officers may reject the thought that "research" can apply to such studies as "command relations" or "tactical or logistical concepts" or the "arts of military decision or military planning."

In recent years there has been great emphasis placed on technical research aimed at the improvement of weapons and weapon systems. Technical research—or the search for better "hardware"—is and will continue to be of vital importance. *However, the need for continued technical research should not obscure the need for research in the realm of ideas.* The intangible nature of "idea research" makes it particularly elusive when we try to plan or program it. In military research, studies of "strategy," "logistics," and "tactics" in the abstract sense are largely "idea research"; studies of weapons and equipments and their operation are largely "technical research." It seems neither possible nor profitable to state precisely where one leaves off and the other begins.

In meeting the challenge posed by the complexity of modern warfare and urgency of the situation, two major factors are important—

(1) The problems are so big that no one individual

can be expected to grasp their major interrelations and at the same time be familiar with more than a few of the innumerable technical details. Further, due to the size of the problems, it is even possible that various research groups may be working on the same problem without knowing the interest or progress of other workers in the same field. Another result of the size of the problem is that the official correspondence dealing with these matters is too extensive for any single individual to read, let alone to grasp.

(2) Successful research is based on skepticism. Samuel Eliot Morison says, "Every honest historian has, time and again, rejected the theory or 'frame' with which he started his research, and has built another to suit the facts that he plows up." [5] Therefore, in true military research, no organizational concepts, military policies, or rules should be considered sacred.

Administration has the task and obligation to lay down policies, operating procedures, and rules based on the best possible application of the truth as it is known at any one time.

Research, on the other hand, has the obligation to search for truth regardless of, and sometimes in spite of, official acceptance of, or insistence on certain ideas or dogmas. It is a process of constant examination and reexamination. After the results of research have become known it then becomes the task of administration to evaluate these results in terms of practical application and to take appropriate action.

The point is that study and research must go forward in the fields of both technology and ideas. The alternative is smug stagnation and defeat.

Danger of Self-Deception
Many of the requirements for organizations and personnel that are herein stated as necessary to logistic effectiveness and

---

[5] Presidential address at dinner of American Historical Association in Chicago on 29 December 1950.

efficiency in wartime may be considered to be too costly for our peacetime establishment. This is a matter in which official opinion and decisions will vary in accordance with the degree of apprehension as to our national security which may exist at any particular time. Regardless of what the decisions may be it is still important that the military professional have a clear idea of the manner in which various deficiencies affect our combat strength.

In particular, the professional should not fall a victim to the facile assumption that combat strength can be increased by the simple expedient of arbitrary reductions in logistic forces. There is an important distinction between the rigorous elimination of waste or unwarranted luxury, and the mirage of false economy. The first is merely the application of a strict logistic discipline. *The second is a delusion based upon a failure to understand the nature and magnitude of the logistic base on which the combat forces must rest before they can begin to fight.* High military commanders may be called upon to accept many arbitrary and unsound political decisions but they themselves must not fall into the trap of self-deception.

The Man for the Task

In concluding this exploration of the fundamentals of logistics it is well to discuss the type of man who should exercise major responsibility in the vital area of logistics.

The perspective of command in logistics discloses a pattern of the management of a vast flow of primarily technical information and decisions. This management effort is accompanied by the generation and control of material and a supply of personnel, all of which are directed toward the enormous variety of special technical projects that are required to create and to support military forces and to sustain operations. There are requirements at every level of planning and operation both for over-all management and for technical management. At every level the over-all management or command problem is to direct and supervise the combining of a variety of technical

tasks, *all to the end that specific combat forces can conduc,
military operations directed toward the achievement of specific
strategic and tactical objectives.*

This pattern sheds light on the question of the degree to
which major logistic work should be considered as a specialized type of duty for officers. Here we can learn a good deal
from business and industry. In these fields top management
also controls and coordinates the work of specialists in many
technical fields toward the achievement of non-technical broad
ends. Frequently in the top management group we see men
with unspecialized general backgrounds; and frequently, also,
we see men who have worked for years in technical specialties.
However, the successful leaders have in common a broad understanding of business and industrial affairs, the ability to use
and to direct technical specialists, the ability to grasp and
evaluate large amounts of information, and the ability to select
correct objectives and to lead men toward their attainment;
above all, they have a drive and a vision which lifts them above
the obstacles that blind and hamper men with little minds. So,
in logistics, technical specialization should be neither a bar
to nor a necessary qualification for major responsibility.

Finally, it is not essential either to good administration or to
good logistics that all logistic functions be grouped under the
heading of "logistics" in the organization and directives which
actually manage our armed forces. However, it is vital to establish common objectives, to recognize the problems and their
relationships, to identify and to provide a free flow of critical
and significant information to those responsible for the management of these problems. It is essential to educate men of ability
in these responsibilities and to assign them to controlling positions. And, above all, it is vital to develop mutual confidence
and loyalty to those professional ideals which more than any
technology or weapons will determine the quality of our national military security.

No one ever stated the fundamental problem more clearly than Mahan:

> War cannot be made a rule of thumb; and any attempt to make it so will result in disaster, grave in proportion to the gravity with which the issues of war are ever clothed.[6]

---

[6] Mahan, *Naval Administration and Warfare*, Little, Brown and Company, Boston, 1918, p. 232.

BIBLIOGRAPHY

Books

Arrow, Kenneth J., Karlin, Samuel, and Scarf, Herbert, *Studies in the Mathematical Theory of Inventory and Production,* Stanford University Press, 1958.

Baldwin, Hanson W., *The Great Arms Race,* Frederick A. Praeger, New York, 1958.

Ballantine, Duncan S., *U.S. Naval Logistics in the Second World War,* Princeton University Press, Princeton, N.J., 1947.

Barnard, Chester I., *The Functions of the Executive,* Harvard University Press, Cambridge, Massachusetts, 1950.

Bragadin, CDR. (R) Marc' Antonio, *The Italian Navy in World War II,* U.S. Naval Institute, Annapolis, 1957.

Carter, W. R. RADM., Retd., *Beans, Bullets, and Black Oil,* Government Printing Office, Washington, 1953.

Churchill, Winston, Speech in House on Army estimates, 1901 *Maxims and Reflections,* Houghton Mifflin, Boston, 1949.

Churchill, Winston, *A Churchill Reader,* Edited by Colin R. Coote, Houghton Mifflin Co., Boston, 1954.

Clausewitz, Karl Von, *On War,* Infantry Journal Press, Washington, D.C., 1950.

Corbett, Julian S., *Some Principles of Maritime Strategy,* Longmans, Green and Co., London, 1918.

Cordiner, Ralph J., *New Frontiers for Professional Managers,* McGraw-Hill Book Company, Inc., New York, 1956.

Cresswell, *Generals and Admirals,* Longmans, Green, New York, 1952.

Earle, Edward Mead, *Makers of Modern Strategy,* Princeton University Press, Princeton, 1952.

Eccles, Henry E., *Operational Naval Logistics,* Bureau of Naval Personnel, NAVPERS 10869, Washington, 1950.

Ehrman, John, *Grand Strategy,* Vol. V., Her Majesty's Stationery Office, London, 1956.

Falls, Cyril, *The Nature of Modern Warfare,* Oxford University Press, New York, 1941.

Falls, Cyril, *The Place of War in History,* Clarendon Press, Oxford, 1947.

Freidin, Seymour and Richardson, William, *The Fatal Decisions,* Foreword by S. L. A. Marshall, William Sloane Associates, New York, 1956.

Hankey, Lord, The Right Honourable. *Government Control in War,* Cambridge University Press, New York, 1945.

Howard, Michael, *Soldiers and Governments,* Eyre & Spottiswoode, London, 1957.

Huntington, Samuel P., *The Soldier and the State,* The Belknap Press of Harvard University Press, Cambridge, Massachusetts, 1957.

Jane, Fred T., *The British Battle Fleet,* S. W. Partridge and Co., Ltd., London, 1914.

Johnson, Paul, *The Suez War,* Greenberg, New York, 1957.

Kaufman, William W., *Military Policy and National Security,* Princeton University Press, Princeton, 1956.

Kesselring, Albert, GeneralFeldMarschall, A.D. *Kesselring, A Soldier's Record,* William Morrow & Company, New York, 1954.

King, ADM. Ernest J., *U.S. Navy at War 1941-1945,* U.S. Navy Department, Washington, 1946.

King-Hall, Sir Stephen, *Defence in the Nuclear Age,* Victor Gollancz Ltd., London, 1958.

Kissinger, Henry A., *Nuclear Weapons and Foreign Policy,* Harper & Brothers. New York, 1957.

Leighton, Richard M. and Coakley, Robert W., *Global Logistics and Strategy 1940-1943,* Chief of Military History, Department of the Army, Washington, 1955.

Liddell Hart, B. H., *Why Don't We Learn From History?* George Allen & Unwin Ltd., London, 1944.

Liddell Hart, B. H., *The Rommel Papers,* Harcourt Brace and Company, New York, 1953.

Mahan, A. T., *Naval Adminstration and Warfare,* Little, Brown and Company, Boston, 1918.

Mahan, A. T., *Naval Strategy,* Little, Brown and Company, Boston, 1911.

Mahan, A. T., *The Influence of Sea Power,* Little, Brown and Company, Boston, 1893.

Mao Tse-Tung, *On the Protracted War,* Foreign Languages Press, Peking, 1954.

Maugeri, ADM. Franco, *From the Ashes of Disgrace,* Reynal and Hitchcock, New York, 1948.

Mises, Ludwig Von, *Human Action,* Yale University Press, New Haven, 1949.

Montgomery, Field-Marshall, *The Memoirs of Field-Marshal Montgomery of Alamein, K.G.,* The World Publishing Company, Cleveland, 1958.

Morton, Louis, *The Fall of the Philippines,* Office of the Chief of Military History, Department of the Army, Washington, 1953.

Napoleon, *Napoleon and Modern War,* His military maxims, revised and annotated by Col. C. H. Lanza, USA., Military Service Publishing Company, Harrisburg, 1943.

Naval War College, *Sound Military Decision,* Newport, R.I., 1942.

Nelson, Otto L., Jr., *National Security and the General Staff,* Infantry Journal Press, Washington, 1946.

Novick, David; Melvin, Anshen; and W. C. Truppner; *Wartime Production Controls,* New York, 1949.

Osgood, Robert Endicott, *Limited War,* The University of Chicago Press, Chicago, 1957.

Pogue, Forrest C., *The Supreme Command,* United States Army in World War II, the European Theater of Operations, Office of the Chief of Military History, Department of the Army, Washington, 1954.

Risch, Erna, *The Quartermaster Corps: Organization, Supply, and Services,* Volume I, Government Printing Office, Washington, 1953.

Rosinski, Herbert, *The Evolution of the Conduct of War and of Strategic Thinking,* Naval War College: Newport, R.I., 1955.

Rosinski, Herbert, *The German Army,* The Infantry Journal Press, Washington, 1944.

Roskill, Capt. S. W., DSC, R.N., *The War at Sea,* Volume II, *The Period of Balance,* Her Majesty's Stationery Office, London, 1956.

Ruppenthal, Roland G., *Logistical Support of the Armies,* Volume I, May 1941-September 1944, Chief of Military History, Department of the Army, Washington, 1953.

Shaw, Lt. Colonel G. C., *Supply in Modern War,* Faber and Faber, Ltd., London, 1936.

Smith, Brig. Gen. Dale O., USAF., *U.S. Military Doctrine,* Duell, Sloan and Pearce, New York, and Little, Brown and Company, Boston, 1955.

Smith, General Walter Bedell, *Eisenhower's Six Great Decisions,* Longmans, Green and Co., Inc., New York-London-Toronto, 1956.

Stanley, Timothy W., *American Defense and National Security,* Public Affairs Press, Washington, 1956.

Thompson, J. M., *Napoleon Self-Revealed,* Houghton Mifflin Company, Boston and New York, 1934.

Thorpe, Colonel Cyrus, *Pure Logistics,* Franklin Hudson Publishing Company, Kansas City, Mo., 1917 (Out of print).

Wardlow, Chester, *The Transportation Corps: Movements, Training, and Supply,* Office of the Chief of Military History, Department of the Army, Washington, 1956.

Whitehead, Alfred North, by Lucien Price, *Dialogues of Alfred North Whitehead,* Recorded by Lucien Price, Little, Brown and Company, Boston, 1954.

Lectures

Badger, ADM. Oscar C., USN, Retd., "The Influence of Logistics on Strategy," at the Naval War College, 23 September 1954.

Carney, R. B. ADM., USN, Ret'd., Address before the Executives Club of Chicago, 23 April 1954.

Carney, R. B. ADM., USN, Retd., "Principles of Sea Power," an address at the Naval War College, 7 June 1955.

Conolly, ADM., R. L., USN, Retd.:
"Principles of War," at Third Naval District Reserve Officers Seminar, 13 November 1951;
"Sea Power," at Naval War College, Newport, 20 May 1952;
"The Exercise of Command," at Naval War College, 27 January 1953.

Dulles, John Foster, address to the Annual Luncheon of the Associated Press, New York, 22 April 1957.

McKean, CDR. J/S., USN, "Naval Logistics" at the Naval War College Extension, Washington, D.C., 10 March 1913.

Meade, Randolph Jr., CAPT., USN, "The Service Squadron," at the Naval War College, 20 November 1956.

Morison, S. E. RADM., USN, Retd., Presidential address at dinner of American Historical Association in Chicago, 29 December 1950.

Owens, Charles H., Jr., "The Logistical Support of the Army in the Central Pacific: 1941-1944," a dissertation submitted to the Faculty of the Graduate School of Georgetown University in partial fulfillment of the requirements for the degree of Doctor of Philosophy, Washington, June, 1954.

Sims, W. S., RADM., USN, at the Naval War College, December 1919.

Vogelgesang, CDR. C. Theo, USN, "Logistics—Its Bearing Upon the Art of War" at the Naval War College. Published in *U.S. Naval Institute Proceedings,* Vol. 39, No. 1, March 1913.

Wilson, Charles E. (Secretary of Defense), graduation address, 11 June 1957 at National War College.

Periodicals

Atlantic Report on World Today, Washington, *The Atlantic Monthly,* October 1957.

Air Power—Report of the SubCommittee on the Air Force, 85th Congress, 1st Session, Senate Document No. 29, February 20, 1957.

Baldwin, Hanson W., "The New Face of War," *Bulletin of the Atomic Scientists,* Volume XII, Number 5, May 1956.

British White Paper of April 4, 1957 as published in abridged form in the *N.Y. Times* of April 1957.

Business Week, April 13, 1957, pp. 63-74, "Consolidation Adds up to Fatter Profits for Safeway."

Bureau of Supplies and Accounts (Planning Division), "The 'Modern Air Logistic' Concept and Project 'FAST'—Fleet Air Support Test," 1957.

Bureau of Supplies and Accounts, NAVSANDA Publication 340, "Supply Support of the Navy," September 1957.

Bureau of Supplies and Accounts, NEWSLETTER, "Concept of Navy Logistic Organization," September 1958.

Bureau of Supplies and Accounts, NEWSLETTER, "Concepts of Navy Logistic Organization," May 1958.

Congressional Record 1st Session 85th Congress. Vol. 103—Part 8 Senate, July 1, 1957.

Ferguson, Allen R., "Air Force Logistics," in January 1957 issue of *Aeronautical Engineering Review*.

Fesler, James W., "Administrative Literature and the Second Hoover Commission Reports," *The American Political Science Review*, Vol. LI. No. 1, March, 1957.

Finletter. September and October 1954 articles in *The Atlantic Monthly*.

Forbes, Malcolm S. *Forbes*, November 1958 issue.

Garrett, CDR. J. H., SC, USN, "Characteristics of Usage of Supply Items Aboard Naval Ships and the Significance to Supply Management," *Naval Research Logistics Quarterly* Vol. 5, No. 4, December 1958.

Hart, B. H. Liddell, "The Defense of Europe," *New York Tribune*, 19-21 March 1957.

Hunt, CAPT. R. B., USN, Retd., "Definitions of Logistics," The George Washington University Logistics Research Project, April 1956.

Huston, James A., Dr., "Korea and Logistics," in *Military Review* of February 1957.

Japanese report of operations of their First Striking Force in the SHO Operations, October 16-28, WDC 161641 NA 11839.

Johnson, Ellis A., "The Crisis in Science and Technology and Its Effect on Military Development," *Operations Research Society of America*, Vol. 6, Number 1, January-February 1958.

Keightley, General Sir Charles F., "Operations in Egypt—November to December 1956," Supplement to *The London Gazette*, 10 Sept. 1957.

Kaufmann, William W., "The Crisis in Military Affairs," *World Politics*, a Quarterly Journal of International Relations, Vol. X, Number 4, July 1958.

King-Hall, Sir Stephen, *News-Letter*, Nos. 1070 and 1079, London, 1957.

King, James E. Jr., "Nuclear Plenty and Limited War," *Foreign Affairs*, January 1957.

Krause, Captain R. E., USN, "The German Navy Under Joint Command in World War II," *U.S. Naval Institute Proceedings*, Vol. No. 73, No. 9, September 1947.

Mahan, A. T., "Blockade in Relation to Naval Strategy," *The Journal of the Royal United Service Institution*, Vol. XXXIX, No. 213, London, 1958.

Meier, R. L., "Beyond Atomic Stalemate," *Bulletin of the Atomic Scientists*, Volume XII, No. 5, May 1956.

Morgenstern, Oskar, "Note on the Role of Follow-Ups in the Naval Supply System," George Washington University Logistics Research Project, File PAM-43-1, 1 December 1952.

Murray, Thomas E., "Reliance on H-Bomb and Its Dangers," LIFE, May 1957.

National Defense Transportation Journal, Volume XIV, No. 6, Nov.-Dec. 1958, National Defense Transportation Association.

New York Times, November 15, 1957, p. 26, lead editorial.

Officer's Call, published by the Department of the Army Troop Information and Education Division, 1951.

"Operation Musketeer," in November 24 1956 issue of *The Economist*.

"Operation Overlord," an historical analysis by the U.S. Army Transportation School, Monograph No. 3.

Osmanski, Colonel Frank A., "A Fourth Service of Supply?" in June 1958, issue of *Military Review*.

Palmer, Lt. General, W. B., "Commanders Must Know Logistics," *The Quartermaster Review*, July-August 1953. (Reprinted from the April 1953 issue of the Army Information Digest.)

RAND Corporation, "Report on a Study of Non-Military Defense," Santa Monica, California, July, 1958.

Raymond, Jack, "U.S. is Debating Two Defense Issues," in July 22, 1957 *New York Times*.

Slessor, Sir John, "The Great Deterrent and Its Limitations," Bulletin of the Atomic Scientists, Volume XII, Number 5, May 1956.

Solomon, Henry, Joseph P. Fennel, and Marvin Denicoff, "A Method for Determining the Military Worth of Spare Parts," George Washington University Logistics Research Project and Bureau of Supplies and Accounts, April 1958.

Strausz-Hupe, Robert, "Protracted Conflict: A New Look at Communist Strategy," in ORBIS, published by the Foreign Policy Research Institute, University of Pennsylvania, Volume 11, No. 1, Spring 1958.

Weichold, Eberhard, VADM, Commander German Naval Forces Mediterranean 1941-43, *ONI Review,* September 1946.

Wermuth, Anthony L., Lt. Colonel, "Can't Live Without Them," *Military Review,* U.S. Army Command and General Staff College, Volume XXXVIII, Number II, February 1959.

INDEX

331

The Eccles Papers

Henry Eccles enjoyed a long and close relationship with the U.S. Naval War College, and in his later years donated his personal papers and records to the College's Naval Historical Collection. His estate also donated additional material after his death in 1986. The holdings now fill over 100 archive boxes, the contents of which span his life from early childhood to his last months in a retirement community in Needham, Massachusetts. This extensive collection tells the story of this remarkable naval officer's significant contributions to the nation in war and peace, at home and abroad, in senior leadership positions, and as a world renowned educator. Researchers interested in reviewing this historic collection should contact the Head, Naval Historical Collection, U.S. Naval War College, 686 Cushing Road, Newport, Rhode Island 02841-1207. A detailed register of the contents of the Eccles Papers has been compiled by Dr. Evelyn M. Cherpak, and a copy can be requested from the above address.